Terrence Malick's Unseeing Cinema

James Batcho

Terrence Malick's Unseeing Cinema

Memory, Time and Audibility

James Batcho
United International College
Zhuhai Shi, China

ISBN 978-3-319-76420-7   ISBN 978-3-319-76421-4 (eBook)
https://doi.org/10.1007/978-3-319-76421-4

Library of Congress Control Number: 2018936609

© The Editor(s) (if applicable) and The Author(s) 2018
This work is subject to copyright. All rights are solely and exclusively licensed by the Publisher, whether the whole or part of the material is concerned, specifically the rights of translation, reprinting, reuse of illustrations, recitation, broadcasting, reproduction on microfilms or in any other physical way, and transmission or information storage and retrieval, electronic adaptation, computer software, or by similar or dissimilar methodology now known or hereafter developed.
The use of general descriptive names, registered names, trademarks, service marks, etc. in this publication does not imply, even in the absence of a specific statement, that such names are exempt from the relevant protective laws and regulations and therefore free for general use.
The publisher, the authors, and the editors are safe to assume that the advice and information in this book are believed to be true and accurate at the date of publication. Neither the publisher nor the authors or the editors give a warranty, express or implied, with respect to the material contained herein or for any errors or omissions that may have been made. The publisher remains neutral with regard to jurisdictional claims in published maps and institutional affiliations.

Cover credit: Samara Doole via Unsplash

Printed on acid-free paper

This Palgrave Macmillan imprint is published by the registered company Springer International Publishing AG part of Springer Nature.
The registered company address is: Gewerbestrasse 11, 6330 Cham, Switzerland

For my father, David John Batcho (1935–2017)

Preface

This book is an attempt to create a work of original philosophy. It is not a book on film theory. As a work of philosophy, it does not aim to summarize or advance contemporary trends of scholarship but, rather, to invent new concepts. Terrence Malick's films provide the experiential lines of flight and Gilles Deleuze, in particular, provides a conceptual language. Through their work I wish to offer a way of thinking of cinema not on visual or textual terms—e.g., receptive, cognitive, psychoanalytical, or semiological—but through what I name "unseeing." From this approach, cinema—Malick's in particular—is not observed from the distance of screen to viewer, rendering it for analysis as a text, work of art, or mode of spectatorship. Exploring cinema from the standpoint of unseeing requires one to enter the life that unfolds, to treat cinema as a real experience for those who live its reality. This is the philosophical work I am attempting through my engagement with Malick and Deleuze.

I believe that philosophy, at least in the post-Nietzsche European tradition, is as much a reflection of a writer as of his topic. Therefore, while this book is a philosophical work about cinema, it is also personal. It was written during a time when I witnessed my father succumb to the anguish of Alzheimer's disease. In January 2017 he died of a heart attack before the effects of the disease could completely incapacitate him. What I witnessed was the slow, incalculable process. I remember several times sitting with him late at night when he couldn't sleep, haunted by dreams as vivid as waking life. I listened to him recount memories that overlapped in illogical recreations. These late-night tales would always end the same, in tearful pleas to "go home," wherever that was. These nightly gatherings came in moments of quiet and stillness. During the day was another gathering, a demand to know and a failure to understand what was slipping away. This, I imagine, is a familiar story to family members who have lived it and who themselves have felt powerless to come to terms, let alone to help make amends for the darkness that accompanies it. I have written nothing about this beyond this paragraph. But I mention it because it is here throughout this work, unstated within the statements. Memory, reborn in recollection, becomes an act of imagination and creation, a striving to *make* what is continually in a process of unaccountable loss. As this book moves through Malick's cinema, these aspects of memory and imagination are expressed as an audible gathering in the moment that opens to the newness of time. This account culminates with *The Tree of Life*, a work that *reforms* Malick's characters through such gatherings. Love, redemption, and forgiveness are not the words spoken but, instead, the movement itself—a process, another listening, a new expression being made. This is cinema's power, which Malick expresses in *beatitude*, a Spinozan beatitude.

Another personal reflection I wish to offer is that I met Malick when he came to teach a seminar at my university, an indirect result of the research I was doing on him at the time as a PhD student. During the time of my dissertation defense, I attended his lectures and spoke with him briefly outside of class. I found him to be anything but the recluse I had read so much about. Instead, he was in person warm, kind, and open, even enthusiastic. One might think I would take such an opportunity to ask him questions pertinent to my research, but I resisted, less out of reverence and more because I did not want to know whether he read Deleuze or what he had to say about his use of sound. (I told him briefly about my research and I believe his response was a simple, *Yes, sound is important.*) I wanted his films to express themselves *to* and *for* me, without the burden of explanations about his artistic and philosophical intentions. It became clear during my time with him that he felt the same. Whenever students tried through their questions to draw him into recollections about technique, casting, or life on the set, his response was always a polite variation of *I don't remember; it was a long time ago*. He seemed uninterested in interpreting his own work, which to me was for the best. Instead, he took a Socratic approach to class time, politely shifting any probing questions back onto what the students felt about topics such as redemption, authenticity, and friendship.

Or at least this is my recollection. I try to imagine, to recreate, July 2015, listening to Malick's recurring lectures about Plato's two winged horses that every rider attempts to steer in her chariot of reason. One lifts its rider toward the heavens while the other pulls the whole vehicle (the soul) down to the earth. During these class sessions, Malick requested that nothing be recorded, nor anything written down. The seminar was to be lived in the moment and in the future only in its capacity for remembering and forgetting, two "currents" of memory living in mutual need, as Kierkegaard suggests. I remember the books he asked us to read: the *Phaedrus*, *The Letters of Vincent van Gogh*, *The Gospel According to Mark*, and Epictetus's *Discourses and Selected Writings*. I remember the films he screened for us: Kurosawa's *Seven Samurai*, Mizoguchi's *Ugetsu*, Olmi's *Il Posto*, and Fellini's *La Strada*. I remember that the one film of his that he chose to screen was *The New World*. I remember that this theme of redemption, this theme that became mine as I rewrote my dissertation into this book, was his theme that he returned to with the most frequency. I remember that he seemed most concerned in hearing the students' thoughts on these questions, through these films he screened and the books he offered for reading. As for everything else, I'm trying to remember but I cannot. I wrote nothing down. My writing now cannot bring it back. It can only express in recollection and forgetting, the film that I play back in myself.

For many of these same reasons, I avoided reading analyses of Malick's films during my three years of research for this book. This also applies to recent works on film theory and film philosophy, most of which came late in the process. Although I address film semiology and sound theory, my purpose here is to move through a different process. There is a wealth of great scholarship on Malick, Deleuze, and cinema. But the majority of film theory and philosophy sees and listens to film from the distance of reception, a distance taken and analyzed as visual (spectatorship) or textual ("readings"). I wish instead to take the films *as they are* and work through them on their own philosophical terms. My conscious effort, therefore, is to remove myself from film analysis in favor of penetrating cinematic experience. I hope this keeps me true to the two central figures of this work: Deleuze and Malick. Deleuze's mission in writing his two books on cinema was not film criticism or theory but proper Deleuzean philosophy. The intensity with which he writes about time, memory, sense, and difference, and his emphasis on a transcendental immanence, reveals the craft of a metaphysician more than a scholar referencing prior scholarship. Similarly, much of Malick's uniqueness comes from it being nonreferential, nonlinear and noncategorical, which is one of the central themes of Deleuze's metaphysical and ethical *oeuvre*. In the spirit of Deleuze's monographs, this is mine on Malick, yet one written from a particular rather than total perspective. It is not a comprehensive work on "Malick's cinema" but, rather, a particular way of philosophizing Malick's *unseeing* cinema, offering new concepts *informed by* cinema and philosophical texts. And like Deleuze, I wish at the same time to offer concepts that bring cinema together with questions and problems of experience, audibility, memory, and ethics that go beyond cinema, living as we are in a time of visual and textual noise.

One such problem explored is the epistemological, nonbinary relation of sound and audibility. Sound theory and film sound theory tend to move toward and along the object of analysis, even as scholars occasionally write of the importance of *events*. Readers of Deleuze (specifically his writings with Félix Guattari) tend to couch hearing and listening in musical terms, as the two writers themselves often did. I wish to unsettle the study of what is named "sound" by giving emphasis not to music (aesthetic), nor to objects that make sound (phenomenological, empirical), nor to recordings or representations of sound (technological, historical, representational). Instead, this work gives thought to *audibility*: the experience of hearing and listening. As phenomena, "sound" is the unseen manifestation of what the Greek tradition has named, in a visual bias, as "appearances." Audibility is then the experience of these unseen appearances, which I offer to reconceptualize cinematically as expressions of *unseeing audibility*. Because "understanding" in the philosophical tradition is grounded in images and statements, unseeing audibility gives time to different faculties and potentialities. Their expressions, cinematically, emerge in durations and resonances of imagined memory and the time that unfolds them in a coexisting multiplicity. This is a *lived* relation. And conceptually, it is a much different exercise from that of "observing" sound—studying it, analyzing it, and interpreting it from frontal, proximal, and distal perspectives.

The arc of the book reflects the process of usurping distance and extension with the aim of entering. It begins with analysis in order to progress gradually toward moving within cinema as itself, as immanent to nothing but itself. The first chapter opens a discourse on unseeing as a relation of memory, time, and audibility, which in the same effort addresses my challenges to analytical, representational, and textual/linguistic thinking about cinema. The second chapter offers a means of penetrating into unseeing. It applies Deleuze's conceptions of cinema to the audible dimension and the *logos* made of its relations within, culminating with a description of Malick's *logos*. The next three chapters progress chronologically through four of Malick's films, beginning with *Days of Heaven* (*DoH*) and concluding with *The Tree of Life* (*TToL*). I emphasize these four films because, taken together, they are a progression of the more ethical themes offered here—unseeing as a manifestation of *repetition*, which invites an opening to unspoken expressions of redemption and forgiveness. Malick's first film *Badlands*, which preceded *Days of Heaven*, is a rather straightforward film as pertaining to the thematics offered here, and is acknowledged only for its voice narration. Malick's post-*TToL* films, beginning with *To The Wonder*, fragment his unseeing to the point of destruction, a destruction that will be addressed as well. The four films spanning *DoH* to *TToL* present their own evolving arc, a widening *logos* that moves from linear to multiple in its temporality, from presentation to audience to the unraveling of thought within, allowing for a widening of unseeing coexistence. These films are not so self-contained as they might seem, based on appearances alone. With unseeing as the philosophical theme and the immanent condition, each film comes to inform the others that follow, while those that follow repeat what came before. Through these four films, we therefore open to a repetition in progress. This *repetition* is a philosophical concept. Although central to Deleuze, my appropriation of the concept is primarily informed by Kierkegaard. His repetition is a revisiting of what progresses, recreates, and in many ways reforms what has occurred before. My philosophical aim is to move these themes into areas of unseeing and audibility. My ethical wish is to give attention to Malick's increased opening of hearing, allowing for another kind of listening that expresses a gathering and taking account *as logos*. *The Tree of Life* culminates themes of unspoken redemption that began with *Days of Heaven*. For this period, Malick is the philosopher of spirit, not a transcendent otherness but, rather, spirit born of those who need to gather, take account, *reimagine*. Perhaps, for one can only speculate, he is attempting his own redemption, a re-listening to himself through his persona-as-filmmaker, who takes account through the listening of his living intercessors.

I owe a tremendous debt to so many who have helped me along this path, often with research and editorial suggestions and advice, but just as often with support, friendship, and conversation that had lasting effect on this work. This book was written on the move—in Busan, Berlin, Basel, Salento, Beijing, Zhuhai, San Francisco, and (mostly) Chiang Mai—and I am grateful to those who helped me to make homes of all of them. It is impossible to name everyone who assisted, guided, and encouraged me along the way, but I wish to express my sincere thanks in particular to Hubertus von Amelunxen, Elie During, Shimin Bie, George Khoury, Jonathan Bennett Bonilla, Yanyun Chen, Nicole des Bouvrie, Gabriel Yoran, Jeremy Fernando, Geoffrey Bell, Dina Jost, Euna Kim, Terrence Malick, Drew Burk, Pilaipan Norapanya, Vincenzo De Masi, Yamile Yemoonyah, Clara and Anne Dufourmantelle, Christopher Fynsk, Lim Lee Ching, Adam Staley Groves, Cody McKibben, Kelsey L. Smith, Brent Malin, Minju Park, Michael MacArthur, George Baca, Simone Lee, Chris Souza, Zachary Stockill, Suphak Chawla, Sebastien Tayac, Michael Medley, Wayne Deakin, Judith Mandel, Martin Matuštík, David McPhee, and Jacob Miller; to my professors, in addition to those already mentioned, in particular, Bracha Ettinger, Avital Ronell, Pierre Alferi, Graham Harman, and Siegfried Zielinski; also to Lina Aboujieb at Palgrave-Macmillan; and most of all to my family, Carole Batcho, Linda Christian, and Katherine Hill.

Zhuhai Shi, China   James Batcho

Contents

1 **Introduction** 1
   Unseeing, Audibility, and Logos 5
   Deleuze and Kierkegaard: Repetition and Unseeing 8
      Logos, *Ethics, Faith, and God* 15
   The Audible Faculty in Repetition 18
   References 22

2 **Unseeing** 25
   Problems of Language and Representation 29
      Film Semiology and Its Structures 30
      Deleuze's "Utterable" 32
   Sound Theory and the Hegemony of the Material Image ... 35
   Unseeing: Deterritorializing Space, Reterritorializing Time ... 38
      The Matrix of Events 39
      An Immanent Gathering 44
   References 45

3 *Logos* **of Cinema** 49
   The Transcendental Immanence of Thought 50
      A Cinematic Empathy 52
   Beyond the Audiovisual: New Dimensions in Unseeing ... 56
      Audible Threads: Subjectivity, Madness and the Fold ... 58
      "Life Within the Folds" 62
      Kierkegaard's Anxiety of Subjectivity 65

Opening Unseeing to the Crystalline and the Hodological   68
   From Simultaneity to Coexistence   71
   Coppola's The Conversation: *Simultaneity and Crystalline Audibility*   74
Terrence Malick's Logos   77
   Malick's Expressions of Nature   81
   Creating the New from the Past   83
Cinema as Logos   86
References   87

4 Days of Heaven and Hell   91
Mixing: The Process of Differentiation   92
   Audible Differentiation in Malick   95
A Heraclitean Lesson   98
   First: Hearing   100
   Second: Listening   104
   Third: Nomos   107
References   113

5 Malick's Temporal Shift   115
Repetition and Coexistence: Malick's Expressions of Immanence   117
   Cinematic Leaps in Time   120
   Dreaming and the In-Between   124
Malick's Time and Becoming   127
   Fragments of Unseeing: The Thin Red Line *Through* The Tree of Life   130
   Pages of a Life: Memory and Dreams in Coexistence   133
   After The Tree of Life: *Adrift in the Repetitions of Habit*   138
Narration: Layering Time, Speaking the Unspoken   143
   Malick's Voices   144
   Rupturing the Authority of the Voice   148
References   151

6 Listening to the *Logos*   155
Hearing that Listens; Listening that Continues to Hear   155
The Thin Red Line: *Listening for the Now*   159
The New World: *Listening to Meaning*   162
   Tendere *and Tension*   168
The Tree of Life: *Listening Beyond Memory*   173

The Act of Transferring and the Limits of Logos	179
Malick's Ethics: A Time of Forgiveness	183
References	186
7 Continuer	189
References	196
Index	197

CHAPTER 1

Introduction

A story begins in the midst of its continuance. "'...*and then.*' A storyteller only knows these two words. I walk here, elsewhere, it doesn't matter, and then the encounter happens. It changes the world. Rebirth" (Serres, 2012, p. 148). Cinema's continuance drops you, like Alice, directly into sensation. Any film has its world of hearing, listening, and seeing that precedes its beginning and transcends its sequence as the drop begets its continuance: "*and then....*" You've never been in this world, not quite. Yet you have. Because you have lived, because you have preceded and continually transcend what you see, you can begin at the drop. Only then can "*and then...*" continue itself. Filmmakers imagine this; they imagine your drop. They know you've not only lived but also have been here before, *in cinema*, as they craft the newness of this particular time—*this* beginning in the midst of continuance. Every film is a movement forward, an imagining of the future from the past, a making and a living of the future—in short, a *repetition*.

To enter into this notion of repetition, let us relinquish cinema from its boundaries—as something outside of us, something made, even as a work of art. One stops thinking not only of beginnings and endings but also of borders and frames, analyses and readings, representation and form. One stops thinking about what a film is and thinks instead about *thinking*, cinematic thinking, the thinking that Terrence Malick and his characters make. One has already entered when one lets go of the familiar academic discourses of cinema as a phenomenon to be understood on textual, symbolic, technological, or material terms. These efforts to understand, this is not what moves us. Cinema instead moves through conditions of memory and experience in their fragmentations, as does the one who experiences the film's unfolding.[1] This is why cinema is so ripe for philosophy—not because one can analyze it but because it continues *one's own* fragmented sense of self, one's feeling of time and presumed understandings of things. Philosophy works in these arenas as well. Cinema is an empathetic relation exchanged in signs, associations, images, and threads.[2] It is not a language; it is a way of thinking continuance.

In conversation with Andrew Klevan, Stanley Cavell says that a film "thinks" (2005). One might expand this and suggest that cinema gives "bodies" to thinking, to lives who think. It does not produce thought but, instead, provides bodies, beings, subjects who (and which) express the very process of thinking—a series of gatherers whose thought unfolds. Or, rather, certain films do. Malick's films can be thought in many ways, but a theme offered here is that what one may name as his images and sounds are together expressions of unseeing and hearing. Given that films are audiovisual, one might think that the "other" to images is sound. But this would be another way of regarding cinema in its distance, that we as filmgoers, transcending the apparatus, *receive* images and sound. Instead, I suggest that a Malick film belongs to his characters. There is no camera that shows; there is memory. There is no sound that projects through speakers; there is hearing and listening. Malick's films at this level of engagement are about the limits of memory, time, and audibility. What unfolds cinematically in Malick increasingly becomes an activation of unseeing that opens to expressions of thinking born of these limitations. Unseeing turns objects and sounds into gathering relations of time, opening a field of thought to relations as *logos*.

This does not mean that Malick injects philosophical problems or direct mentions of philosophy into his films (although he occasionally does), nor is it that his films are reflexively calling attention to the form and its process.

---

[1] See, for example, Elsaesser & Hagener, who, even though they place experience in the past tense, recognize that cinema lives, haunts, and influences us "in much the same manner as past memories or actual experiences. Neither fully external nor entirely 'in the mind's eye,' films are complexly woven into time, consciousness and self" (2010, p. 151).

[2] Cognitive film theory often refers to a "paradox of fiction" regarding the emotional bond of audioviewer and character. (See Sinnerbrink, 2011.) But I agree with Sinnerbrink that any such stance cannot cope with ineffable layers of involvement one has in a film. Cognitive and reception theories tend to place the emphasis of experience on a divided audience's visual perception, while unseeing offers a different mode.

Instead, one finds a cinema that *does* philosophy but through the *thinking of its characters* more than through plot or dialogue.[3] If you were to describe the plot of a Malick film, particularly after *Days of Heaven*, you would struggle to say much beyond something like: *people struggling to take account of their time of living within the world in which they are thrown*. A Malick film neither states nor presents philosophy; instead, it offers an opening to the philosophical work going on within itself. He expresses thought through his "intercessors," the personae who think. This is different from Plato's Socrates and Socrates's interlocutors. Rather than working through philosophy in dialogues, Malick's cinematic intercessors think and engage with the gathering of time. We as experiencers of the film then engage in the time of thought that is nothing like a reading but more a search along the tendrils of its limits. In Cavell's terms, philosophy is not what is "in" a film but only what is discovered in it. His interlocutor Klevan adds that "films are not simply prompting clear thoughts in us, or even clear ambiguities. They encourage us to take notice of those feelings that have yet to be voiced, which are 'awaiting' their 'voice.' They encourage us to keep a hold of that sense, not to lose it, or forget it; to keep a hold of the murmurings, the rumblings, that are the route into discovery, not simply the discovery in itself" (Cavell & Klevan, 2005, p. 193). To open such movement, Goodenough suggests that such a film must enable one to see beyond appearances to the "real" structure behind them (2005).[4]

Yet even here, in Cavell's conception of cinema and the scholarship that has followed him, we still have not entered. We must move beyond *mimesis* and *diegesis*, showing and telling. If the ongoing Platonic tradition *says* in reasoned dialogue and *shows* in knowledge and understanding, cinema in Malick brings the process inward. Rather than showing or sounding, his immanent expressions of seeing and hearing take flight *from* what shows or sounds, from that which is causally or materially determined. There is an

---

[3] This aligns, at least somewhat, with Jerry Goodenough's fourth distinction of film philosophy (2005). For more on this, see as well S. Mulhall (2008) and R. Sinnerbrink (2011). Mulhall has his own categories on the relationship between film and philosophy: film as philosophizing, the philosophy of film, and film in the condition of philosophy. A welcome argument is his prioritizing of the particular (see 2008, Chap. 5.), a concept Sinnerbrink extends into his concept of "romantic" film philosophy, often played out through writings on Malick.

[4] Goodenough is also working here through notions proposed by Bernard Williams and Julian Baggini.

unseeing to any seeing, and this is where memory and the audible come to resonate each other in time. Within the moment of any seeing there is *life* in what is unseen—an audible life, but also an *audibility* that opens to new seeing.

This is as true for lived experience as it is for cinema. The audible is a forgotten element of philosophy, which as writing tends to concentrate on knowable statements and visibilities (Deleuze and Foucault), the sayable and the picturable (Wittgenstein), or the statement that discloses the image of truth (Heidegger). And yet in all four philosophers just mentioned, particularly late in their careers, there is a striving to go beyond these limits, limits that cannot be achieved through philosophical prose. Malick, as he moved into the mature stage of his filmmaking, brushed these same limits, often through unstated repetitions of the ideas of those writers just mentioned. Cinema that shows and speaks, such as in a "philosophical" filmmaker like Christopher Nolan, who is often badly compared to Malick, is devoted to camera, exposition, and screenplay. We may think of his process as the reverse: screenplay is rendered as exposition that unfolds profilmically for the camera. Why do Nolan's films talk and show so much? Perhaps because his ideas cannot be gathered and therefore must be clearly explained in statements and revealed in things. Cinema in its unseeing and unstated movement works instead through relations, signs, and silences that give *time to thinking*, rather than a presence with the ceaseless procession of objects, symbols, and language.[5] This imagined and created time is lived, even if it cannot be directly seen nor stated. This duration is lived by poets who both conjure and gather in resonances of thought, or by one who struggles with faith, who both *makes and feels* a divine actuality.[6] Malick's cinema unfolds the time of this experience, bringing it closer to a Kierkegaardian thinking: an expression that in itself strives along the infinite within the finite, thereby bringing *us* within the inferences of faith and belief housed in those who hear and imagine.

---

[5] Sinnerbrink writes of the importance of considering how a Malick's films "thinks," as itself, although he couches it in visual and narrative terms (2006).

[6] We may consider William James here (2002), that the thought of a religious experience is actual because it is experienced. Similarly, a duration of thinking given rise in unseeing, its poetry and divinity, is made actual through the cinematic image.

Unseeing, Audibility, and *Logos*

This text, being as we are in writing, aims to situate Malick's cinema in a manner that is different from its recurrent discourses. To move outside of film theory's representational and analytical readings of dialogue, images, and symbolism, it proposes a series of interconnected cinematic concepts that lead into the unseeing overlaps of memory, time, and audibility. This requires some necessary exposition:

- A film is an expression of a world that is real to its characters. *World* is used here in it broadest possible connotation as inclusive of its own entirety.[7]
- Within this world is its *logos* (λόγος). As conceived cinematically, *logos* is the unseeing relational element of a film's world.
- *Unseeing* is not a blindness but an everyday condition in which one's consciousness is open beyond the field of one's present seeing. Absent a visual object-event of understanding, unseeing invites one to strive along a multiplicity of time. It thereby opens one to other faculties or paths of experience—namely, the audible.
- Unseeing is particularly attuned to *audibility*, which is one's interplay of hearing and listening as *logos*.
- *Hearing* in this connotation is not "understanding"; rather, it is a continuing, unmediated openness of audible awareness. *Listening*, by distinction, is the specificity of thoughtful engagement.
- Seeing as one hears forms a referential recognition or understanding of the event. Not seeing what one hears opens to a duration of unseeing.
- Because a state of unseeing cannot see its present visual phenomena that sounds, *unseeing audibility* has the power to move along the faculties of memory and imagination, engaging one's fragmented past and reformed future within the present. It is a hearing of and listening to time.
- Unseeing is the condition, *logos* is the gathering relation, and audibility is the field and the opening to potential expression.

---

[7] "World" is a contentious term in philosophy, often finding some division, such as the totality of appearances, perspectival aspects such as *Weltanschauung* and *Weltbild*, language, or narrowing into an emergence born of some action or gesture. I mean it here and throughout in its most colloquial connotation, which is also most appropriate for cinema: the entirety of what is and may be.

- Through a character's attentiveness to *logos*, the unseeing aspects of her or his experience are expressed. These expressions born of unseeing are a different faculty of understanding and belief from those gained through visual appearances and language, yet they are not independent of either.
- Unseeing is capable of dividing time into multiple and interrelational durations of *actuality* (present formulation/manifestation) and *virtuality* (the infinite potentiality of memory and experience).
- Through states of unseeing, audibility is able to be present with appearances (a *simultaneity*) or to move free of present appearances (a *coexistence*).
- In so doing, one's audible faculties gain independence from presence while maintaining its inseparability from *logos*. This *independence and inseparability* opens new circuits or threads of thinking that form new time-image durations in cinema. To make audible is to express an idea that has not been actualized outside of its otherwise everyday continuation. To make audible is to feel and think the unformed idea in a resonance of repetitions. In this way, unseeing creates new images from the past and projects new ideas forward into the future.
- Unseeing audibility is a relation of time more than space, one that moves beyond references to form *inferential* relations with time and the possibility of a different unfolding of present understanding. Audibility is an ability of the audible, a means of turning such inferences into decisions of belief.[8]
- An *unseeing cinema* is that particular aspect of cinema that expresses a character's relationship to memory and imagination, one that is given life through the activation of her or his audible faculties. As Malick's films progress, this unseeing comes to gradually replace seeing. Unseeing becomes the foundation of his unfolding, as his films shift from present time to the time that struggles between recollection and repetition in the Kierkegaardian sense. This is not reflexivity, because that would place it outside both *logos* and world. The thinking and deciding that arise from unseeing occur within the world of the film and through the *logos* relations formed by its characters.

---

[8] See Kierkegaard's *Philosophical Crumbs* (2009) in which he writes that belief comes ultimately in a decision. "The conclusion of belief is not an inference but a decision, thus doubt is excluded" (p. 150). I am modifying his process to suggest that the inference shapes the belief that gives rise to action.

- Each film has its *logos*, but also its *nomos* (νομός) or nomadic law expressed through its characters' successes or failures to take account within it.
- Unseeing, audibility, *logos*, and *nomos* come together when one considers that unseeing audibility is an engagement that is inclusive of but not reducible to prior categories of sound such as speech and music. Because unseeing audibility has neither prior system nor visual reference, any present *gathering* is an expressive relation with memory and signs. Such a *logos* relation must move along a nomadic, distributive engagement that ties together the virtual field of memory with the actual field of present activity: a *nomos*.
- A film does not have to maintain its logic to an audience, only to its characters. If its logic fails or is altered, its characters take account (or fail to) as *logos*. Therein lies cinema's creative potential and its ability to evoke new thinking.
- The final claim is that there are several filmmakers who create in brief durations of unseeing as described here. Yet Malick is the only filmmaker who has developed it into a form of pure expression.

All the terms defined here will be expanded through the course of this work and through Malick's films. The concept of *logos*, however, requires immediate attention. It is a historically contentious, untranslatable word that has drifted in meaning since Heraclitus introduced it sometime around 500 BC. As applied here, *logos* is not the same as what we find in its contemporary philosophical connotations of language, statement, word, ratio, or reason. Nor is it defined by or reducible to an *a priori* substance, *demiurge*, or Christian *Word of God*. Taking from its early use, *logos* is an activity of *gathering*, *taking account of*, and *making from* all that is presently unseen. It is an engagement with signs that resonate the echoes, attributes, images, thoughts, and feelings of what was once lived and lives again in one's fragmented account. This is different from remembering, withdrawing, or dwelling in the past; it is a coexistence within lived experience, one that has been ignited under the influence of signs. *Logos* as an engagement of unseeing is a relation with time, memory, and hearing, particularly in *how one attends* to its plurality of streams, tethers, circuits, or planes within any such coexistence. Beginning from this standpoint of *logos* changes the question: What happens when one begins with the resonance of thinking rather than an image in appearance? This is a different question of creativity and reason, and is a difficult cinematic task. A film is typically composed in accordance with the dominant codes that unify cinema's two arrows of time: linear montage and linear speaking. Malick's films are exceptional because they fragment the ideology of linear progression. But the dyadic unity is ruptured less through its imagery as given to a viewer and more in its gathering of these resonances within his characters. True to Deleuze's cinema, images in Malick are not the prior of thought but, rather, the unfolding of thinking within such resonance, both in the activity and in the effect. Malick does not construct images. Rather, his characters resonate life in a gathering that makes the *logos*. His films unfold through one's taking account of the multiplicity of thought that must be attended to in an active engagement. In this, his *logos* unfolds not as a work of art but as expressions of life.

Deleuze and Kierkegaard: Repetition and Unseeing

Malick is known to have an affinity with three philosophers mentioned already: Kierkegaard, Heidegger, and Wittgenstein. All inform this writing as well. What is perhaps out of place for Malick is the mention of Deleuze, who has been deeply influential to me, although there is no evidence that Malick has read him. Deleuze's two cinema books are not analyses of form or theory as much as they are works of philosophy, ones that offer some of the clearest prose available for his complex cannon of metaphysical terms. Such terms are employed liberally in this text, even if they are not always directly cited: his openness and immanence; his resonating interrelations of images, signs, and circuits; his movement, action, and de/reterritorializations; his unseeing depth that emerges in material and sensory events; and above all the thinking that is born of differentiations in the virtual/actual flux of experience and memory. One of the great treasures of Deleuze is the many ways to think through him. The Deleuze I employ for Malick is the solo writer more than the writer who partnered with Guattari. And for my part I do not pick up from contemporary materialist or mechanistic readings of him, nor do I find them relevant to what Malick does. Malick's cinema is the *immanence and actuality of thought* and thinking in a relationship with signs, images, matter, memory, and the folding of subjectivity. All this gives birth to the unseeing that sees anew. Deleuze's concept of the *virtual* is key to this process. For the uninitiated, "virtual" here is not some digital or nonreality, but is the pure memory of experience that meets a pure transcendentalism, a mutual folding that is *actualized* in a singular thought that unfolds in a creation of something new. This is just one of Deleuze's dizzying mélange of concepts and terms that lays fertile soil for the generation of new thought and new cinema. For readers unfamiliar with Deleuze, I hope my application of his terms is employed in such a way that one need not intimately know his work to follow the trajectories—and divergences, for I diverge often from Deleuze—offered here. His concepts will be expressed as we go, sometimes explicitly and other times implicitly. For those who are readers of Deleuze, I employ footnotes as a means of working through his concepts in more detail. (This applies as well to other, denser streams of philosophical thought, leaving the reader to follow or pass over such lines of flight.)

There is another reason for invoking Deleuze: to give thought to his *oeuvre* that he never explicated, that of this connection between "unseeing" and "audibility." His ontology of images, even in their lack, evidences an ocular bias and yet his metaphysics of *difference* and *events* describes the activity of unseeing as offered here. He appealed widely to notions of signs, forces, and "the whole," but he does not offer a conceptual tissue of the "outside" of discourse and images except to say that from this unmentioned idea, actualization comes in a thought, movement, image, object, or event. In *Difference and Repetition* he writes of difference in invisible and sonic terms: "amplitude," "resonance," a "dark precursor." Resonance and "noise" are also themes in his other great work of philosophy, *The Logic of Sense*. Yet he wrote almost nothing, save a few sideward considerations, about the *hearing of* and *listening to* this invisible activity in its formless, sightless, unspoken, and chaotic state. Even in *The Logic of Sense*, he discounts noise to give thought to speaking, avoiding the audibility that is free of language's prior structure. This is surprising for a philosopher whose concepts strive along an array of interconnected effects, producing an open, temporal topology that overlays chaos and invites a journey along the infinite.

While this is a book about Malick's cinema, therefore, its other aim is to open and encourage an examination of the audible in Deleuze's implied unseeing. In the process, perhaps it can address another problem in Deleuze's cinematic effort: his dependence on images. Any image, whether mirror, window, or recollection, is still an image; and the problem of images even in their generative capacity is how they imply or even necessitate a distance. Such distance is important for Deleuze, both in *The Logic of Sense* and in his cinema books—works that in certain respects are complementary. The nonsense of "noise" is explored in the former at the level of language; but his "surface" is paramount as this deeper disorganization remains for him submerged. Pertaining to cinema, his focus struggles to penetrate surfaces and because of this he is incapable of surpassing this distance. Even though he fights against a semiology of a film, and even as he blurs the delineations of subjectivity and objectivity, his image relations, as ocular, still conceive of cinema from an external perspective. For *whom* is the crystal-image, the affection-image or the recollection-image? For him it is given for the audience, not lived by the inhabitants of the film world.[9] These concepts align with his effort to conceive cinema *as art*, as blocs of sensation that stand on their own terms.[10] This is just one of the aspects in which Deleuze and I (and I believe Malick, too) differ, and where other paths become necessary. Yet in addition to images, Deleuze tells us that cinema is also made of *signs*, which is in many ways the very heart of unseeing audibility. This book aims to move to the *inward* relations of signs—to penetrate the film's surface and find a reality of the movement and thinking inside it. This existence within allows us to explore the distances and relations of its *logos* rather than its surfaces. A crystalline unseeing, for example, is the audible duration belonging to lives who live within, not the *audioviewer*.[11] Because of this, I conceive Malick's films not in cinematic images but in movements of a life, the lives of those who attempt to enter into new relations of thought, drawn forth by a hearing within oneself. Such audibility breaks not only objective and subjective binary distinctions but also the presumption of images and their dogmas, presuppositions and identities.

This unseeing, occasionally opening to divine possibilities, relieves thought from the incessant logic of objects and words. This other relation is not apprehension but a gathering and an account, which returns us to a *logos* before Aristotle got hold of it. This nonlexical *logos* appeals to no Aristotelian ground, not even to *his logos* of man's reason. It offers another opening, a silence to hear and listen along potential planes of the infinite within finitude, an immanence that offers the *cinematic maybe* of transcendence. Such a way of thinking necessarily includes bodies, motion, activity,

---

[9] For another perspective on this, see Teresa Rizzo's *Deleuze and Film: A Feminist Introduction* (2012). She provides a different argument from what I offer here, one based on the body of the spectator. For Rizzo, Deleuze and Guattari offer a conceptual means to overcome binary distinctions that otherwise render women as the other to male perspectives.

[10] See Deleuze & Guattari (1991).

[11] "Audioviewer" is an admittedly cumbersome noun, but I require a noun for when "audience" and "viewer" presume too little or too much. "Audioviewer" has gained some traction in film theory, so I am employing it here as well.

signs. Heidegger called *logos* the *laying that gathers*, while Deleuze considers thinking as laying along an immanent plane. While there are deep distinctions, these notions are not in conflict—neither with each other, nor with *logos* as conceived here.[12] Thinking transcendence folds its *thinking* back into life, becomes creativity itself—a theater of thinking.

For this reason, Kierkegaard becomes just as important as Deleuze in conceiving Malick's unseeing cinema. Rather than a projection of light and sound, cinema as *logos* proposes that Malick's characters live the film. They create how they live by their thinking and through their actions. In this, Malick and Kierkegaard are aligned in several key aspects: (1) Kierkegaard works his most literary ideas through pseudo/heteronyms: Johannes de Silentio, Constantin Constantius, Johannes Climacus, and others.[13] Ostensibly writers, these are the narrators of Kierkegaard's concepts, but "they" also develop their arguments through a cast of characters who play out various roles—Abraham, Victor, "A," William, the Young Man. Deleuze, sometimes writing with Guattari, conceives of such individuals as various kinds of personae. De Silentio and Constantius, the conceptual personae of Kierkegaard, then write through other personae—e.g., the intercessors Abraham and the Young Man.[14] (2) From his 1998 work onward, Malick, like Kierkegaard, is not interested in following the uni-

---

[12] Yet there are distinctions to address. Heidegger's and Deleuze's notions of *logos* evolved over time. Heidegger's "laying that gathers" is concentrated in his mid-period *Early Greek Thinking* (1984) and is an effective conception of *logos* on those terms. However, his wider use is not advocated here because it relies too much on an Aristotelian conception of a *logos* that reveals the image of existing truth (*aletheia*) in a *statement*. For Deleuze's part, his development and critique of *logos* is also based in Aristotelian/Heideggerian terms. He conceives *logos* as *a priori* and preconditional to thinking, and he often thinks of thinking itself as lying between statements and visualities, not so distant from how Heidegger thinks of *logos* as between the statement and its image. To reiterate, briefly: *logos* as used here is an engagement with unseeing and its signs—*logos* through immanence, which, perhaps, carries the idea of transcendence. This brings it to a pre-Aristotelian, Heraclitean, nonlexical relation, but one that does not discount language or images. As will be repeated later, *logos* is itself but only because it is made in its making.

[13] *Heteronym* comes from Fernando Pessoa but applies to Kierkegaard and is mentioned as well by Deleuze and Guattari. This word has another, more common, meaning, which will be explored in the conclusion.

[14] The distinction between these terms *intercessor* and *conceptual persona* are not always consistent in Deleuze. In some writings he seems to make them synonymous, while in others the persona is one through whom the philosopher *becomes* while the intercessor is the character or other entity that acts out the philosophy. It seems that an intercessor is one type of persona and a persona is one type of intercessor.

versal conventions of form. The cinematic/narrative norm is to feature a hero who walks a path and gains help from others along the way who share in the same sense of aesthetics or a universal ethics. But for both thinkers, these stages of aesthetics and ethics must be surpassed to reach the plane of faith. Kierkegaard wrote that for one to become a knight of faith, he must pass through a conflict with himself. This knight finds himself eternally tested and gains little help along the way. And as with Kierkegaard's intercessors, Malick's characters struggle to come to truths other than those of universal ethics. (3) This struggle of ethics and truth is one of authenticity, which requires a disruption of the mind. Such disruption comes from within and "excites anxiety," as Kierkegaard writes. It is not entirely a relation with present events and more a present relation with time, with one's own past and future that lives within the moment. Kierkegaard's *knight of infinite resignation* is constantly looking back in recollection, which threatens to lead one away from oneself, in what Heidegger later called *Verfallen*, or "fallenness." Kierkegaard's knight of faith, however, deterritorializes time in a forward progression, which he calls *repetition*. Within this personal, inner battle between resignation and faith, one finds Malick's characters engaged in recollection and repetition, beginning with *The Thin Red Line*. (4) All this is evident in Malick through his increasingly temporal cinema. His images are made from the very uncertainty of time. What binds his cinema together is a *logos* that builds a temporal matrix of unseeing.[15] *Logos* is not a simple subjective reasoning but is a relation that is made from one's engagements with the outside—what Deleuze calls the "fold" of the outside within a subject.[16] It is involvement in the immanent field of memory and audibility—an interplay of virtual and actual signs that come to the fore in sensation, reverie, remembrances, and recollections, and which may be projected cinematically as images and sound but which subjectively emerge through one's faculties of audibility that give thought to time.

---

[15] Roger Munier also conceived of cinema as a *logos*, writing that its "'world, in its own terms and in the immanent expression of itself, puts itself at the service of a logos'" (Mitry, 1997, p. 374). Yet he also places *logos* in structuralist terms as a "discourse" through which consciousness structures objects. Mitry, commenting on Munier, comes closer to a *logos* as offered here, in that "reality organizes *itself* into a *logos*" (p. 375, emphasis added).

[16] To be clear: The fold is Deleuze; but again, his adoption of *logos* is different from that offered here.

Repetition, Kierkegaard's response to Plato's "recollection,"[17] effectively expresses the theme of authenticity along a path of faith, grace, and redemption. Recollection and repetition are the same movement, Kierkegaard writes, just in opposite directions, with repetition as a future-oriented creation of the blissful moment rather than the sorrowful past. "The dialectic of repetition is easy, because that which is repeated has been, otherwise it could not be repeated; but precisely this, that it has been, makes repetition something new" (2009, p. 18). All that has existed becomes again but not as it was before. Recollection, by contrast, is not in itself a negative movement, but it is also not new. Recollection begins with loss because in its gathering it has already anticipated and found comfort in it, Kierkegaard's Constantius claims, while repetition is both a gathering and a movement forward. Repetition is a willful act that requires the courage to gather a deeper sense of oneself. In his writings, Kierkegaard often conceives of the two in audible terms, and Malick expresses this conflict through the audible gatherings of his characters. Kierkegaard writes that when one is devoid of either, life becomes noise: "When one lacks the categories of recollection and repetition, all of life is dissolved into an empty, meaningless noise" (p. 19). At the level of ethics and faith, Malick's cinema can be conceived as a struggle between the two, with repetition being the cinematic concept (or idea) that prevails as authentic. After *Days of Heaven*, repetition is the ethics that redeems in its unfolding.

Deleuze puts Kierkegaard with Nietzsche in writing that they, along with Péguy, give repetition a power but also make it into "the fundamental category of a philosophy of the future" (1994, p. 5). All three couch the concept of repetition in characters and in theatrical terms. (We can think of Nietzsche's Zarathustra as much as Kierkegaard's Young Man.) Through their intercessors, the three offer repetition as a means to oppose "*all forms of generality*" (p. 5). He adds that they go so far as to work repetition into their style. (We might say that both Deleuze and Malick do this as well—advancing certain themes through repetition in each new work.) Deleuze proposes four points here: (1) They all make something new of repetition. In Kierkegaard, one is not "extracting" something new from repetition—

---

[17] He adds that this is Plato's concept, not Socrates's. Socrates, Kierkegaard writes, was more interested in the moment. In Plato's *Meno*, "Recollection" (*anamnesis*) is described by Socrates as learning and inquiry that emerges through the truth that resides already within due to the immortality of the soul, and is for him proof of its immortality. This, Kierkegaard notes, makes recollection a "backward reference."

for as he says, only the contemplative mind extracts: "It is rather a matter of acting, of making repetition as such a novelty; that is, a freedom and a task of freedom" (p. 6). (2) Repetition is in opposition to the laws of nature. Repetition is not nature, like the cycle of seasons. In Kierkegaard, one does not obtain repetition from nature. Repetition involves "the interior element of the will…because everything *changes* around the will, in accordance with the law of nature."[18] (3) Repetition is in opposition to moral law; it suspends ethics and becomes an inner *logos*: "Repetition appears as the logos of the solitary and the singular, the logos of the 'private thinker'" (pp. 6–7). In Kierkegaard and Nietzsche, the private thinker of repetition is in opposition to the daily "mediated" discourse of one's profession. (4) Repetition is opposed to "the generalities of habit" and "the particularities of memory" (p. 7). In Nietzsche and Kierkegaard, they fade in the face of repetition, which is the thought of the future, a positive power: "When Kierkegaard speaks of repetition as the second power of consciousness, 'second' means not a second time but the infinite which belongs to a single time, the eternity which belongs to an instant, the unconscious which belongs to consciousness, the 'nth' power" (p. 8).

Through Kierkegaard's and Nietzsche's repetition, Deleuze writes, a work takes on "a movement capable of affecting the mind outside of all representation; it is a question of making movement itself a work, without interposition; of substituting direct signs for mediate representations; of inventing vibrations, rotations, whirlings, gravitations, dances or leaps which directly touch the mind" (p. 8). Here he might as well be describing Malick, even though he never mentions him in any of his writings.[19] Deleuze continues: "This is the idea of a man of the theatre, the idea of a director before his time. In this sense, something completely new begins with Kierkegaard and Nietzsche. They no longer reflect on the theatre in the Hegelian manner. Neither do they set up a philosophical theatre. They invent an incredible equivalent of theatre within philosophy, thereby founding simultaneously this theatre of the future and a new philosophy" (p. 8). This is evident in Malick as well, who constructs his *logos* as an interlacing of repetitions in various applications of the term. Repetitions of thought, world, and theme create a cinema of repetition that reaches out along a *new ethics* of forgiveness and even redemption. His cinema as a

---

[18] For more commentary on this by Deleuze, see Deleuze (2015).
[19] He does in a footnote; his reading of Heidegger's *Essence of Reasons* in *Difference and Repetition* is Malick's 1969 translation. See also: Malick (1969).

whole is itself variable movements through experience in their particular scenarios, while each film is a repetition (a new repetition) of these repetitions. Taken altogether they become a movement toward something beyond the conventions of cinema, beyond a popular ethics. His films reach out toward a new plane of thought, an infinite time that offers a place of unity, redemption, and forgiveness. This is not a material plane nor does it live in Idealism. It is an immanence and an ethics that comes through *logos*—the gathering and the account as one's relation to others and the world. "In the theatre of repetition, we experience pure forces, dynamic lines in space which act without intermediary upon the spirit, and link it directly with nature and history, with a language which speaks before words, with gestures which develop before organised bodies, with masks before faces, with spectres and phantoms before characters—the whole apparatus of repetition as a 'terrible power'" (p. 10).

Logos, *Ethics, Faith, and God*

We may speculate here on the reasons Deleuze then leaves Kierkegaard behind to embrace Nietzsche in Deleuze's own metaphysics of repetition. To some degree it is born of his admiration for Nietzsche's *activity*—his "dancing" as a creation of worlds. But pertaining to his rejection of Kierkegaard, I propose three main reasons: God, subjectivity, and possibility over actuality. These aspects will be addressed fully in this work, and to a certain extent are at its core, given Malick's own faith and the kind of subjectivity he seems to embrace. Regarding the question of God, I read in Deleuze an implicit distaste for Kierkegaard's *identity to*—"identity" being a major problem for Deleuze—a Christian God, a transcendent and determining *beyond*, which Deleuze opposes. Deleuze is an atheist, not only in an areligious sense but also in an ethical one. He is resistant to any appeal to fixed and divine prior structures and the essentialist thinking that results. A Spinozan immanence is therefore advanced instead of a divinely separated transcendence, one of expression rather than the Word of Scripture.[20] For this same reason he also resists adherence to *logos*, which

---

[20] See Deleuze's monograph on Spinoza and the Scripture and its Word concept of God, which Spinoza sets aside in favor of immanent expression. As Deleuze writes, for Spinoza "The concept of expression, at once speech and manifestation, light and sound, seems to have a logic of its own" (1990, p. 53).

for him is a structure to rise above or escape.[21] But by his description, it seems this resistance to *logos* is based on his readings of Heidegger and Aristotle, which have come to dominate its familiar contemporary connotation, which has turned the word into denotation. I am proposing that while *logos* may be conceptually prior, it is only expressed in its relation and *through the expression*. In this it is not fixed but, rather, is both real and made through a fluidity of relations. To employ three of Deleuze's terms, *logos* is "folded" from the "outside," becoming an experiential rather than an exclusively artistic, "apprenticeship" with signs.[22] In Heraclitus, *logos* folds and unfolds through listening as opposed to seeing, and is thereby expressed as a condition of unseeing. This is how *logos* and *nomos* stop being oppositional concepts; as audible, they become not order versus movement (as in Deleuze) but, rather, as a cohabitation of engaged relations and fluid understandings.

Deleuze's aversion to transcendence and *logos* arises from an objection to anything separated from the virtual and actual potentiality of lived thought and lived experience. This does not mean that he is opposed to notions of spirit, essence, the outside, and the infinite. Nor does it stop him from asking questions about Kierkegaard's theatre of faith, in which the Dane "dreams of an alliance between a God and a self rediscovered" (Deleuze, 1994, p. 11). We must remember that Kierkegaard's knight is not a "Knight of God." God may be the "Wholly Other" of love, but *faith* is the paradoxical relation. Kierkegaard's literary existentialism finds its

---

[21] In *Proust and Signs*, Deleuze claims that "there is no Logos that gathers up all the pieces, hence no law attaches them to a whole to be regained or even formed" (2000, p. 131). As with this passage, his use of the term often presumes an *intelligence* that is prior. However, this is not *logos* but more aligned with what the Greeks referred to as *nous*: divine thought, the mind of God. Deleuze's thinking on *logos* evolved somewhat through the course of his writing. In *Difference and Repetition*, *logos* takes on a distinction from *nomos* as that which *allows for* a rupture of thought. And in his final work with Guattari, the two write that the "sieve" along the plane of immanence is a pre-Socratic *logos* that is not aligned with reason. "If we call such a plane-sieve Logos, the logos is far from being like simple 'reason' (as when one says the world is rational)" (1994, p. 43). They imply that *logos* in the ancient Greek sense, which is advocated here as well, was the means of taking from the flux of chaos in its immanence. *Logos* is now the other to a transcendence of the sages that is imposed from beyond. While maintaining an entity status as itself—a sieve as a *thing* that gathers rather than the *activity* of gathering—it at least moves Deleuze toward a kind of relation that engages in potentialities not reduced to the rational and analytical, nor the visual and stated.

[22] For context, see Deleuze, 2000 (apprenticeship) and 1988 and 1993 (the fold and the outside).

field of struggle here in the question of faith and resignation. It might seem as if Deleuze and Malick are on opposite ends of the spectrum when it concerns God, owing to Deleuze's resistance to fixed preconditions and transcendent identities. But Kierkegaard's writing is primarily about the struggle of faith rather than the fact of God, which is anything but fixed.[23] And is this not Malick's cinema as well? Malick, it seems, also embraces a Christian God. But as with Malick the philosopher, as a Christian he is never explicit about it. Malick's divinity is immanent, Spinozan even, in that it does not depend on exposition, morality, dialogue, or scripture to express God's infinite attributes of thought and extension. Malick's God unfolds not in transcendence nor through *logos as Word*; rather, it is through the univocity of nature's expressions—thought, extension, images, memory, movement, sounds, hearings, and listenings. His characters, inseparable from nature, work through struggles, not finalities. The solitary non-hero in constant movement searches within the turmoil of ethics and faith, seeks within natural time-spaces that are free of such concerns, imagines the idea of spiritual transcendence within an immanent transcendentalism: mind and body, nature and grace, earth and cosmos, past and future. Is Malick not asking the same questions through his own theater that Deleuze asks of Kierkegaard's? "All sorts of differences follow: is the movement in the sphere of the mind, or in the entrails of the earth which knows neither God nor self? Where will it be better protected against generalities, against mediations? Is repetition supernatural, to the extent that it is over and above the laws of nature? Or is it rather the most natural will of Nature in itself and willing itself as *Phusis*, because Nature is by itself superior to its own kingdoms and its own laws? Has Kierkegaard not mixed all kinds of things together in his condemnation of 'aesthetic' repetition: a pseudo-repetition attributable to general laws of nature and a true repetition in nature itself; a pathological repetition of the passions and a repetition in art and the work of art?" (p. 11). Deleuze says he cannot answer these questions; neither can Malick. In theater as in cinema, transcendence becomes a maybe of thinking and fictional imagining that stretches philosophy beyond its limits while maintaining a devotion to truth—the truth of fiction. The question of God need not be stated nor answered and can instead be expressed within Malick's cinema that *moves through* shifting accounts and states of wonder about such questions.

---

[23] Indeed, Kierkegaard is radically opposed to attempts of the church to ossify faith.

As for the particular question of repetition, in all three thinkers it is a creative force and activity. For both Deleuze and Kierkegaard, repetition is not subordinate to identity, and in this, there is more affinity than dissonance between the two when it comes to the application of repetition advanced here.[24] Kierkegaard, Deleuze, Malick: each paints repetition using a different palette.

The Audible Faculty in Repetition

How does any of this pertain to audibility and the concept of unseeing? By first recognizing a backward account—to concrete references and the causality that so dominates theories of sound—in order to reverse it and advocate instead a movement forward. In his book on his friend Foucault, Deleuze writes of the power that is the condition that resonates Foucault's two regimes of knowledge: visibilities and statements (1988). Audibility, as an epistemological field of play other than statements and visibilities, finds itself sometimes within these two regimes of knowledge and sometimes independent from them. One is within when one hears someone speak (statement) or when one sees and hears a motorcycle (visible) drive by; one is independent when one hears but does not see what one presumes from the sound that is neither a statement nor visibly present for verification (i.e., hearing a sound nearby that one *believes* to be a motorcycle). This independence is the condition of unseeing: the seeing that does not see and the hearing of nonstatements. Statements and visibilities determine knowledge along the stratum, but nonstatements and nonvisibilities engender another fold.

Here we come closer to Deleuze's *other* relations and forces. The gap here again is that Deleuze did not write about sound-audibility-unseeing within this key aspect of his metaphysics—chaos and its hearings, indepen-

---

[24] The following quote from Deleuze reads to me more of a Kierkegaard than Nietzsche influence, and it illustrates the complexity of his metaphysics and his movement on matters of subjectivity: "The role of the imagination, or the mind which contemplates in its multiple and fragmented states, is to draw something new from repetition, to draw difference from it. For that matter, repetition is itself in essence imaginary, since the imagination alone here forms the 'moment' of the *vis repetitiva* from the point of view of constitution: it makes that which it contracts appear as elements or cases of repetition. Imaginary repetition is not a false repetition which stands in for the absent true repetition: true repetition takes place in imagination" (1994, p. 76).

dent of any language, music or system.[25] Although sound is spatial, as itself and as *given to* audibility, through time and memory it gives rise to a nonplace that is possible in cinema, a form of expression unique in creating time. This nonplace that Deleuze describes lies above the mechanisms that marshal knowledge into use, creating an outside zone of ephemeral collisions, opening time forward into repetition. "The informal outside is a battle, a turbulent, stormy zone where particular points and the relations of forces between these points are tossed about. Strata merely collected and solidified the visual dust and the sonic echo of the battle raging above them. But, up above, the particular features have no form and are neither bodies nor speaking persons. We enter into the domain of uncertain doubles and partial deaths, where things continually emerge and fade" (1988, p. 121). His "sonic echo" is not what is here conceived as audibility; rather, it is a statement on the echoes of *statements* and therefore within the built strata of knowledge even as a kind of residue. What is germane instead is what follows, this Leibnizian domain above.[26] Although this is not for him the zone of audibility, it aligns with Deleuze's many writings that test the border spaces of what does not fall into the stated and the seen.

Unseeing audibility as a creative force *is repetition*. "Sound design" in cinema interjects durations within any moment—durations that make thought and make images as thought. What interjects is time or, more specifically, durations as expressions of time that intercede and define the moment. This interjection can either be mirror or window as it lives within the audible moment. As a mirror, sound as heard reflects back on the past, becomes representational; as a window, sound as heard becomes repetition in audibility, surpassing its representational *regard* which aims to objectify itself. Yet the mirror or window maintains an element of each other by sustaining the question of what is the degree of creation (window) that lies in an understanding (mirror), and vice versa. And further still: window

---

[25] With Guattari, he wrote of Kafka's audible characters, who hear not a "systematized music" nor "a composed and semiotically shaped music…rather a pure sonorous material" (1986, p. 5). This concept of sound reflects writings at the time about *musique concrète*, fluxus and experimental music. And in *A Thousand Plateaus* (*ATP*), they write of the deterritorializing effect of ambiguity in the audible relation: "sound invades us, impels us, drags us, transpierces us. It takes leave of the earth, as much in order to drop us into a black hole as to open us up to a cosmos. It makes us want to die" (1987, p. 348). Yet even here, as elsewhere in *ATP*, the context of their writing is the de/reterritorialization of music and the refrain.

[26] See Deleuze's book on Leibniz: *The Fold* (1993).

and mirror are always in front, offering what is seen at a distance. Audibility has no such limitation. In the nonspaces of audible experience, a new duration of thinking, a time of thinking, opens to a coexistence of past and future in an interplay with each other, a question of understanding that does not yet understand. Sound and seeing are associated with objects in space, the fixity of present time and achieved understandings. But unseeing audibility—the thinking that *continues* a relationship of hearing and listening—is a relation with the multiplicity of time. It works between the recollections of the knowable and the projection into future ideas. *Un*-seeing is an *other*-seeing, an imagining that is not dictated by the distance of objects in space. In their joining and their fragmentation, unseeing and audibility at their most powerful allow what Kierkegaard and Deleuze describe and what Malick makes: to open to a new plane of actuality. Hearing and listening that legitimizes the world of things reinforces convention. But audibility in a relation with memory and time ruptures identities of visibilities and statements and invites a new path that works along the limits of understanding, the zones of faith and belief, the infinite within the finite: "If seeing and speaking are forms of exteriority, thinking addresses itself to an outside that has no form. To think is to reach the non-stratified. Seeing is thinking, and speaking is thinking, but thinking occurs in the interstice, or the disjunction between seeing and speaking" (Deleuze, 1988, p. 87). In this, Malick's cinema accomplishes what Deleuze can only implore, to split from the strata of presumed causality, with its determinate objects and its sounds: "Thinking does not depend on a beautiful interiority that would reunite the visible and the articulable elements, but is carried under the intrusion of an outside that eats into the interval and forces or dismembers the internal" (p. 87). A Malick film lives on these interjections that invite another plane, a plane that explores the furthest reaches of the *logos* his characters make or, to their peril, ignore. His characters at their most authentic break from the present and think their movement toward a not yet defined zone of new actualization. Such actualization does not end but continues to express the intermingling of faith and ethics within themes of redemption, forgiveness, love, God and family. So often in Malick's characters, these zones were previously closed but can now move forward into new relations. "In this way the outside is always an opening on to a future: nothing ends, since nothing has begun, but everything is transformed" (p. 89).

Wittgenstein writes that the sense of any sentence must obey its logic, and that when language goes on holiday, philosophical problems emerge

(2009). Audibility and unseeing blur the sharp lines of propositions and are therefore worthy problems to explore. Deleuze and Guattari write that propositions are often confused with concepts; the former are discursive and the latter are expressions of bodies and events, inextricable from their history (1991). Concepts are vibrating centers that resist coherence and correspondence with each other and instead meet up in zones where they "freely enter into relationships of nondiscursive resonance" (p. 23). The confusion of concept and proposition is manifest in a prevailing and problematic "language of cinema," which applies a propositional method to a conceptual field. In the audible relation there are no propositions, no signifiers, no referents, nor even a language. Unlike music and speaking, audibility has no *a priori* system to contain it and from which it gives expression. Audibility is the capacity in oneself for thinking, which *may then* utter the statement or find the representation. But it is also a capacity that may continue to think rather than to land, to maintain the question.

Consider cinema's three classes of sound: dialogue, music, and sound effects. Of the three, only the last has no grammar, no syntax, no form. In lived experience it does not even have a name. It is the repetition of chaos. As such, it is often discounted as "noise" or, if given present attention, named as "sound," usually in a *secondary* status as the "sound of" something which is phenomenologically or empirically higher.[27] In unseeing audibility there is no answer, no *of*, unless one decides as such. Deciding is not audibility but its outcome, not *logos* but its outcome, not Kierkegaard's moment but its outcome. Yet, more often than not, sound and hearing share the hiddenness of being ignored through the neglect of acceptance and habit. There is nothing to hold unless one takes hold in thought, in audibility. Sound can be kept in memory as *echoic*. But the aspect of memory offered here is something else. Rather than objectifying sound through capture, one regains the events of the past through the coexistence of audibility and unseeing that repeats forward. Audibility is an actual duration that resonates the virtual, but the coexistence holds only so long as the virtual continues to live within the actual. This durational coexistence is the repetition. Rather than a passive virtual, audibility is one of receptivity, activation, and creation that seeds the unfolding of time. This is Malick's unseeing cinema. With its time that thinks comes the chance for redemption, forgiveness, or something else that has no name.

---

[27] Sound theory is often consumed by this phenomenological, empirical or empiricist "sound of." From the secondary qualities of Locke to the "aural objects" of Metz and continuing into more contemporary scholarship.

REFERENCES

Texts Cited

Cavell, S., & Klevan, A. (2005). What Becomes of Thinking on Film? In R. Reed & J. Goodenough (Eds.), *Film as Philosophy: Essays in Cinema After Wittgenstein and Cavell* (pp. 167–209). New York: Palgrave Macmillan.
Deleuze, G. (1988). *Foucault* (S. Hand, Trans.). Minneapolis: Minnesota University Press.
Deleuze, G. (1990). *Expressionism in Philosophy: Spinoza* (M. Joughin, Trans.). Brooklyn: Zone.
Deleuze, G. (1993). *The Fold: Leibniz and the Baroque* (S. Hand, Trans.). London: Athlone.
Deleuze, G. (1994). *Difference and Repetition* (P. Patton, Trans.). New York: Columbia University Press.
Deleuze, G. (2000). *Proust and Signs: The Complete Text* (R. Howard, Trans.). Minneapolis: University of Minnesota Press.
Deleuze, G. (2015). *What Is Grounding?* (A. Kleinherenbrink, Trans.). Grand Rapids: &&& Publishing.
Deleuze, G., & Guattari, F. (1986). *Kafka: Toward a Minor Literature*. Minneapolis: University of Minnesota Press.
Deleuze, G., & Guattari, F. (1987). *A Thousand Plateaus*. Minneapolis: University of Minnesota Press.
Deleuze, G., & Guattari, F. (1991). *What Is Philosophy?* (H. Tomlinson & G. Burchell, Trans.). New York: Columbia University Press.
Elsaesser, T., & Hagener, M. (2010). *Film Theory: An Introduction Through the Senses*. New York: Routledge.
Goodenough, J. (2005). Introduction I: A Philosopher Goes to the Cinema. In R. Read & J. Goodenough (Eds.), *Film as Philosophy: Essays in Cinema After Wittgenstein and Cavell* (pp. 1–28). New York: Palgrave Macmillan.
Heidegger, M. (1984). *Early Greek Thinking* (D. F. Krell & F. A. Capuzi, Trans.). San Francisco: Harper.
James, W. (2002). *The Varieties of Religious Experience*. Mineola: Dover.
Kierkegaard, S. (2009). *Repetition and Philosophical Crumbs* (M. G. Piety, Trans.). Oxford: Oxford University Press.
Malick, T. (1969). Translator's Introduction. In M. Heidegger (Ed.), *The Essence of Reasons* (pp. xi–xviii). Evanston: Northwestern University Press.
Mitry, J. (1997). *The Aesthetics and Psychology of the Cinema* (C. King, Trans.). Bloomington: Indiana University Press.
Mulhall, S. (2008). *On Film* (2nd ed.). New York: Routledge.
Rizzo, T. (2012). *Deleuze and Film: A Feminist Introduction*. London: Continuum.

Serres, M. (2012). *Biogea* (R. Burks, Trans.). Minneapolis: Univocal.
Sinnerbrink, R. (2006). A Heideggerian Cinema?: On Terence Malick's *The Thin Red Line*. *Film-Philosophy, 10*(3), 26–37.
Sinnerbrink, R. (2011). *New Philosophies of Film: Thinking Images*. New York: Continuum.
Wittgenstein, L. (2009). *Philosophical Investigations*. Malden: Blackwell.

CHAPTER 2

Unseeing

A photograph—as a technological reproduction and a material object—has no sound embedded within its form. Materially devoid of its own motion, time is nonetheless ingrained in what constitutes its moment, an overlapping of durations that joins a history beyond the frame of its capturing, an activity of capture, and as one captures a referent in an activity of viewing. With time comes the possibility of implied audibility owing to the image's temporal and historical dimensions that transcend it and make it what it is. Because the image is still, one's experience of it is entirely reflective, an extended moment of a more extensive time. One brings an imagined narrative to this point between a past prior to its capture (the referent's history) and another past that is in the viewing (the image's history that includes its being viewed). In the viewing is a coexistence of this dual history and an assumption of the referent's continuance into a prior future that continued beyond its capture. A photograph is not only an image of what happened but also an imagining of what happened after that—together engendering a sense of wonder that creates a fiction. As imagined, this narrative act is neither told nor entirely seen. There is an *unseeing* that imagines events beyond what is seen, which makes the image meaningful. This coexistence of history, reverie, and imagination is, when one gathers it, what constitutes the photograph.

Many have written about the ability to live inside what one personally seeks and presumes to find in the image. Walter Benjamin takes note of the "image worlds, which dwell in the smallest things—meaningful yet covert enough to find a hiding place in waking dreams, but which, enlarged and capable of formulation, make the difference between technology and magic visible as a thoroughly historical variable" (Benjamin, 1999, p. 512). This dwelling and dreaming is the measureless time of suspension, one that allows the spectator into it. Gaston Bachelard writes that brilliant photographers are able to offer a "*duration of reverie*" to an image's viewership (1960, p. 120). "With an image which is not ours, sometimes with a very singular image, we are called to dream in depth" (p. 125). Victor Burgin writes of the signification in the joined duration of photographer and viewer: "The signifying system of photography, like that of classical painting, at once depicts the scene and *the gaze of the spectator*, an object *and* a viewing subject" (1982, p. 146).

Roland Barthes situates his gaze as that which engages in the time of discovery, most sharply with his *punctum* as one's own participation in its event. Such a find lies within a broader ontology expressed so evocatively in his *Camera Lucida* (1981). One of Barthes's intriguing themes in this work is to recognize that I (he) am the one who discovers while the thing (the referent) is what is discovered, without creating a subjective/objective duality. His act of discovery within the photograph is almost like the act of discovery in the world, except that there is *this* representation as the enabler of one's act. For the active viewer, the representation (the photograph) disappears and one goes straight to the referent. As he firmly states: "the referent adheres" (1981, p. 6). Barthes does not want to reduce the image solely to a photograph, a representation. He wants to find something that resonates—we might say, not the photograph but something independent of it, something within the event and its history that is personal to him. The referent, the object, is the "*necessarily* real thing which has been placed before the lens, without which there would be no photograph" (p. 77). The photograph doesn't show the referent; the referent is what constitutes the photograph, the latter being "an emanation of the referent" (p. 80). "The image, says phenomenology, is an object-as-nothing. Now, in the Photograph, what I posit is not only the absence of the object; it is also, by one and the same movement, on equal terms, the fact that this object has indeed existed and that it has been there where I see it. Here is where madness is…a bizarre medium…hallucination: false on the level of perception, true on the level of time" (Barthes, 1981, p. 115). Barthes here is likely responding to Jean-Paul Sartre's phenomenology, which states that an "image" is that of memory, as distinct from its actual object (2004). The image, Sartre writes, therefore presents an empty intentionality—nothing, or no thing. Yet Barthes is suggesting that the photograph carries its own contradiction, as memory whose referent remains and continues. The madness of contradictions in the still image, as Barthes writes, is that it is fixed in time, as itself and as a moment; yet it bears time, both in itself and in its active reception. To suggest that a photograph is without time is to claim that memory does not exist. Because we do have memory, and a capability for recollecting, the photograph exists—and sanity can contemplate madness.

Memory and time are the seed and its fertilization of one's *audibility*, which is the engagement with the moment that opens to the time of oneself. Within unseeing, audibility complicates the present and poses a challenge to the signification and significance of the moment.[1] In the actuality of a present unfolding, a virtual field of potential relations becomes available for a gathering. Sound in the world and audibility as one's actual relation require a time that is shared, a *simultaneity*. But audibility is also a virtual relation of past and future, and here lies a potentially infinite *coexistence*. This actual/virtual milieu comes from Deleuze's readings of Bergson, who writes of the mirror image that not only reflects but also *envelops* the real. Deleuze adds that in the actual/virtual relation, it is as if "a photo or a postcard came to life, assumed independence and passed into the actual" and then back into the photo again (Deleuze, 1989, p. 68). Yet, unlike the photograph, there is no instant of capture in the sonic or the audible. There is no phenomenology at all in a state of pure hearing (hearing as immediate perception without idea). One cannot pick up an image of sound, hold it, isolate its time. In Barthes's use of the term, there is no referent. There is instead an *inferential condition*—like cinema, a gathering of durations in a *logos* not limited to language.

Reverie, understanding, and comprehension require the injection of a *new* time, a time for these faculties to do their work. In Ridley Scott's *Blade Runner* (1982), this concept is offered beautifully in a close-up of a photograph. It is a picture of Rachel's (Sean Young) childhood, one that never existed. As Deckard (Harrison Ford) gazes at it, there is a quick, barely perceptible moment before the cutaway. We can just barely hear the sound of children's laughter while a shadow moves across the photo. One might say that this briefest of shudders is Deckard projecting time into the referent that this photograph, as false evidence, lacks. Perhaps it marks the

---

[1] For more on this signification and significance, see Manuel Delanda's lecture "Deleuze, Subjectivity, and Knowledge" (2011).

time of his first unthought expression of love—a hope of *giving* her time, a history, born of his belief in her humanity. In any case, there is hearing that draws forth a recollection—not real, but hoped for—*imagined* as a projection forward. We can therefore also reverse this equation, but with a variation: audibility is the time of reaping what has been sown as memory. The materiality of what is named "sound" is irrelevant to what audibility gathers in thinking. This temporal moment is an illusion in Scott's film itself. One might claim that in this shot the referent moves, but it does not. The shadow shifts across the *photograph*, not the image. What gives the image time is this barely audible laughter—a moment of audibility, forgettable as sound—that gives the *impression* of movement.

This necessitates an important distinction in whose phenomenology is at work in this reverie. We do not hold the photograph; Deckard does. The audioviewer beholds *his* reverie, his hearing of time. While he holds the object of a photograph and seeks within it, his attentive act sees neither object nor referent. The object disappears to emphasize the image, here "image" being the thinking or *imagining* of time that we often name as memory. He is not seeking her but is seeking her time, asking the wordless question: Is this time of hers real? What is initially apprehended becomes an imagining through this audibility within him, through the time that his audibility gathers to make the imagining. In this act, cinema takes on a thinking within itself; it has a way of expressing what needs not be stated or understood. The unstated and imagined, the felt and recollected, the hearing and listening—all gather and shape what rides along the borderlines of knowability: what is, what may have been, and whatever is unseen in the seeing.

This experience Scott gives to his character Deckard lasts for an instant—in fact, only a few frames. In Malick it is not an instant; rather, it is the experience that carries his cinema. If Deckard is seeking in the photograph a time that was once real intersecting with this time that is undoubtedly real, Malick finds this image through the opening of an audibility that has nothing to look at and has not yet been seen. Hearing and listening engages one's faculties of memory and imagination, allowing one to open to an image of thinking. This was the oral tradition of poetics, *poiesis*—that the story as gathered in listening opens one's mind to the creation of imagery. Where Malick is different from Scott is that the former *opens* this imagery that is thought. As Deckard hears, we imagine that he imagines, that he creates imagery in his mind. But Malick reveals this thinking, the thinking of his characters, *through his very imagery*. We see

Deckard himself experience this in a later scene. His plucking at the piano opens his thought to a unicorn, and here we do see the image of thinking. But it is only for a moment and then it is gone. Both the photograph and the unicorn are reveries, but with Malick, it eventually becomes his entire cinema. He builds in extended, overlapping durations of coexistence that his characters unfold. This was first explored through the soldiers in *The Thin Red Line*. It becomes more prevalent in the films that follow, and by the time Malick gets to *The Tree of Life*, almost the entire film is a coexistence of durations, in which memory is not only recalled but also becomes a *repetition*, a future recollection in the spirit of Kierkegaard.

Problems of Language and Representation

Cinema can be theorized or philosophized in many ways, reaching back in Western thought to Plato and Aristotle. Both worked through questions of art and poetics that continue to be studied today. Plato's distinction of *mimesis* (representation) and *diegesis* (narration) was picked up by Aristotle, whose codification of the elements of theater informs the dramatic structure of contemporary cinema. At the level of *mimesis* one can claim, as is often the case, that a film is a series of images, with its objects and events representing nature and ideas. A more "diegetic" perspective is one that analyzes a film at the semiological level—both in the Greek sense "as spoken" and in the more structuralist adoption of the term in the context of language, text, readings, and speakings. Indeed, *diegesis* has become the theoretical framework for determining an audible ontology in contemporary discourses on film sound. The problem with such theories, as applied to cinema, is that they prioritize audience and reception over immanent experience.

Conceived at the level of experience, the discussion may turn instead from what cinema is to the life that is lived by those within it. This reaches back even further to Homer, Anaxagoras, Heraclitus, and Parmenides and the question of the "made" world. The *demiurge*, for example, is not God but the creator god, while *nous* is God's floating intelligence that seeds the mind. Then there is *logos*, which is perhaps the most enigmatic of concepts, appropriated in various ways to systematize, *a priori*, logic, reason, God's transcendent "Word," or the truth waiting to be revealed through language. Yet unlike the transcendence of *demiurge* and *nous*, Heraclitus's *logos* is neither internal nor external, but made in one's immanent, unseeing audible relations. All such concepts are developed to come to terms with the uncertainties of lived experience. Before the dogmas of religion, philosophy formulated concepts about how the world was made and what was the right way to live. The matter as it pertains to cinema is this: perhaps the world is made, and that is a speculation for other writers, but there is no doubt that cinema is *actually* made. When one takes a step outside of cinema as mimetic, diegetic, or textual and asks the question from here, at the level of real experience, the discourse changes to what is involved in its making.

Unseeing cinema does not aim to overturn representation and language, but it opens to a different relation—that of *logos* and, another Greek term, *nomos*. These two words are not normally associated with poetic theater or contemporary cinema because, at least in the older Greek use, neither adheres to the *observable* knowledge/aesthetic conceptions of Greek *eidos* (appearances) or *techne* (art). But they do reside at the level of experience when one conceives of a film as its *own world of relations*, binding the flux of life in a way that is other than art, statement, or appearance. *Logos* here is not statement, nor is it prior to its own unfolding. It is the gathering of memory within the audible moment of real life, engaging one's faculties of listening and hearing that are given thought in unseeing. It is not a dualism, not restricted to mind, but is relational to a mutable, distributive, nomadic conception of laws, which the Greeks referred to as *nomos*. *Logos* together with *nomos* become an engagement of thinking that is mutable and relational, not only to each other but also for the person who listens to what is always being heard. This *relational* aspect is key to the concept. *Logos* is not private, as Heraclitus reminds us, but, rather, thinks in a way other than appearance and representation—in effect, deterritorializing and reterritorializing what is presumed as understood. These two concepts fall under neither *diegesis* nor *mimesis* because, again, in Greek poetic conceptions, such terms lie at the level of audience, voice, and representation—narration *to* the distant listening of words and imitating *for* the distant seeing of things. *Logos* is thinking as a relation to life and its time of living—its present, past, and future actions, events, and situations, neither mimetic nor diegetic to any other object, action, or statement; rather, it is *real to its inhabitants*. The emphasis is not what cinema is but how cinema unfolds lived experience in the creation of new images.

Film Semiology and Its Structures

Before going too far into the world of a film and the *logos* that binds it in unseeing, it is important to address these acts of distancing that are often at the forefront of discourses on cinema. Here the notion of a film language runs deep. We find it in Béla Balázs's "form-language," D. W. Griffiths's "syntax," and Christian Metz's semiology and psychoanalysis, and it continues today. The reasons for maintaining a distance are vast, but for the scope of this work we can highlight first the problem of claiming, with its loaded implications, any *reality* to cinematic imagery. Cinema is, among other claims, an associational art. Giving cinema a language relation absolves one from making assertions about what it *is* ontologically from what is *seen* and therefore capable of analysis. To write "This film is" is considered bad analysis, but to write that "This film says" or that "One can read from" the film provides the safety of analysis and interpretation. In a cinema as language, one endows it with a familiar constructive, referential component and a way of thinking *about* a film. Jean Mitry, in writing about Ferdinand de Saussure, states that linguistics is the "ideal reference" for experience (1997). It endows that which is not language with an analytical framework. The presence of language is so ingrained, so knowable a function of reasoning and interpretation, that it provides a useful model for nonlinguistic structures of expression. The difficulty of such a conception is evident in writers like Metz and James Monaco. Metz claims that one can justify a cinematic language without having to apply it to a *langue*, or some system of language (1974). Monaco similarly wavers—on the one hand claiming it is not a language but on the other "like a language," even though he admits, like Metz, that it has no system (2000).

Although he uses the word *language*, Balázs comes closer than the others mentioned here to describing *experiences* that some filmmakers are able to express cinematically. His "form-language" is nonsystemic, nonlexical, speculative, and experiential, conceiving of a "gestural" expression of movement (1952). "Understandings" come not through any referential system but, rather, because it is learned and must be learned to be understandable. He emphasizes that the silent film returns us to our "aboriginal mother-tongue" of gesture and affect, the language before words and speaking. Through Griffith and others, the division of associations came with the cut. But rather than forming into a syntactical system, Balázs finds a living montage that unfolds as a "mosaic," and it is through this that cinema's form-language can be learned. The distancing that is evident in stage theater "fades out of the consciousness of the spectator" in film experience (p. 48). A film's fragmented montage holds together because this mosaic is "an association of ideas, a synthesis of consciousness and imagination" (p. 53). For semiologists like Metz, montage is a syntagmatic arrangement, akin to that of a phrase or a sentence (Metz, 1974).

Balázs's mosaic is not linguistic, but is experiential and nonreductive. What Balázs does not say is that this cinematic learning is in fact simply learning, since cinema is *also* an extension of our lived relations.

For Mitry, there is no one language; rather, there are different systems for organizing thought. Film, he writes, is "*first and foremost*" grounded in images (1977). Images come from reality but have the possibility to become signs. In doing so, images act as a means of "expression" while their *organization* takes on the language function. This organizational language is an "organic structure" that enables such expression. In this way, cinema is not a discursive language—not predicated on some preexistent system of discourse—but instead a developed language. He mentions that prior to spoken language, early human beings thought in "mental shapes." Early directors had no film language, and so they constructed associations. Insofar as it expresses its language, cinema's is necessarily vague, which for Mitry is what enables it to rise to the level of poetry. We must question, however, the need to name cinema as language at all, given all the prostrations it wades through.

Deleuze's "Utterable"

We can find a better conception of cinema's relational engagement through Deleuze. In his reading of Metz's semiological framework, cinema is language in (1) its factuality, its having become a narrative art; and (2) its syntagmatic instances of "approximation," with the shot as the smallest "oral utterance" in any narrative (Deleuze, 1989, p. 25). For Deleuze, images are not narrated; rather, narration is a consequence of the images as "initially defined for themselves" in their activity (1989, p. 27). Here Deleuze is elevating the status of the image but also extending his work from *Difference and Repetition* (1994)—that is, his resistance to any act or event that falls back onto a preexisting analogy or resemblance. To reverse the pole and put it another way, he resists any prior identity that dictates what unfolds in thinking—in this case, art and in this particular case, cinema. His problem with a semiology of film is that it reduces the image to an "analogical sign belonging to an utterance" and consequently some structure that underlies it (1989, p. 27). For Deleuze, what is expressed is the process of differentiation that is within the image in its movement: the movement-image that constitutes its significance in the event. In his concluding chapter in *Cinema 2*, Deleuze returns to this issue and addresses more specifically whether cinema can be thought of as a language. In so doing, he reveals his particular outlook on experience itself. "Cinema is not a universal or primitive language system [*langue*], nor a language [*langage*]. It brings to light an intelligible content which is like a presupposition, a condition, a necessary correlate through which language constructs its own 'objects' (signifying units and operations)" (1989, p. 262). Cinema builds this inseparable correlation in "movements and thought-process (pre-linguistic images), and points of view on these movements and processes (pre-signifying signs)." Taken together, its whole constitutes a "'psychomechanics,' the spiritual automaton, the utterable of a language system which has its own logic. The language system takes utterances of language, with signifying units and operations from it, but the utterable itself, its images and signs, are of another nature" (p. 262). This "utterable itself" is a network of images and signs distinct from, and lived prior to, any statement. In cinema as well as—and as an aspect of—experience, there is no *a priori* system of signification in our encounters with phenomena. Where language may enter is in the utterance, written and spoken through language itself, in applying *its* system as a means of expression entering into concepts and discourse about the utterable. But this is not cinema; it is discourse *about* cinema or, for the characters of any film world, discourse *within* cinema.

Deleuze is offering an experiential *semiotics* rather than a semiology. This places emphasis on the motivation of any expression or affect rather than identities from the relation that becomes codified into images and statements. It relaxes any structure of Saussurean signifier, signified, object, or referent in favor of the actuality of relations, which as themselves emphasize what is unseen and not yet known. This distinction is particularly relevant in audible encounters, something Deleuze largely ignores: unseeing audibility is linked by presupposition and precognition. *Unseeing* sees what is present and thereby presupposes one's understanding. *Audibility* is a precognition that makes no supposition; it unfolds what is unseen before any linguistic or rational signification takes hold. To put this another way, what one sees dominates present-actual processes of understanding. But within such seeing there is also unseeing thought, whose own actuality is free to draw from a virtual temporality, which coexists within the moment. Audibility invites and unfolds this coexistence.

Returning again to cinema's utterable, Deleuze writes that even when it speaks verbally, cinema "is neither a language system nor a language. It is a plastic mass, an a-signifying and a-syntaxic material, a material not formed linguistically even though it is not amorphous and is formed semiotically, aesthetically and pragmatically. It is a condition, anterior by right to what it conditions. It is not an enunciation, and these are not utterances. It is an *utterable*" (1989, p. 29). We can think of the utterance as what becomes sound-as-discursive, or what is said. Only then does thought enter into reference or analogy—an understandable matter about which one speaks. The utterable, however, is that which may give rise to *any* potential engagement. One such engagement is audibility. This ability is not a given, but is that which may emerge from within that which is available insofar as one is open to it. In other words, if language as sonic is the utterance, audibility is the utterability—a plane of potentiality within the encounter, which may or may not give rise to an utterance. The problem is that once language lays *claim* to the utterable, Deleuze suggests, such utterances come to "dominate or even replace" what previously embodied its own matter (1989, p. 29).

For Metz, turning the assembly of images into a language is what shifted film from a visual medium to a narrative one. Language and sight thereby become embedded in the art of montage. For the Russian revolutionary filmmakers, montage was cinema's art, but was also its weapon, a visual means toward conceptual argumentation.[2] Supposing one were to grant a grammar to montage—a shot is a word, a sequence a sentence, a scene a paragraph—perhaps it is appropriate given that both montage and language are linear.[3] With the coming of sound to cinema, a new question arises: If the collision of image associations forms an argument or poetic statement, what is the discursivity of footsteps, a distant train whistle, the hum of a factory, or the noise of some indiscernible variable in an unseeing?[4] Are they merely adjectives and adverbs to montage's nouns and verbs, or are they something other than this presumed language? The early writers about the sound film proposed that sonic elements form the antithesis of a dialectical relation in montage, often stated as "counterpoint," and

[2] The "principle means of influence," as Eisenstein, Pudovkin, and Alexandrov called montage (1988).

[3] Sinnerbrink as well mentions the implausibility of comparing a shot to a word (2011). Images, he notes, are more complex than words. What he does not mention is that sounds and one's audibility raises the complexity beyond even referentiality.

[4] Rick Altman writes about "discursification" in film and television (1986). For him, the sound of TV is "far more discursive as a whole, openly interpellating, addressing the audience, and thus involving spectators in dialogue, enjoining them to look, to see, to partake in that which is offered up for vision" (p. 597). Film, by contrast, is nondiscursive, he writes, because it presumes a secure, predictable voyeur who simply watches. Yet even this viewer who watches could be considered a "reader" by way of Altman placing the viewer at an observable distance. I reject the voyeuristic viewer in favor of an empathetic engagement.

reside in their symbolic reference. But as the craft of its design grew over the decades that followed, sound, and hearing, gained independence from the montage while maintaining inseparability from the world. Hearing moves across, within, and outside of montage, not only conceptually but also as itself in the event of sounding that joins with hearing. It is today neither anti- nor counter- but, rather, finds its own expression, as Balázs hoped. Michel Chion writes that even if one can conceive of a visual language, "an *audiovisual language*, if there is one, cannot be envisaged or encoded like a visual language" (2009, p. 231). In fact, it should not be encoded as language at all. Sergi Eisenstein, Vsevolod Pudovkin, and Grigori Alexandrov were astute in their warning in 1928 that sound should not fall into a supportive relation with montage but, instead, should be antagonistic to it, as a means of constructing new ideas (1988). Yet even here one can borrow from feminist theory and ask why the audible must be the "other" to a dominant visual lexis. Even if one were to accept a visual grammar of film, sound cannot function solely to maintain the ideology of linear montage, its objects, and its methods of analysis. It must emerge as its own expression and seek out its own time.

Sound Theory and the Hegemony of the Material Image

With a language of cinema, we are only facing the film; we have not yet gone within. To do so we must break the distance of the gaze. Taken visually, any film invites a form of textuality, as well as objective considerations of things and their spatial relations. Taken as audible rather than visual or sonic, the soundtrack has the capacity to live outside of present space and independent of the distance of sight. While the meeting of sound and hearing may occur in space, this constitutes only the direct, present relation. Time is the audible involvement that stretches into a *durational* relation with memory, thought, and signs. Conceived in such a manner, cinema finds itself in a semiotic unfolding, born not of identity (*mimesis*, representation) nor from preexistent systems (language, music) but, instead, emerging as differences, associations, and a kind of thinking that maintains rather than answers its questions. An audible design as a semiotic relation is a relation of experience. It has the capacity to evoke one's unseeing associations born of lived experience. One need not recall any specific visual memory for it to occur but, rather, have lived within the sensory world, where one accepts, rejects, and engages its fragmented suggestions. These unseeing states are the reason why such codes work, but also the reason they should aim to be broken. Cinema is the life of a world that intimates in sensation.[5]

Sound theory regularly addresses the lie of synchronization that creates the ideology of audiovisual unity. But its methods are just as often dealing with matters of spatial distance, affirming this ideology. Distances demand analysis and prehension in order to overcome the dual divisions of sound/image and screen/audioviewer. Cinema as reception, representation, cognition, and semiology place the audioviewer at a privileged level in this distance. This sets up a conjoined bias of cinema as exclusively visual and lexical. Such thinking is also found in sound studies, which often conceive sound as a duality of diegetic and nondiegetic. *Diegesis* in Greek means "narration." But during the 1970s and 80s, film theory devised a reversal: *diegesis* took the place of *mimesis* and became the film's "real" world.[6] It was decided then that through narration, images arise. There are four interrelated problems with this *diegesis* as applied to film sound: (1) it proposes a *material* duality that dictates what is real (diegetic) and what is unreal (nondiegetic) to itself, grounding endless arguments that analyze what is or is not sounding from *within* the film world; (2) it is a *lexical* concept that presumes a film is read in a linear fashion; (3) most problematic is that it reinforces what is visual and material in its presence or its absence in a spatial conception; and (4) all of this is for the benefit of the audioviewer, who sits outside of what is real.

At its core, this contemporary conception of *diegesis* establishes a materialistic duality by spatial ontology. The structural elements of cinematic narrative, such as sound (or music), is either physically present in the world, and at least *accessible* to its characters, or it is not. If there is a so-called blending or ambiguity between the diegetic and nondiegetic, it is only possible because the film establishes a *material* point of reference and the ambiguity approaches or departs from such a visual, spatial point. In other words, a matter–space ontology is established and ambiguity becomes a kind of variation on states of awareness to it. This ties sound to some preexisting space regardless, once the question of ambiguity arises.

---

[5] The "life of our soul in its very intensity is much more adequately expressed in a glance, a sound, a gesture, than in a speech" (Arendt, 1978, p. 31).

[6] See for example Doane (1985), Bordwell & Thompson (1985), Gorbman (1987), Chion (1994, 2009), and Taylor (2007).

And because it is tied to space, its ontological negation is only accessible via the privilege of the audience, thereby creating a divide—in other words, a distance. An example of this is Wagner's *Die Walküre* theme in *Apocalypse Now* (Coppola, 1979). Many film sound theorists have written about this scene as a blending from diegetic to nondiegetic music. But such a blend still moves along the yes/no binary of audience, leaving out all other potentialities. One might, for example, open instead to questions of time, the *when* of hearing rather than the *what* of sound. Or perhaps music never sounds and is instead some other expression, a way of thinking. In both of these examples, music is an immanent expression, regardless of what is spatial or sonic. With space as the ground of music's ontology, nondiegetic can connote only one thing: a transcendent spectacle for audience.

Since the coming of sound to film, nearly every theory of sound has found itself consumed by spatial and visual concerns. Two other familiar concepts found in film theory are "synchresis" (synchronized sound) and "offscreen sound" (or "acousmatic" sound). *Synchresis* is Chion's neologism for synchronization plus synthesis in which the coupling of image and sound, unrelated ontologically, takes on a dialectical third meaning in their combination. *Acousmatic* is sound that as heard is uncoupled from its visual verification. Both are in fact problems of verification based on a need to visually understand. Chion's thesis is that there is creativity in *synchresis* because the application of an object or image to an unrelated sound creates an affective disharmony. We can think again of *Apocalypse Now* and the classic shot of a ceiling fan accompanying the sound of a helicopter. Neither image nor sound alone produces the meaning that is born in the joining of the two. In offscreen or *acousmatic* conceptions, the creativity comes in the object-event being visibly absent in the hearing of the sonic-event that is normally *identified* with it. The familiar example here is in *The Wizard of Oz* (Fleming, 1939), in which a literal Pythagorean curtain opens to reveal the monstrous voice of authority as a timid man with a microphone. In both concepts a *meaning* is applied because in both there is a present *visuality*. The disharmony of *synchresis* comes from the sound being applied to the object (seen presently); the ambiguity of *acousmata* comes from the sound being applied to the object (not seen presently).

Unseeing: Deterritorializing Space, Reterritorializing Time

Unseeing as a concept and as a condition is different in two ways. First, it uncouples a *hearing* from its object-subject duality and necessity, as found in a present seeing (*synchresis*) or present not seeing (*acousmatic*/offscreen). Second, *synchresis* and *acousmatic*/offscreen are audience-directed concepts and are related to sound as given to audioviewer in the presumed audioviewing. Unseeing turns cinema away from spectatorship and into the overlaps of character and world. Since the emphasis is audible rather than sonic, time is emphasized over space. Time calls into question the identifiable and the universal to open up a lived relation, a connection to one's individual past as a movement into the future. In unseeing, one's gathering of one's own memory is an account with the past and future, through present durations of thinking, dreaming, imagining, projecting. This brings the cinematic audible into affective, resonating dimensions that do not need to be shown in the present moment. An expression of audible unseeing is an expression of one's gatherings, one's fragmented and significant associations with the past. It is a present negotiating of memories and recollections that imagines the future by reimagining the past. This opens hearing to a coexistence of times, a coexistence of durations. Following Bergson, duration as a concept frees time from its objective measure because any action, movement, or thought creates its own time. The ambiguity of *what is* therefore is not *what is this thing*, this object, but *what is this time*; it is not this thing being heard but, when is one hearing, what is one working through, what is being made.

Malick's films express this multiplicity of durations through an audibility that seeks along the various threads of thought that fragment time, allowing his characters to break from objective demands. He or she has not entirely left behind the mediation of the objective within temporality, but strives along another thinking, opening a resonance. Kierkegaard writes that "objective uncertainty" frees one from the fixity of time in a movement of passion that excites anxiety and turns one toward decisiveness (2009). Jean Wahl writes that Kierkegaard's conception of time is that of "discontinuous becoming," which counters Hegel's time as absolute. This fragmentation and emergence is "made up of crises, advancing by leaps and bounds; it is an inexplicable becoming, containing irreducibly novel elements—the upshots of our decisions" (Wahl, 1969, p. 50). This is not born of mere chaos but, instead, of the paradox of *the eternal within the moment* that cannot be understood but only expressed. Coexistence becomes an unbinding, opening to movements outside of the linearity of time and encompassing thought of the infinite or perhaps, if one wishes to name it as such, ideas of God. Deleuze's Spinozism suggests that the idea of God is an expression of the infinite, but one that has gained its power through thinking. Such shifts, flights, and other fragmentations in Malick come in repetitions of hearings that form into new images. The audible returns and repeats to divide time, to create the objective uncertainty that aims to reform a lost unity.

This takes cinema beyond Deleuze's time-image into something new. In resisting the bias of cinema as a language, Deleuze conceives it as a relation of images and signs. For him, cinema is not narrated. There is no prior structure, nothing underlies images. Images *make* narration. Malick's unseeing cinema takes this further: For him, images are not making narration but, rather, the very *activity* of creating thought, a thinking that neither speaks nor narrates nor even sees, but that listens and imagines forward. Audibility in Malick is therefore not a prehension but a return of thinking that creates its new thought.

The Matrix of Events

Conceptions of distance are not limited to film sound, but extend to a more recent trend of sound phenomenology and materialism.[7] Here we find a methodological thinking that often references Aristotle, Edmund Husserl, and Pierre Schaeffer. Again, the need here is to capture sound, to fix it to its object and its name. Through such phenomenological and nominal efforts, *sound* becomes functional and understandable through an object relation ("sound of") or by being granted an object status ("sound" or "sound object"). The familiar move is to follow Aristotle, who conceived a duality between "sonance" and "audition" (1991, p. 294). While he does conceive the latter as the "being-at-work" of consciousness, his principal interest is the motion of objects. Schaeffer, one of the more influential contemporary writers on sound, followed Husserl's phenomenological reduction to propose a "reduced listening," which placed an emphasis on the *sound object*. His *Guide Des Objets Sonores* aims to bracket our "natural attitude" of listening in order to go straight to the

---

[7] For relatively current discussions, see Nudds & O'Callaghan (2009).

sound itself.[8] His interest was in finding new methods of musical notation and expression by breaking apart the objects of sound into their "concrete" nature. Sound becomes both systematically managed and materially objectified by intending not its relational and semiotic aspects but moving toward their eventual use value.

The problem in objective considerations of what is audible is that neither sound nor hearing is an object. They comprise both a simultaneity and a coexistence of events, conceived neither as subjective nor as objective. Following William James, what we find is the overlapping of relations that themselves have a reality.[9] *Continuity*, as James conceives of the word, is one that is not occurring but *being made*. Such a "conjunctive transition" is James's counter to Kant: rather than a leap into *a priori* categories, we ride along a virtual, transitional continuum. Relations are not just relations *in* the world but also relations that *form* the world.[10] Further, there is no "bedding" on which events fall back to: "it is as if the pieces clung together by their edges, the transitions experienced between them forming their cement" (2003, p. 45). This, for James, is how experience grows by its edges both in the durations and the relations that come to be expressed. This comprises for James the flux of relations, its conjunctions, continuations, and separations. "The great continua of time, space, and the self envelop everything betwixt them, and flow together without interfering" (2003, p. 49). For James, as for Deleuze, reality is as much in the relations as in objects or things. The flux gains its reality in relations rather than in its components. Similarly, we do not find any "reality" in any object, sound, or audibility as each stands alone. Whatever is conceived of as real is in their temporal relations.

To conceive of an object is to conceive of fixity. Yet what we name as "sound of" occurs in interactions of multiple events. An *event* as applied here is a simple concept compared with Deleuze's or other contemporary uses in philosophy. An event is something like an effect, attribute, or affect that constitutes a relation that is real by the relation made *in the overlap*, and is not reducible to any one thing or object. Event does not exclusively reside in categories of force, matter, rupture, or idea but may be any of them or a combination. In thinking of events rather than objects or things,

---

[8] For an English translation, see Chion (1983).

[9] See the various essays in James (2003).

[10] Again, "world" has a range of connotations. What James names as "world" I name cinematically, and pertaining to audibility, as "*logos*."

one welcomes the notion that whatever occurs will not remain, may not appear, and is rarely entirely knowable. But its effect resonates world, *logos*, and thought.

To begin from the *sonic* is to work through a method, such as phenomenology, ontology, or materiality. Sound resides in the realm of, in the Greek sense of the term, appearances. But an epistemology of *audibility* requires a synthesis in which the time-event of the real, the time-event of the sign, and the time-event of thinking all meet in a shared duration. These three overlapping events are delineated as follows: First is the *object-event*, which is the activity of two or more objects in collision. With this, the object loses its primary and reflective stasis and is put into uncertainty through action. This is what gives rise to sound in its present-actual emergence. This conjoining—the object-event that sonifies—produces another series of complex material interactions of frequency, amplitude, and the feedback of various harmonic collisions. In this interaction—a *sonic-event*—sound ceases to be fixed and is granted its continual change even if such change constitutes a microphysics or a micropercept. A sonic-event denies that there is anything one can name as a "sound object," which is nominal, not actual. A sonic-event is a *sign* working within a semiotic, matrixial flux. Finally, the audible component is the most complex of all, the activity that one personally experiences within one's lived time—relational as *logos* in a present-actual condition. This is the fragmented unity of body, mind, and world that makes a *logos* relation: the *audible-event*. In an audible-event, one hears and listens in an actual duration that ignites a multiplicity of virtual potentiality into a circuit—the past-future and inside-outside of thinking the now.[11] Consider as well that the audible-event is the development of a thought; but more, it is the germination of what Deleuze and Guattari call the concept, "both absolute and relative" (1991). Audible thinking is relative to the plane on which an event occurs, with its array of problems; it is absolute in how it resonates as itself within a totality. This is the relationality that maintains its actuality—the wholeness of the sonic and the fragmentation of the hearing that together constitute the audible-event.

We can isolate each of these terms, as each event possesses its own infinite series of physiological and at times psychological *micro-events*, composed of and composing into singularities. At the level of attention, the event of audibility commonly subsumes all the various parts into its relation.

---

[11] For more on this taxonomy of audibility, see Batcho (2017).

But *logos* is manifest only as one maintains the various *relational* aspects of events. The flux of overlaps complicates thinking and composes new thought. This is the critically important point of what is named here as audibility, particularly as it concerns unseeing: any object, sound, or audible state is a repetition that is not a copy. Ontologically, only this tree falls in this forest and, because of this, is only this original sound. It is a repetition because the event of each has happened repeatedly—other trees have fallen and made other sounds—but not in this particular combination, at this time. Each fall (object-event), each sound of a fall (sonic-event), and each hearing of a fall (audible-event) is its own new creation as a repetition; but the three *together* are what create a complex state of newness. Audibility is the core element that is the relation both actual in the moment and virtual of the time that cycles, conditions, and shapes the moment. The entirety of one's experience comes to inform this instant that projects forward. It is the idea of the idea, as Deleuze wrote about Spinoza's power of thinking (1990). One's knowledge is not an understanding of the thing; rather, understanding is composed out of one's particular gathering of the conjoined event. So while we may be able to divide each event category nominally, we cannot divide them existentially.[12] The emphasis cannot be in the isolation of each. Instead, we concern ourselves with the *haecceity* of the relation of any two or three, particularly the existential involvement with the event that is audible. This and only this event of falls/sounds/is-heard is the conjoined repetition. This has never occurred before and never will again. We name it as "the sound of a tree falling" because of the general necessity of habit and naming, but it itself is a new repetition. Just as any single event is original, the complexity of its originality is even deeper in the flux of relations. Where things become cinematically interesting is when something in the flux is out of joint: sonic-/audible-event without object-event, audible-/object-event without the sonic-event, etc., or when one aspect resides on a different temporal plane from another. This is where one finds another repetition, a repetition that loses identity and comes to play more strongly with the forces of the virtual and questions of transcendence within such actual events. Here in the repetition, circuits fluctuate as concepts resonate and vibrate new thinking—inferential and nondiscursive. This is the repetition of Kierkegaard and Deleuze—a memory of the future.

---

[12] Here I'm borrowing from Kierkegaard's language (2009). What I mean here is that one can categorize something as object, sound or audible, but we cannot categorize how it is experienced in any moment.

Rather than a flux, I propose that audibility engages in a matrixial relation. This is borrowed from Bracha Ettinger, for whom the term "matrix" is central to her conception of the generative, spatiotemporal womb of creativity and imagination (2006). *Matrix* etymologically is "womb" and what is matrixial lives within a borderspace that for Ettinger is female in its generative capacity. I employ this term to hearing because in Ettinger's creative works, the matrixial describes *becoming* in ways that are *not* bound to visual, objective, or subjective identities and prehension. Conceiving of a semiotic matrix of audibility therefore addresses another problem of distancing in film sound theory—that of a subject/object duality, employed in cinema as yet another material and visual distinction. We can think of the objective aspect as a universal acceptance of a film world's objects: a rational continuity that establishes a believable world. In practice, objectivity in cinema comes through its developed conventions of visual-spatial camera positioning, invisible editing, and continuity in sound. Film subjectivity is by opposition a means of using the apparatus of film to shift from a self-independent (objective) position to a personal and embodied one in order to connect an audience more directly to a character's condition.

Taken to the level of hearing, an objective/subjective duality implies materiality by temporary negation, wherein for the moment our hearing is other than objective truth—i.e., thought or consciousness. Yet as applied in a film, such subjectivity remains tied to the character who sees. If one wants to place an ontology of hearing to any shot, it lies generally in a relation to the camera eye. At its most common, hearing then assumes an *identity*, as identical, with the camera. But audibility is the aspect of cinema uniquely capable of escaping such identity. Hearing is always there, hovering, moving, existing, projecting, not because of the camera but in an acknowledgment that audibility *also* exists and offers a disclosure in its own manner. This breaks from these adherences to space, visuality, and audience given in terms such as *synchresis*, *diegesis*, *acousmatic*, and *off-screen*. Audibility has the power of not showing up, of extending any seeing into a time given birth in unseeing. It can move through some elsewhere in another, perhaps indeterminate, time. Through this, another plane is made, a coexisting audible one that can disjoin or delegitimize images from their presumed time. This is not a division such as with *diegesis*, for any hearing must maintain itself within the *logos* of the film. But even in its inseparability, it can seek out its own independence. The camera cannot do this; once the camera gains independence from a space, it has separated itself from where and when it is.

An Immanent Gathering

Cavell writes that a film offers *this* view and not another, *this* place and not another, *this* time and not another.[13] This is visually accurate, but audibility is not so confined to place and its space, particularly for its characters, for whom audibility is a means of dividing or moving outside of time without needing to divide space. The mind's ear and its virtual gatherings grant a particular agency to a character, an individual, to move within her world and reach outside of any spatial specificity. We can think again of Deckard viewing Rachel's photograph in *Blade Runner*. Through Kafka's characters, Deleuze and Guattari make a distinction between one's head bent to the photograph and one's head raised up to the sonic (1986). This is a good start for thinking audibility. Yet in Malick, the rising of his characters is less an ascension to some sonic *otherness* to the visual; rather, it opens to another field of play. We find this expressed in different ways through Kierkegaard, Heidegger, and Deleuze—the *springing* and *leaping* of thought that is ungrounded to language and things. We find this in various gatherings of *logos*: the overlaps of dreaming, recollection, and reverie and the opening of new planes of thought given flight. Audibility in a matrixial relationship with this moment of unseeing does not discount the present and the actual, but it means that one is no longer bound to it. The striving is not phenomenological *to* any identifiable place or image. And once we reach *The Tree of Life*, it is neither semiological nor semiotic, as there is no sign to signify. The call of audibility itself opens. Its unseeing expresses a *possibility* of time—its *own* time—when *now* functions as a maybe, owing to its ability to move across visual depiction and its objects. This is the unseeing aspect of audibility that takes on shifting durations of simultaneity and coexistence, hodological and crystalline, that are prevalent in Malick's cinema. There is no *diegesis* needed and the question of subjectivity opens to the folds of the experiential and the existential.

As *logos*, cinema's distances lie entirely within its world, in the fragmentations of memory and time that reach along the boundaries of the knowable and the uncertain, the recalled and the forgotten, the finite and the infinite. *Logos* gathers in immanence while transcendence takes on another question based upon the real lived experience of a particular character or entity engaged in unseeing. The variable threads of uncertainty and certainty within the engagement problematize the relation and give rise to its

---

[13] See Cavell (1979) and Cavell & Klevan (2005).

tensions. We find such tensions in the characters of the Farmer and Bill in *Days of Heaven*, the soldiers of *The Thin Red Line*, the two lovers in *The New World*, the adult Jack in *The Tree of Life*. It is not a question of what they are hearing but whether and how they come to hear, and through this, what each chooses to listen to. In Malick, immanence and transcendence become a part of film's intriguing *maybe*, which invites (in some cases forces) an act of seeking along new threads. The great ambiguity of experiential cinema is that meaning may be tremendously important to a character; but it is unimportant as a universal because there is no universal in cinema, only relations. Once meaning is decided, the engagement is lost. Their struggle—their attention and lack, their seeking that does not find—resonates the existential condition with which we as audience come to empathize.

References

Texts Cited

Altman, R. (1986). Television Sound. In T. Modleski (Ed.), *Studies in Entertainment* (pp. 566–581). Bloomington: Indiana University.

Arendt, H. (1978). *Life of the Mind*. San Diego: Harcourt.

Aristotle. (1991). On the Soul. [abridged]. In R. E. Allen (Ed.), W. S. Hett (Trans.), *Greek Philosophy: Thales to Aristotle* (pp. 292–306). New York: The Free Press.

Bachelard, G. (1960). *The Poetics of Reverie: Childhood, Language, and the Cosmos* (D. Russell, Trans.). Boston: Beacon Press.

Balázs, B. (1952). *Theory of the Film* (E. Bone, Trans.). London: Dennis Dobson.

Barthes, R. (1981). *Camera Lucida: Reflections on Photography*. New York: Hill and Wang.

Batcho, J. (2017). New Understandings in Hearing. *The New Soundtrack, 7*(1), 1–14.

Benjamin, W. (1999). Little History of Photography. In Michael W. Jennings (Ed.), *Walter Benjamin: Selected Writings, Volume 2 (1927–1934)* (pp. 507–530). Cambridge: The Belknap Press of Harvard University Press.

Bordwell, D., & Thompson, K. (1985). Fundamental Aesthetics of Sound in the Cinema. In E. Weis & J. Belton (Eds.), *Film Sound: Theory and Practice* (pp. 181–199). New York: Columbia University Press.

Burgin, V. (1982). Looking at Photographs. In V. Burgin (Ed.), *Thinking Photography* (pp. 142–153). London: Macmillan Press.

Cavell, S. (1979). *The World Viewed: Reflections on the Ontology of Film*. Cambridge, MA: Harvard University Press.

Cavell, S., & Klevan, A. (2005). What Becomes of Thinking on Film? In R. Reed & J. Goodenough (Eds.), *Film as Philosophy: Essays in Cinema After Wittgenstein and Cavell* (pp. 167–209). New York: Palgrave Macmillan.

Chion, M. (1983). *Guide Des Objets Sonores: Pierre Schaeffer et la recherche musicale* (J. Dack & C. North, Trans.). Paris: Institut National De L'Audiovisual & Éditions Buchet/Chastel. Retrieved online, January 24, 2014 at http://www.ears.dmu.ac.uk/spip.php?page=articleEars&id_article=3597

Chion, M. (1994). *Audio-vision: Sound on Screen* (C. Gorbman, Trans.). New York: Columbia University Press.

Chion, M. (2009). *Film: A Sound Art* (C. Gorbman, Trans.). New York: Columbia University Press.

Deleuze, G. (1989). *Cinema 2* (H. Tomlinson & R. Galeta, Trans.). Minneapolis: University of Minnesota Press.

Deleuze, G. (1990). *Expressionism in Philosophy: Spinoza* (M. Joughin, Trans.) Brooklyn: Zone.

Deleuze, G. (1994). *Difference and Repetition* (P. Patton, Trans.). New York: Columbia University Press.

Deleuze, G., & Guattari, F. (1986). *Kafka: Toward a Minor Literature*. Minneapolis: University of Minnesota Press.

Deleuze, G., & Guattari, F. (1991). *What Is Philosophy?* (H. Tomlinson & G. Burchell, Trans.). New York: Columbia University Press.

Doane, M. A. (1985). The Voice in the Cinema: The Articulation of Body and Space. In E. Weis & J. Belton (Eds.), *Film Sound: Theory and Practice* (pp. 163–176). New York: Columbia University Press.

Eisenstein, S. E., Pudovkin, V., & Alexandrov, G. (1988). Statement on Sound. In *S. M. Eisenstein: Selected Works Volume I, Writings, 1922–34* (pp. 113–114). London: BFI.

Ettinger, B. (2006). *The Matrixial Borderspace*. Minneapolis: University of Minnesota Press.

Gorbman, C. (1987). Narratological Perspectives on Film Music. In C. Gorbman (Ed.), *Unheard Melodies: Narrative Film Music* (pp. 11–30). Bloomington: Indiana University Press.

James, W. (2003). *Essays in Radical Empiricism*. Mineola: Dover.

Kierkegaard, S. (2009). *Concluding Unscientific Postscript to the Philosophical Crumbs* (A. Hannay, Trans.). Cambridge: Cambridge University Press.

Metz, C. (1974). *Film Language*. New York: Oxford University Press.

Mitry, J. (1997). *The Aesthetics and Psychology of the Cinema* (C. King, Trans.). Bloomington: Indiana University Press.

Monaco, J. (2000). *How to Read a Film: The World of Movies, Media, and Multimedia* (3rd ed.). New York: Oxford University Press.

Nudds, M., & O'Callaghan, C. (2009). *Sounds and Perception: New Philosophical Essays* (pp. 1–25). Oxford: Oxford University Press.

Sartre, J. (2004). *The Imaginary: A Phenomenological Psychology of the Imagination* (J. Webber, Trans.). London: Routledge.

Sinnerbrink, R. (2011). *New Philosophies of Film: Thinking Images.* New York: Continuum.

Taylor, H. M. (2007). The Success Story of a Misnomer. *Offscreen, 11*, 8–9.

Wahl, J. (1969). *Philosophies of Existence* (F. M. Lory, Trans.). London: Routledge.

Films Cited

Coppola, F. F. (Director). (1979). *Apocalypse Now* [Motion Picture]. USA: Paramount Pictures / American Zoetrope.

Fleming, V. (Director). (1939). *The Wizard of Oz.* USA: Metro-Goldwyn-Mayer/Loew's.

Scott, R. (Director). (1982). *Blade Runner* [Motion Picture]. USA: The Ladd Company, Warner Bros.

CHAPTER 3

Logos of Cinema

A *logos* does not speak; people speak. A world does not present; it exists. A Malick film does not produce sound; its characters hear and listen. Unseeing is the condition and activity of gathering and taking account as *logos*. In a Malick film, a character finds herself already in an unseeing condition of gathering in a *logos* relation. But an audioviewer is not held to the level of mere spectatorship or phenomenological distancing; rather, she enters into an existential, mnemonic, sensory, and empathetic relation with what unfolds. At the level of perception, the distance between spectator/hearer and screen/speakers is indeed insurmountable. But the vital *experiential* distance is that of engagement within itself among its characters, which engages an audioviewer when he lets go of the actuality of perceptual distance. In a *logos* of cinema there is no film but, rather, a field of engagement, a lived series of overlapping durations. The architects of any *logos* are the characters who think, live, and act within their worlds. They "make" the film by the act of being alive.

Because we are so accustomed to regarding a film as something observed or read, this might at first seem abstract. To think of cinema as *logos*, one abandons the dominance of the gaze and its lexical/visual structures. *Logos* cannot be conceived in the distance of objects, signifiers, or referents. Rather than images, a cinematic *logos* manifests in durations and events, which may then give rise to images in their creation. *Logos* is the relational component of virtual unseeing that shares its durations with actual, or present, seeing. Its primary channel is audibility, whose openness lies in *hearing*. This verb, "to hear," carries multiple meanings in different languages. Typically, "to hear" means to understand, "to *obey*."[1] But "hearing" in another connotation is the openness of availability, the unmediated, the transcendental, and the unconscious.

THE TRANSCENDENTAL IMMANENCE OF THOUGHT

This "transcendental" requires clarification. *Transcendence*, *transcending*, and *transcendental* are deep and complicated topics in philosophy. These terms will be explored as we go, but here are some introductory distinctions: *transcendence* is a realm or entity, immutable and separate from everyday reality; *transcending* is an existential act of exceeding one's limits. Both open the question of Kierkegaardian possibility and paradox, of whether one may transcend reality or one's current situation. *Transcendental* as offered here is immanence that is transformational, the potentiality of the virtual and actual, and the maybe of any experience. It is not limited to mind, spirit, or matter, but it does not discount any, wrapped as each is in the same moment of significance.

Transcendental for Deleuze was matched with empiricism as a response to Kant's transcendental idealism. But as applied to unseeing, transcendental is closely aligned with Deleuze's *virtual*. We may think of the virtual as the entirety of what may become as actual. Any actual event maintains an element of the vastness of the virtual field. The virtual and actual react and respond together, changing both an event and the whole. The virtual thereby transforms and becomes transformed by any actual and vice versa. This is informed by Deleuze's adoption of "univocity," or the immanent inseparability of thought and matter—no outside attributes, causes, or modes. Put another way, nothing is outside of transcendental reality. We can then think of the virtual as the matrix or flux of activity that may become actualized in newness, and the actual as maintaining its connection to the virtual, which together contribute to the transcendental. For the Catholic Church, the danger in such thinking was pantheism, a critique leveled at Spinoza for his univocity. The church demanded an entity beyond who judges. But for Spinoza and Deleuze there is no beyond, nothing *transcendent to* immanent reality. All is immanent within the transcendental flux of virtual and actual relations, which for Deleuze

---

[1] This is central in Heidegger's later period conception of *logos*—the laying that gathers—as the hearing that understands. See Heidegger (1984). See also Brann (2011).

manifests in difference (being) and repetition (time).[2] This is an aspect of Deleuze's philosophy that is often forgotten: any becoming or, as I call it, any *event*, is resonated by *and resonates* the whole. This applies to memory as much as to material and metaphysical relations. Any sonic- and audible-event alters and is altered by the vast matrix of life's activity. One gathers *as logos* the overlap, not as any duality. Hearing, as offered here, is the virtual aspect of audibility, which precedes and resonates any actual listening that engages within the interplay of object-, sonic- and audible-events as repetitions of time.

What we find in a *logos* is that these various time-events form a matrixial interplay of signs, which themselves give rise to image-events of pure memory that cycle and resonate the complexity of lived experience. We may then think of these image-events in Malick as the thinking that unfolds by its characters, which are then given life as well in the audioviewer. Image-events are not exclusively audible, but in Malick they are in a near continual seeing/unseeing relation. We may conceive this philosophically as disclosure and withdrawal, but it is better thought of as a present moment in which the virtuality of memory in its potential durations has multiplied into events of actuality, forming a coexistence. The time-events are the actuality of the *logos*, while its image-events are the thought that becomes the film. Consider the familiar notion of cinema as dreamlike. We say this because the audioviewer becomes engaged in another's *logos*. More to the point, the oneiric aspect of cinema is that we come to relate to a *logos* that is another's *reality*. I might have certainty that the characters' world is objectively, empirically unreal, but in their certainty it is real and in this sense is actual to their consciousness.[3] The *logos* is *logical*, not necessarily to the audioviewer but *as itself* and *to* its characters; and when its events are not logical, nonsensical, it calls into question the audible paradoxes that lie between self and world.

For Deleuze, the problem arises when one claims an identity—an "immanent to" or "transcendent to" that conceives life as referential to something other than what is lived.[4] A film's characters carry on with their

---

[2] I am greatly assisted in my reading here by Daniel W. Smith's "The Doctrine of Univocity: Deleuze's Ontology of Immanence." See Smith (2012).

[3] The HBO series *Westworld* approached this in an interesting manner by breaking the *presumed logos* and thereby widening the sphere of *its own* actuality. Through reverie they come to self-awareness and remake their world because of it. In this, they transcend.

[4] For more on this in a noncinematic, metaphysical sense, see Deleuze (2001) and Agamben's interesting meditation on that essay in his "Absolute Immanence" (1999). For

lives within the logic of that world and in this world they are absolutely real. They exist, they feel their condition. In a Malick film there is no immanence *to* anything but itself, its own thinking that unfolds. Transcendence meanwhile is not the transcendent audience, but within itself—a "maybe" of the lives who live and make *logos*. Transcendence for them becomes not an entity beyond but a maybe that comes alive cinematically. This transcendence is at the very least a possibility, a thought, a movement—in Kierkegaard, the possibility of eternity within time.

Yet, much as how Malick's characters imagine transcendence, we imagine immanence. We who experience *the film* are visitors, not observers. We know we are folding ourselves into the world of others. We thereby have the capacity through empathy to overcome the gap and feel within the film rather than outside it. Cinema in this way gradually effaces this distance, as our physical measure gives way to empathy. The point of connection is belief: just as she believes in logic and gathers as *logos*, so do I. Here, I as audioviewer do not suspend disbelief but, rather, ignite my belief in immanence that continues to think through immanence. This is one of cinema's many reversals: immanence, not transcendence, becomes the idea, the belief. In believing, I am not so distant as *observing* another's dream but instead am in an active engagement of reverie. Bachelard writes that "the memory dreams, and reverie remembers" (1960, p. 20). Memory constitutes our own distant relations that nevertheless live in nearness—an ongoing struggle with availability that somehow resides in a self within oneself that is also an *other* to oneself. A reverie activates the memory, drawing it closer, taking account and gathering forward in a state of imagining that builds the memory.

A Cinematic Empathy

While Bachelard here does not write of cinema, his poetic reverie is one way of conceiving the cinematic condition. The nocturnal dream, he writes, is a disorganizing of the soul, while the reverie is an act of binding the soul, an idealizing and imagining of the *anima*. This is *our logos* relation that feels another's. One can imagine the cinematic condition when Bachelard states that "by transporting the dreamer into another world, reverie makes the dreamer into a person different from himself. And yet

---

Deleuze, to think "immanent to" is to give life over to something that is not itself. Life does not depend on and is not determined by anything other than or outside of life.

this other person is still himself, the double of himself" (p. 79). This is how we become the double to Deckard.[5] As he views the photograph so do we, as an empathetic tether begins to build, a folding into the *logos* that folds. Reverie within becomes reverie of the audioviewer, developing into a circuit: empathy–*logos*, *logos*–empathy. Furthermore, Bachelard suggests that reverie must be attended to in listening. "In order to know ourselves doubly as real being and an idealizing being, we must *listen to* our reveries" (p. 58). All this is rooted in memory. There are many philosophical ways to conceive memory and its present thinking *as cinematic*: Bergson's virtual, Deleuze's recollection-image, Kierkegaard's instant-repetition, Heidegger's *thanc*. All will be explored here through various aspects of Malick's cinema, which houses no single thesis on the subject. The case of Bachelard's *reverie* is particularly conducive to the engagement of the audioviewer, who is neither distant nor inside. Indeed, Malick seems compelled not to distance his audioviewer, as we find our reveries intertwined with his characters' reveries. Dream, reverie, and thought become indiscernible and any film theory concept of subjectivity evaporates. In a cinema of reverie, one falls into an already active gathering that is the *logos* of any film world. The emotions of its inhabitants come alive through our own acts of imagining and the conjuring of empathy. We find an empathetic relation with its particular world that is made by hearing and listening. This cannot be done if one is simply designing sound as overlays to a series of visual elements, objects in motion, capturing, etc., but only by giving characters the capacity to gather and make. As the cinematic fire illuminates, the *cosmos* churns, the *logos* murmurs, the *unseen* conceals and reveals. Unseeing audibility finds itself present in other durations—emergences of activities whose existence has no predetermined allegiance to known things. Audibility as matrixial is not a container for things, as Plato's *Timaeus* might suggest. It is another power. It not only finds itself within a set of cosmic or natural laws but also its *thought* that permeates, adheres to, and fades from everything, from the simplest object-event relation to the most preternatural audible hallucination or transcendent call. Unseeing opens this audible channel to what is other than seeing, an *other* that has the capacity to transcend present objects, space, time, language, and convention without leaving the world.

A conception of cinema-as-*logos* therefore proposes that a film breathes its own infinite, virtual field through the actualities that emerge in their

---

[5] See Chap. 2.

gathering. A *logos* discloses in a way that conceals its own larger world, and in doing so, resonates its own unseen infinity. Every film world has its knowable horizon, its "limit"—a temporal *terminus* beyond which a film's characters cannot go. Yet the time of a film world goes beyond the time its characters spend within it. The sphere of temporal engagement finds its narrowest limit with the audience, wider with its characters, and vastly, incomprehensibly wider as *world*. Yet if we think in terms of *logos*, this infinity, the whole, resonates back to audience in circuits that may become for an audioviewer wider than for any character, or may for a character become wider than its world.[6] When one conceives a film world through its *logos*, one infuses it with its own history that need not be shown. *Logos* provides a larger culture, a vaster universe, a long draw of time, both into the past and forward toward the future, beyond the film's ostensible end. Its attentiveness by its characters draws it into life and creates repetitions that open a new field of ethics or faith. None of this need be shown or stated.

One's audibility is particularly tuned to such indeterminate and indeterminable durations of creative thought and experience. In one of his cinematographic notes, Robert Bresson writes: "The eye (in general) superficial, the ear profound and inventive. A locomotive's whistle imprints on us a whole railroad station" (1977, p. 39). It is more than simply *a* railroad station; rather, it is this *particular* one, which in its sounding has opened an auditor to its entire history that can only offer *this* singular moment of hearing. This train whistle has sounded thousands of times, but this *haecceity* is a present relation of oneself to one's place, in time. This is the *world* aspect, what Deleuze might call the whole that mutates through its specificities, and what I am offering as the *logos* that is this gathering within the world that has always been, a drawing forth in particularities, a process of taking account.

To think in terms of a *logos*, hearing underlies any dominant discourse of listening. One draws forth aspects that do not adhere to the dictates of reason, the residues and resonances, the traumas and discoveries—remembered, forgotten, and conjured—of a lived life. Audibility is a meeting that envelops the larger scope of any dominant listening within the larger scope of oneself. In every conversation, one does not simply encounter another's

---

[6] An example is an implied transcendence, in which a character believes in a deity whose reality remains an open question. To borrow from James, this belief in the unseen may be as real as anything one sees (2002).

spoken words, but instead engages with and gathers from everything that she and the other have been.

To think of this audibly, consider Andrei Tarkovsky's film *Stalker* (1979). There is the famous scene in which the men cross between worlds and their hearing shifts. Not a word is spoken during the journey. They hear the rhythmic clacking of the train, and it becomes audibly more strange. It is not the object or subject that changes; there is no diegetic shift, or change in objective to subjective sound, as film theory often conceives it. Thought of as a *logos* relation, there is also no reflexivity in this scene, no breaking of space, nothing transcendent to its events.[7] The change is the transition within *logos*, manifest as a changing relationship of attention for a character and his setting, one that constitutes an infinite and ineffable condition that wordlessly expresses this audibility. While the train moves visually along a horizontal plane, the audible emerges as a stretching beyond horizontal associations and into "attentive recognition."[8] In such a perceptual state, any object remains unchanged while the film, as *logos*, shifts between planes.[9] Every detail of a film has a time element within that has given it *itself*, and as such the possibility of an extended discovery beyond the sensory-motor condition, as a lifting forward from the *logos as logos*. The world remains intact, but the relationship to a specific, particular entity or event has changed the whole, giving birth to an audibility tied up with the uncertainties of the actual and the virtual. Here we have a shock to the system that invites the audience, the audioviewer, to the attention of the *logos* in the same moment as it threatens to rupture it. Tarkovsky's shaking of the *logos* is more like Deleuze's free-moving, pure image or sonic situation, which is "condemned to wander about or go off on a trip" (1989, p. 41). This occurs by taking flight from the actual, when the purely virtual aspect of the time-image allows audibility to open a relation to the actuality of thought.

---

[7] I will later argue that Tarkovsky's use of sound is transcendent to its *logos*, but here it is audible.

[8] This is Deleuze's term (1989), borrowed from Bergson. He writes that this change to attentive recognition is one of "description." The time-image decouples the thing from its sensory-motor aspect and becomes "pure" optical/sound. It is not description in a narrative explanation or diegetic delivery; description, rather, is a way Deleuze conceives of pulling out that which is more than the thing perceived in an otherwise sensory-motor framework. Description replaces the object to make something new.

[9] "In this case, instead of an addition of distinct objects on the same plane, we see the object remaining *the same*, but passing through *different planes*" (Deleuze, 1989, p. 44).

Beyond the Audiovisual: New Dimensions in Unseeing

When *listening* is unseeing, devoid of visual verification, there is the question of what one makes of this duration. Contemporary sound theory often attempts to give sound its own legitimacy as itself, independent of images or objects. This is valuable concerning questions of sound, but any state of *audibility* is not independent of imagery and instead makes use of it when affect combines with a need to understand.[10] At its most creative, sound design aims to push the ambiguity of the narrative question: What is that sound? But this is not really the question. It is, rather, What event is making this sound? What things are making the sound here and now? It is a question not of sound but of causality. In attempting to answer this question of *what* one is listening to, one must make an image association from what is unseen—the imagining of memory. This is not, to borrow another Wittgenstein phrase, a "private language"; it is a private affair housed upon the gatherings of memory. *As audible*, therefore, one achieves or appeals to no consensus or universality but only gathers through one's own repetitions.

As much as Aristotle wants us to be creatures of rationality, rhetoric and sight are not the only faculties that direct or motivate thinking. "Thinking" comes in many forms that are difficult to categorize. Nonconceptual thought, in which audibility is engaged, is a resonance of an incommunicable array of effects, not causes. What audibility *makes*, therefore, is a fluid series of fragmented relations. In this, unseeing audibility shares something of its own dreamlike state, as one builds in circuits of images and infinite, affective resonances of nonconceptual thought, to understand what cannot be seen in the moment. The making from hearing and listening is on the one hand a series of images. But on the other, one may better conceive it as a condition that, as *logos* suggests, gathers and takes account through virtual and actual repetitions. Repetitions of audible experience give one a sense of one's condition—the *haecceity* of this place, this time, this feeling. This audible ability to construct from memory enables one to apply various combinations to new settings, environments, and states of being.

Audibility in *unseeing*, therefore, requires a different way of thinking about the narrative relation of characters and setting, one that deals with the invisibles of any relation with place and time and the *logos* that gathers

---

[10] There are various modes of listening (see Chion, 1983 and 1994). One can listen to sound for itself, but this is different from one's audible engagement.

what it does not see and therefore cannot "know." Audibility works through conditions and local environments more than places. Such relations can be thought of in what Deleuze considers "forces" and his readings of Nietzsche's and Foucault's conceptions of power. But we must also reach into areas that he does not explicate but only intimates. Foucault conceives "knowledge" not as something gained but as something put to use, which he divides into statements and visibilities. This opens the question of what may be actualized in neither statement nor visible thing. Deleuze writes of Foucault's two regimes of knowledge as "audiovisual," a relationship that is disjunctive (1988). However, Deleuze's "audio-" is not what is named here as audibility because, for him as for Heidegger, it lies in the statement, in speaking. However, audibility as another epistemological field—we might say, as a power or force outside these regimes of knowledge—is broader than speaking and it incorporates and organizes what is often discounted as noise. There is a folding of the sonic to audibility, even as only imagined, recollected, or hallucinatory, which then unfolds in thought, as events akin to "repetitions" in the manner in which Kierkegaard and Deleuze employed the word—repetition as the new, thereby distinct from recollection as the old. *This* "audiovisual" is a different disjunctive relation. The question here becomes: What of the audio that is not a statement? What thought or idea does the audible engender within any particular event in which it emerges as its own event? Such *audibility* aims rationally to reconnect with some lost visual and a lost time. In this sense, the audio is stripped of what Deleuze and Foucault consider it to be (the statement) and instead finds itself in a further divergence that expands into a new relation—that of an independence from the visual that maintains an inseparability from *logos*. As Deleuze and Foucault might say, this audibility is capable of adhering rationally to a dogmatic image or of disengaging from any such prior image or statement. Audibility either adheres to convention or conjures another thinking.

There is therefore in the cinematic a different linking and relinking activity that is audibility. Consider the following: "As long as we stick to things and words we can believe that we are speaking of what we see, that we see what we are speaking of, and that the two are linked: in this way we remain on the level of an empirical exercise. But as soon as we open up words and things, as soon as we discover statements and visibilities, words and sight are raised to a higher exercise that is *a priori*, so that each reaches its own unique limit which separates it from the other, a visible element that can only be seen, an articulable element that can only be spoken. And yet the unique limit that separates each one is also the common limit that links one to the other, a limit with two irregular faces, a blind word and a mute vision" (1988, p. 65). Deleuze continues by suggesting that this is what makes Foucault cinematic. But more germane here is the question of this limit, both common and distinct in each. What arises from the folding of the sonic is *the audible*, which becomes the unfolding of new thought from the interplay of events. It shares the same condition but it also has its own limit. It arises to thought neither as statement nor as visibility but within another diagram, another spatiotemporal topology that finds a different set of limits—a different within and a different outside—that is also not independent of what gives rise to statements and visibilities. To think, then, of the relational element of character and her world, the seeing that unsees, we need to bring *logos* together with the fold of subjectivity.

Audible Threads: Subjectivity, Madness and the Fold

In Bresson's *A Man Escaped* (1956), the question of freedom or death lies in a capacity for hearing what is unseen. Fontaine's (François Leterrier) and his captors' unseeing constitutes the site of conflict. An audioviewer moves along the empathetic bond of shared audibility. We hear and listen for the guards' feet upon concrete, their sound of scraping, their feet upon gravel, etc. We might say it is a bodily relation to world as exhibited through sound; but more to the point, it is a *logos* relation to the world through the sonic-events, audible-events and the touch of bodies in their activity. Such effects are not simply a film-subjectivity—suggesting a spatiality, from his perceptual point of view/audition—but, rather, a particularity of being in this world and its audible horizon. As audioviewers, we are granted some POV shots, but more important, we feel everything from his *condition*. It is less important that we see and hear from his location; we see, but especially *hear as*, this man inside this cell. *Fontaine-in-his-cell* is the empathetic condition that we feel. When Orsini (Jacques Ertaud) is beaten across the hall, the camera and microphones do not change to that cell but, rather, stay with Fontaine; when Orsini is executed outside, we see and hear not *from* but *as* Fontaine's condition within his cell. Neither incident is revealed in the way cinema might normally "show" such an incident, and instead are brought forth from the *logos* as Fontaine's situational audibility. He learns through his hearing and listening, as we do. His audibility opens the condition of his confinement.

A Man Escaped is an example of what is conceived here as audible simultaneity, the now that sees and unsees what is heard. In simultaneity, there is in a single duration of time the present, actual seeing within one's field of vision that also imagines what is not seen from one's memory of unseen spaces. It is a remarkable film because its most intense moments involve unseeing rather than seeing. Fontaine's seeing is only his cell, but what offers a means of escape is his capacity for unseeing, for imagining what he cannot see from his audibility. It is not the opening of another time (coexistence) but, instead, a single time that opens to the invention or recreation of another space or object as an *image*. Psychologist Kurt Lewin writes of a mathematical boundary between a person and environment, and uses the example of a prison cell. A prisoner's space is conceived and built on the knowledge (by both prisoner and guard) of its impassable boundaries. Yet Lewin adds that "The solidity of the boundary of the prison is different for bodily, for social, and for mental locomotions" (1936, p. 44). He never mentions audible locomotions, yet the audible psychology is what gives the prison its permeability, both as space and as time. Fontaine's audibility widens the spherical, temporal boundary beyond the walls of his cell and offers the sense of anticipation of future events. His hearing of the guards' movements of approach, departure, and various distancing thereby also establishes an awareness of the guards' borders as well, opening potential hearings of *his* activity. In listening, he must judge their capacity for hearing him through his hearing of them. Even as we follow Fontaine during his escape, his audible sphere or matrix moves with him and expands. It changes from narrow confinement, with threatening footsteps and voices, to a wider one with more distant sonic-events that he must attend to and navigate in order to escape. It is not simply a matter of widened space and spatial navigation, however; it is that of a different listening to time. Outside the cell but still within the prison there is a squeaking sound that he and the audience hear in unseeing at timed intervals. The empathetic bond between him and us is that both ask the same unstated question. The film eventually reveals that the sound is a soldier riding a bicycle along the perimeter. Also, there are the timed footsteps of a guard he can only hear and not see, whom he must kill. These hearings of and listenings to intervals in repetition are critical to his timing his bodily, tactile movements through space. The body must stand in waiting, resisting the impatient eye that is born of the ear being left alone, as

Bresson wrote in his *Notes on Cinematography*.[11] Audibility is the element of the film that Fontaine attends to, and this attentiveness within *logos* is why he is able to escape. Through his attentiveness, the audioviewer is invited to attend with him and travel along on his journey.

Fontaine is a character who listens to the *logos*. But for listening to be learning, he first needs to become aware of his hearing. This faculty helps him to construct a semiotic web both spatial and temporal. Later, we will explore how this spatiotemporal matrix becomes a multiplicity in Malick, but for now we remain with this linear topology of simultaneity. Fontaine's liberation comes in his ability to attend to his matrix of *indices*. An index in the work of Charles S. Peirce is a sign that points to that which resides in the world. "An *Index* is a sign which refers to the Object that it denotes by virtue of being really affected by that Object" (1955, p. 102). This is important because the index is neither resemblance nor substitute for something else. For these two reasons, it is different from a Saussurean signifier but is instead a sign of experience, a double experience, an attentive activity that one engages with. An index is the very element of simultaneity—the worldly connection of one's unseeing audibility to the logical events in a particular space and present time. Cinematically, an audible index is not an audiovisual match but, rather, a means of connecting what is heard to what is not presently seen. As discussed in the previous chapter, this is often named badly as "offscreen sound."[12] Sound cannot be offscreen because it is never onscreen, which is the place of images. Key to the index is that it is the aspect of unseeing that is causal, rational, unidirectional, and from the perspective of design, ideological. An audible index must be listened to or it is ignored. It moves along the process of *understanding*, which gives rise to a particular line of thought, arriving in a decision. Because its cause is presently unseen, the index is an *inferential* engagement rather than a referential one.

Deleuze conceives of this *visually* as the out-of-field—a connection of sets that together constitute a plane. Conceived as offscreen rather than *unseeing*, the out-of-field has in Deleuze a *relative* relation to the set (what might be otherwise available visually) and an *absolute* aspect (the whole universe that is *not visually available*). The out-of-field thereby constitutes

---

[11] "The eye solicited alone makes the ear impatient, the ear solicited alone makes the eye impatient" (Bresson, 1977 p. 28).

[12] This term, popular in film sound theory, is another example of thinking about sound visually. As Metz correctly noted, there is no such phenomenon as offscreen sound (1985).

an actual relation to other sets and a virtual relation to the whole. Deleuze's cinema conceives of the whole in a Spinozan fashion as a whole whose attributes emerge in "threads." Any thread traverses sets and communicates among them to infinity. "Thus the whole is the Open, and relates back to time or even to spirit rather than to content and to space" (1986, p. 18). His whole/Open, conceived as visually unavailable, relates to that which is invisible in its threads. Conceived as unseeing, the *infinite* is the larger world of the film, its totality. Deleuze does not conceive of this unseen oneness as *logos*, for reasons mentioned previously. But as one is in unseeing, the mode of attention is a *logos* of mnemonic and audible relations, while the threads are its resonant events of activity. Thicker threads connect what is seen to what is unseen, constituting its indexical function of sonic-events achieving a rational corroboration within an audible-event. His thinner threads, however, are the more interesting aspect; here the relations are not confined to an objective accessibility but, instead, cross into realms of the unseen, revealing the whole's temporal quality (as durational) and "introducing the transspatial and the spiritual" element (p. 19). This constitutes a tightening of the spatial—one might say visual—and opens to higher dimensions within a free-flowing, unseeing virtuality. Deleuze uses a metaphor here of a spider, descending into the system as duration. The spider and her web construct a recurring metaphor for Deleuze. For example, in *Nietzsche & Philosophy*, he borrows from Zarathustra, for whom the universal, eternal spider spins its web of reason to hide inside, unseen, awaiting revenge rather than participating in the game of chance (Deleuze, 1983). But in *Cinema 1*, he relates it to the constructing of dreams, which are "like a spider's web" (p. 122). And in two of his early works, *Kant's Critical Philosophy* and *Proust and Signs*, he concludes with web metaphors. In the former he writes of history and nature in their sensory forms, where one finds "pure relations of forces, conflicts of tendencies, which weave a web of madness like childish vanity" (1984, p. 75). In the latter work, he constructs the metaphor of a spider lying in wait, deep in her web (2000). She is the entity that does not see, smell, or taste—nor can she be seen—and instead feels the pull at the farthest edges of her web. She answers only to signs and then emerges to race forward in response. This is how Deleuze considers Proust's narrative search, one that happens not in the chasing of visual things but as an unseeing spider in a web of her own creation. We can then imagine these thicker threads as the "reasonable" appearances of cinema—those that pull together its seeing aspects, within and outside the frame, constituting what we might name as a film's web. But a fly will never approach what it sees as a trap. The thinner, unseen strands are what ensnare without one knowing what is happening—the audible web, a matrix of signs, and the *logos* that encapsulates the relational whole. It is a *logos* of one's own making, made of time. It is neither internal nor external, born of a spider who feels her world as she creates it and *picks up from the logos* those signs that tug at the thinnest, most distant, and forgotten aspects of being.

"Life Within the Folds"

Deleuze writes that Bergson eventually came to the notion that the only subjectivity is time, or more to the point, one's relation as nonchronological time rather than as movement and matter (1989). Returning again to the circuit in Deleuze's thinking, terms like *subjective* and *objective*, *virtual* and *actual* come to chase around each other and complicate each other while the *affect* (what happens) is the disclosure of one's time. Subjectivity is an evolving topic in Deleuze's work, but by the time of his cinema books, it is neither motor nor material but, rather, temporal and spiritual.[13] Key in this is his "recollection-image" as the subjective element of the sensory-motor, or the body and its movement in space. A year later, Deleuze wonders if there is an inside that is deeper than any internal world (as well as an outside farther than any external world).[14] This is what brings him two years after this to expand this concept of "the fold," which for him is subjectivity as a relation far deeper than any isolation. This returns us as well to distances, for in the fold, distance comes close and *moves* inward, perhaps eliminating distance altogether.[15] "The fold" is discussed primarily in Deleuze's monographs on Leibniz and Foucault, but the fold of subjectivity reads as Bergsonian—the folding of the outside that constitutes memory (what Bergson calls "pure memory"), which then unfolds as recollection and forgetting. Subjectivity, inwardness, is

---

[13] "Subjectivity, then, takes on a new sense, which is no longer motor or material, but temporal and spiritual: that which 'is added' to matter, not what distends it; recollection-image, not movement-image" (Deleuze, 1989, p. 47; written in 1985).

[14] "Does this mean that there is no inside? ...*an inside that lies deeper than any internal world*, just as the outside is farther away than any external world?" (Deleuze, 1988, p. 96; written in 1986).

[15] "The most distant point becomes interior, by being converted into the nearest: *life within the folds.* This is the central chamber, which one need no longer fear is empty since one fills it with oneself" (Deleuze, 1988, p. 123).

made as the past is condensed. But the past is not a continuity; it finds its limit on a stratum along which it is recreated. Thought of the past then becomes one of activation in the present, a return that does not dwell but instead turns toward the new.[16]

Deleuze works through Foucault's regimes of knowledge and power and asks: Is there a new dimension to subjectivity available, a third dimension? "How can we name this new dimension, this relation to oneself that is neither knowledge nor power?" He turns again to memory, the folding or doubling of the self. There is "absolute memory…memory of the outside" (1988, p. 107), beyond that which is inscribed. "Memory is the real name of the relation to oneself, or the affect on self by self." Time, Kant said, structures subjectivity. But time as "subjectivation" is memory. It doubles the present and the outside. It is one with forgetting, which for Deleuze is *active*. The folding of forgetting "merges with the unfolding, because the latter remains present within the former as the thing that is folded. Only forgetting (the unfolding) recovers what is folded in memory (and in the fold itself)."

It is a curious move, this *act* of forgetting, but we can turn to Kierkegaard for help. He writes that the entirety of life moves between the two currents of remembering and forgetting. Forgetting is a practice and its ability is conditioned on an ability to remember.[17] "The extent of one's power to forget is the final measure of one's elasticity of spirit" (1946, p. 27). One must forget, must learn to forget; it is not done by making the impressions vanish. Forgetting is not forgetfulness; the former is an art, "a tranquil and quiet occupation." Forgetting only the unpleasant is forgetting badly. "Forgetting is the true expression for an ideal process of assimilation by which the experience is reduced to a sounding-board for the soul's own music. Nature is great because it has forgotten that it was chaos." One must take over the misfortunes, which deprives them of their bitterness. In this, forgetting is done for the sake of remembering. "Forgetting is the shears with which you cut away what you cannot use, doing it under the supreme direction of memory. Forgetting and remembering are thus identical arts," finding "the Archimedean point from which one lifts the whole world" (p. 28).

---

[16] "We will then think the past against the present and resist the latter, not in favour of a return but 'in favour, I hope, of a time to come' (Nietzsche), that is, by making the past active and present to the outside so that something new will finally come about, so that thinking, always, may reach thought. Thought thinks its own history (the past), but in order to free itself from what it thinks (the present) and be able finally to 'think otherwise' (the future)" (Bergson, 1988, p. 119).

[17] Either/or. See Kierkegaard (1946, pp. 26–28).

For Deleuze, forgetting of forgetting places it on the outside, and is therefore death. But in the relation of forgetting and memory, the subjectivity of the fold releases forgetting from fixity. As Deleuze writes, "as long as the outside is folded an inside is coextensive with it, as memory is coextensive with forgetting. It is this coextensive nature which is life, a long period of time. Time becomes a subject because it is the folding of the outside and, as such, forces every present into forgetting, but preserves the whole of the past within memory: forgetting is the impossibility of return, and memory is the necessity of renewal" (1988, p. 108). So long as there is a co-extensiveness with the outside, a folding and unfolding, it becomes life, *a life*, the time of life.

But there is more to Deleuze's question—*Is there a third dimension to subjectivity?*—than memory and forgetting. One must think through the question of signs and the virtual/actual interplay of "power" and "forces"—the folds that occur in relation to the widest reaches of his transcendental empiricism. Deleuze writes that the transcendental field is a topology that lies at its surface rather than its depths, and along this surface runs a "sonorous *continuum*" (1990b, p. 125). While his concept of transcendentalism brackets out subjectivity, this is where we can enter into the question of the *audibility* of unseeing. It has the capacity to enfold another field of forces (to use Deleuze's language) or a neglected aspect of power (to use Foucault's) from within the transcendental.[18] Power relations act in "strategies." Such relations are nonstratified, unknown, anonymous, distinct from knowledge. As Deleuze writes, these "'anonymous strategies' are almost mute and blind, since they evade all stable forms of the visible and the articulable" (1988, p. 73). This falls into Deleuze's "microphysics," which involves connections that are mobile and nonlocalizable, and which "signifies another domain, a new type of relations, a dimension of thought that is irreducible to knowledge." Power, through its relation of forces, does not "know" on its own. Interjecting Foucault, Deleuze writes: "No doubt power, if we consider it in the abstract, neither

---

[18] Again, for Deleuze the *transcendental*, unlike the transcendent, has the capacity for change, mutation, etc. In *The Logic of Sense*, Deleuze seeks "an impersonal and pre-individual transcendental field, which does not resemble the corresponding empirical fields" but is also not an "undifferentiated depth." It is not consciousness, but singularities that are non-personal and non-individual. This occurs on an "unconscious surface, and poses a mobile, immanent principle of auto-unification through a *nomadic distribution*" not fixed or sedentary but also not a synthesis of consciousness (1990b, p. 102). The transcendental for him is therefore not subjectivity, but it is what folds to subjectivity.

sees nor speaks. It is a mole that only knows its way round its network of tunnels, its multiple hole: it 'acts on the basis of innumerable points'; it 'comes from below.' But precisely because it does not itself speak and see, it makes us see and speak" (p. 82). It must be emphasized here that because knowledge is considered in terms of a stratum, it creates a *surface* of knowledge; but again, when he writes of the *outside*, Deleuze conceives it through Leibniz as the above realm of the soul (1993). It is like a blind animal finding its way through other means. In both cases, the strategies of forces may be blind, but folding into subjectivity they resonate with unseeing, which maintains the power to see but is not seeing the event of possible knowing, nor even understanding. We may then conceive of subjectivity in this architecture that Deleuze borrows from Leibniz: unseeing is an interior to the unseen that is exterior, and is only one level of the folding of audibility as subjective, another level being that of the memory and repetition that resonates both territories.

Kierkegaard's Anxiety of Subjectivity

Kierkegaard has his own set of unseen forces to manage. For him, subjectivity is about the choices, paradoxes, and conditions of sin and anxiety related to questions of love and faith. The knight of infinite resignation remembers everything, but it is remembered as pain; yet he is reconciled with existence. The idea becomes curved inward, thereby neither lost nor forgotten.[19] As he recollects his beloved he "keeps the love young…he recollects her in an eternal sense" (1946, p. 124). The ethical dimension applies to everyone and is immanent. There is no *telos* outside the limits of the ethical. The ethical man finds his *telos* in the universal, abolishes the particular in order to become part of the universal. He is therefore mediated in and by the universal. But a path of faith requires an individual to break from mediation and abandon the universal. In doing so "the particular isolates himself as higher than the universal…not subordinate but superior" (p. 130). But he does so only insofar as the particular in the individual "*stands in absolute relation to the absolute*." Kierkegaard's Abraham "transgressed" the universal and stands in relation to it, a personal act for himself and God.

---

[19] "At one moment it is the obscure emotion of the wish within him which awakens recollections, at another moment he awakens them himself; for he is too proud to be willing that what was the whole content of his life should be the thing of a fleeting moment" (Kierkegaard, 1946, p. 124).

Here we encounter a problem of *logos* and a key question in Malick. Kierkegaard's radical faith is a radical subjectivity, in that faith has necessarily given up the worldly relation. The Wholly Other transcends the "coextensive nature," the fold that Deleuze mentions. It is an act of abandoning the transcendental in favor of, rather than an enfolding of, the transcendent. Kierkegaard and Malick's characters seem to struggle with this very problem, and we find it played out in process through Malick's films. In his later films (2013–2017), Malick seems to have abandoned Deleuze's "coextensive nature" in favor of a "private understanding."[20] In a certain sense one may say that *logos* as common (Heraclitus) is disregarded in the seeking along a private faith (Kierkegaard). The question then becomes whether this is an abandonment of the relation or another engagement, another aspect to *logos*—one in which the *telos* of ethics spreads to *encompass* the transcendent, that of faith in God.

Here lies the *aporia* that has delightfully consumed philosophy and inspired literature for 2,500 years, and finds resonance in Malick: What is the limit?[21] Or to echo Heraclitus, What is the listening-to? Kierkegaard wants one to renounce what Heidegger later called "idle talk" for the single voice of the individual self. The leap in one sense requires an abandonment of both *logos* (as common, as relational) and *ethos* (as custom, habit, ethics). But *logos* as gathering, as accounting, takes on a wider scope. It becomes a question again of what the activity of listening is. As *logos*, there is in Malick's Kierkegaardian characters either an expanded aspect that comes to struggle with its limits or an extreme narrowing that denies it. This is why hearing becomes the critical condition of any listening—the openness that has the capacity to enfold what is available in unseeing. Audibility entails this mutual interweaving of hearing and listening; the former is inclusive and open while the latter must close. Listening is deciding what to listen *to*, which in the act must also discount what is unlistened. Hearing is the condition, but listening is the existential struggle, the moment of choice: to seek within recollection, to indulge in dwelling remembrance, to leap along a belief, or to find oneself lifted into the outside, to the wider *logos*, another zone of unseeing. This struggle—the question of whether the outside is

---

[20] "But although the *Logos* is common, most people live as if they had their own private understanding" (Heraclitus, Fragment 2; see McKirahan [2010, p. 112]).

[21] "The question of knowing whether or not the whole range can be attributed to God depends on the separation of whatever is reality in the range from whatever is limitation, that is to say from the order of infinity to which the range can be raised" (Deleuze, 1988, p. 125).

inside— pulls Malick's characters along the various durations of time, as their thinking struggles with where to come to terms with the past as a movement toward connectivity within the vastness of the future.

This is also the zone in which madness creeps in—either the *logos* threatens to say too much or it is abandoned for another gathering. Madness is the certainty of subjectivity—the making from the gathering absent the openness of the virtual. It is less the hearing of delusions (the question) and more the narrow rationalization of listening to them (the answer). Kierkegaard recognized this, which is what makes Abraham so troubling. Voices, sounds, tugs, and leaps of association find evidence in what is not there, a lifting and layering of the past into the present. Time is thereby the locus of the changing ego. Deleuze's readings of Kant describe the ego as a relation of time that produces a division of the *I* (Deleuze, 1984). The actual present meets a prior present and forms a double division. Deleuze conceives of this psychologically as a figure-8. Childhood is not a circle of world formation but, instead, is twisted into two ellipses. The virtual and actual centers, two aspects of the id, are joined by the ego, which is the intersection in the figure-8, the binding of personality. Madness threatens when the relational threads that *bind* and *make* become frayed. Madness is not a separation from the outside, for that is an acceptance of despair in an unwillingness to connect. Rather, madness comes when the "private" has assumed dominance and invents its own other connections. Madness or transcendence is the uncertain path of listening—*Is this a real relation or only myself?*—that becomes the arrival of understanding. This is the anxiety of subjectivity: the self must choose what faith is and what madness is.

Park Chan-Wook's *Stoker* (2013) begins with a voice delivered in a whisper: "*My ears hear what others cannot hear. Small, faraway things people cannot normally see are visible to me. These senses are the fruits of a lifetime of longing, longing to be rescued, to be completed.*" Here we begin a film with a girl, India (Mia Wasikowska), who is in tune with the *logos* in a superhuman sense, someone who throughout acknowledges her separation as a means of coping with the death of her father. In this opening, Park intersperses brief suspensions in the imagery, rendering a still picture, while the ambient sound progresses in time; yet it progresses in mutes of specific sonic layers, as if she herself is suspending sonic-events in the *logos*, or perhaps accessing others through such negation. Her hearing suggests her own private relation. Throughout the early scenes of the film, Park offers various hearings that are not actual sounds to suggest her hyper-receptivity bordering on insanity: her popping a blister, rolling a hard-boiled egg on a table to drown out the whispers of gossiping maids, and the tapping legs of a spider as it approaches her from across the room.

While India's sanity hovers on the border, the titular character in David Cronenberg's *Spider* (2002) is fully mad. All sonic-events that emanate from him are audibly close, personal—his breathing, his clothing, his scribbling in his notebook, his own mutterings—as if he is the only person who can hear (or he is the only person *he* can hear). It is an extreme subjectivity, an enclosure within his own time. Drawing the mental into the material, he builds a web of his past, while the truth inside him hides in wait like Deleuze's spider. He builds and then tugs at his own threads until she emerges, and all is unveiled. The web of signs, its lines and fibers, are for Deleuze both physical and metaphysical, passing through images, objects, thought, art, and politics, tying cinema, society, and self together. These betweens, so critical to Deleuze's whole project, open the doors that may lead to truth or, perhaps in the same instant, the abyss.

Opening Unseeing to the Crystalline and the Hodological

One of Deleuze's more intriguing concepts in *Cinema 2* is that of the "crystal-image," which discloses a point of indiscernibility between actual and virtual. The crystal-image is Deleuze's direct time-image—a momentary emergence of transcendental time, time that has created its *own* circuit. This marks a break or rupture from the organic, sensory-motor of everyday experience. To better understand this "sensory-motor," we turn to Bergson's *Matter and Memory* (1988). For Bergson, any present perception is "impregnated" with memory-images that are themselves fed by pure memory. Perception is a relation to the immediate past, where sensation translates a series of vibrations. This is the *sensory* aspect. The immediate future of any present is continually leaning toward action and movement. This is the *motor* aspect. Sensory-motor is body awareness, which anchors one in the present. One's body as sensory-motor is the center of action, continually in a state of becoming and in a relation with the actual world. Because it is this body relation-awareness, the sensory-motor is not *concerned* with memory; it does not recollect. It is extended, localized, and therein acts as the source of movement. Memory in the sensory-motor is what feeds the body with its unconscious associations and likenesses, informing the body and placing it into all the possibilities of present, future-directed action.

Moving to Deleuze, he divides his time-image cinema into two narrative, descriptive regimes: the crystalline and the organic. He draws Bergson's sensory-motor into his "organic" regime, which is further divided into the real and the imaginary. The imaginary is "actualized in consciousness," the "present actual" (Deleuze, 1989, p. 127). What he means by "actual" here is the actuality of thought that is given rise in present consciousness. As he writes, the interplay involves "linkages of actuals from the point of view of the real, and actualizations in consciousness from the point of view of the imaginary." In this, dreams can also be conceived as organic, and it is possible therefore for cinema to overlap dreams and reality in the organic structure. He does not mention that audibility also functions along the same points of contact when unseeing is the state of involvement.

To illustrate his organic structure, Deleuze cites Lewin, who conceived of a "hodological space" of lived, social relations. From the Greek root *hodos, hodological* means "path" or "way." In Lewin, it describes a mental rather than physical topology—a psychological traversal along discrete regions of consciousness. For Deleuze, "the sensory-motor schema is concretely located in a 'hodological space'…which is defined by a field of forces, oppositions and tensions between these forces" and their resolutions according to their goals. This is conceptually juxtaposed with Euclidean space, which is the area where tensions are resolved. Hodological "narration" for Deleuze is the most economical path, the simplest route, the appropriate detour, the most effective speech, etc.[22] Hodological space is lived while Euclidean space is represented, and both maintain their relation with *chronological* time. This means that time is the constant in a hodological relation, allowing a conscious traversal across space without having to cross all Euclidean points to arrive. Because hodological space is lived, we can think of it as seeing an object and making the hodological leap from this actuality to its virtual potentiality of the past in forming the sensory-motor connection. If we think of the sensory-motor as the body relation in Bergson, we can think of the hodological as the mental activity that includes memory. One travels the path of logic in the instant of capture, sending one's mind along its *hodos* to the law of the object. If we apply this to unseeing audibility, the hodological leap is the activity of the audible-event lassoing an image from the sonic-event within a duration of simultaneity.

---

[22] "This economy of narration, then, appears both in the concrete shape of the action-image and hodological space and in the abstract figure of the movement-image and Euclidean space" (Deleuze, 1989, p. 128).

When Deleuze then writes of a crystalline break in the sensory-motor, he is opening experience to the interruption of time, which summons a different engagement with memory. In the virtual-actual relation, the virtual can be thought of as residing in the pure past as the resonance that lives within any actual thing or thought. Put another way, the actual is what occurs while the virtual is that which differentiates. But in a crystal-image, "the actual is cut off from its motor linkages, or the real from its legal connections, and the virtual, for its part, detaches itself from its actualizations, starts to be valid for itself" (p. 127). The crystal-image forms a duration that gives rise to the indiscernibility of the virtual and *its own* actual, expressed in time and in consciousness. Deleuze describes it as the virtual becoming its own *object*, but it is more that the virtual coalesces into its own concentrated duration, or what I am naming an *event*. Because the crystalline forms its own time, it shares some kinship with Kierkegaard's "repetition," but in a highly concentrated form. In both, the immanent *moment* is the creation of the new from within time as a suspension of time, a timeless time or a reintegration and reformation of time. The distinction is that Deleuze conceives in a virtual relation drawn from time and memory. Kierkegaard's is an expression of faith in which the transcendent eternal has intersected the present: the moment is a state of enfolding and affecting the immanence of time. In both there is then a crystalline-repetition, a new unfolding from the fold of the virtual-infinite. While Kierkegaard's repetition is born of faith, in which sight is not at issue, Deleuze's crystal-image is expressly *visual*. We can think of the familiar connotation of a crystal as a formation that we see—*see through as we see into*—in the event of this birth of time. This constitutes an overlap of time in thought within the same moment. A good example of this is *déjà vu*, itself a form of repetition. Time is no longer the constant, no longer chronological. It is, as Deleuze writes, the "interstice" or the "chronic." As the sensory-motor collapses, "characters, who have become seers, cannot or will not react, so great is their need to 'see' properly" (p. 128). It is a heightened gathering within the event, wherein *seeing* involves seeing something new in what is otherwise organic—perhaps even seeing too much.

Such a concept presents an entry point through which we may conceive the coexistence of actual and virtual as an interjection of the visual and the unseeing audible as an expression of time. Audibility acts as the instigator or agitator of a crystallization within the moment of unseeing. Here we move from simultaneity to coexistence—the audibility that opens to a multiplicity of time. In some respects, this is precisely the activity of unseeing in both lived encounters and cinematic ones. Consider Bergson's description of memory and the virtual as he describes the "living reality" of becoming: "Whenever we are trying to recover a recollection, to call up some period of our history, we become conscious of an act *sui generis* by which we detach ourselves from the present in order to replace ourselves, first, in the past in general, then, in a certain region of the past—a work of adjustment, something like the focusing of a camera. But our recollection still remains virtual; we simply prepare ourselves to receive it by adopting the appropriate attitude. Little by little it comes into view like a condensing cloud; from the virtual state it passes into the actual; and as its outlines become more distinct and its surface takes on color, it tends to imitate perception. But it remains attached to the past by its deepest roots, and if, when once realized, it did not retain something of its original virtuality, if, being a present state, it were not also something which stands out distinct from the present, we should never know it for a memory" (Bergson, 1988, pp. 133–134). Bergson, as Deleuze after him, couches this activity in visual terms, given the imagery of memory; but it is not entirely within the realm of visuality, past or present. What happens in an audible coexistence is that what we gather as the sonic—what we lift from the echoic, what we recollect and recreate in a whisper of the past—lifts us from the temporality of present/material/actual into a matrix of multiplicity. Within its semiotic tethers we take flight along this virtual duration that, given enough intensity, becomes an actual duration. In terms more aligned with Kierkegaard, eternity interjects to give transcendence to immanence. This question of immanence or eternity, time or timelessness, in the crystalline-repetition is the question that opens through Malick. What thought is at work here? What is the present and what is the formulation of the new time that is an interjection? And what is the interjection: thought or transcendence? These questions are left unanswered in Malick, whose uncertainty keeps it safe in the unspoken and the unseen.

From Simultaneity to Coexistence

What is the audible in this crystalline-repetition, drawn from the moment of unseeing? Remember, first, that simultaneity is the establishment of actual time, the sensory-motor association, in the *instant* of unseeing. Coexistence is the unseeing that opens to a layering of multiple durations, allowing thought to traverse along multiple lines of flight. In coexistence, unseeing triggers a rupture that becomes a *moment* through a complication of actual time, drawing a hearing character toward a new time relation. The former is a receptivity to emergence while the latter is the movement of thinking forward. The directionality is important. In cinema, visual montage exists as a linearity of Euclidean coordinates and hodological connections *as given*. The relationships occur in time as an actual progression that includes and in fact encases its own prior. Unseeing works in audible layers of time *in addition to* sequences of seeing time, giving verticality (a virtual coexistence) to the conjoined progression of a multitemporal experience. Deleuze's direct time-image of the crystalline is where audibility is able to both interject and fly free from visuality, space, and language without abandoning *logos*. This is how audibility gains its independence plus inseparability. Sonic-events and their audible-event relation are *usually* organic and usually tied up in Euclidean space—the everyday, the sensory-motor, continuity, familiar associations, etc. Yet as audible and as time *itself*, it also has the ability to move within and beyond space by moving its *time* outside of space. Here we can broaden both the hodological and the crystalline to different realms of audibility.

Cinema sound often centers on two key aspects: synchronization and synchresis. Both concepts are concerned not with audibility but with the sonic and the visual. More important, both are primarily (although not exclusively) audience-determined concerns. Synchronization is the familiar temporal coupling of a heard sonic-event with its seen object-event. The two need not be the same object- and sonic-event. In fact, much of sound design is the decoupling of the two in order to create a stronger cinematic identity. A pedestrian example is an image of a punch to the face with a sound of a frozen cow carcass. Because we have seen the punch *and* heard the cow carcass many times in past films, the audioviewer accepts it as the common cinematic convention of *punch sound*. It is a mnemonic relation (sensory-motor), but one that requires no thought, since the sonic convention is both immediately seen and historically reified. While one could decouple image and sound and maintain identity with the convention, such decoupling is in danger of exposing this cinematic lie. Synchronization is therefore often regarded in ideological terms because one accepts a *synthesis* through a repetition of sameness. And in doing so, the sonic subliminally reinforces the dominant agenda of the image or its object-events.[23] The cow punch is a common example; however, much of the creativity of sound design comes in developing a new idea from the audiovisual fusion.

---

[23] For more, see Doane (1985).

In Chion's concept of synchresis, a new idea arises from the audiovisual dialectic in its disconnectedness.[24] Synchresis is notable because rather than reinforcing identity and the ideology of the visual (synchronization), it introduces difference. Yet, because it is dependent on an *audiovisual* relation rather than an unseeing one, synchresis remains tied to visual understanding and thereby remains on the *plane of reference*. It also, as mentioned, takes us out of *logos* and back to a distancing of audioviewership. It is spectatorship, for the filmgoer, not lived by the characters. Both synchronization and synchresis are therefore different from simultaneity, which is a relation of *logos* and character audibility.

Once we enter into a *logos* within the film, synchronization and synchresis can be replaced by a Euclidean audibility, since all three are about visual, spatial, and instantaneous unfoldings. In a Euclidean audibility, we have a common relation—that of the spatiotemporal, sound-image coordination of oneself within a single environment or space. As *logos*, this is the average open hearing of now in which everything is logical and "sensical." There is an unseeing element here as well—think of an air-conditioner in an apartment—but because no one attends it, it can only be heard. A hodological audibility is a point of *attention* in which one traverses a path that is not presently given in space. It requires a curiosity or need on behalf of the hearer to become a listener. The path that opens is a circuit rather than a traversal. This is where imagination takes hold and one *thinks* by calling forth into listening a need to act or respond based upon the immediate imprecisions of pure memory. One recalls or imagines in fragmented associations of images and environments. Remembering our exploration of Bresson's *A Man Escaped*, we see that Fontaine's audible simultaneity was a heightened hodological state. At a very simple level this is also an everyday occurrence. A dog barks in the neighborhood and I call forth some particularity of dog if I listen. As *logos*, I hold the relation in attention for as long as I am interested. This hodological engagement is one of the ways in which an audible *logos* is made—in particular gatherings of simultaneity.

If we were for a moment to step outside of *logos* to the thought of the audioviewer, cinema can be conceived as a total hodological engagement from start to finish. But here the film image does the work visually that

---

[24] *Synchresis* is a neologism that comes from Chion's fusion of Kantian synthesis and cinematic synchronization. It is a dialectical thesis, antithesis, synchresis activity on the part of the audioviewer accomplished through the collision of a nonequivalent image and sound. So: A + B = C, where C is a new idea formed in the disparate audiovisual dialectic.

audibility does within oneself. If I, in my apartment, hear a dog bark outside, my mind may choose to create the image of a dog barking in my neighborhood. With this thought I have, through audibility, engaged in cinematic thought—I have not only made an image but also moved to it psychologically. Cinema does this visually: it cuts from the image of the apartment to the image of a dog nearby. The sound is unnecessary because the cut dictates the hodological leap. This visual jump is known in film theory as cross-cutting, D. W. Griffith's movement from space to space in montage. Visually, we fully accept our minds being thrust from location to location at the speed of the cut because we can quickly make visual sense of the new arrangement. The visual is more often occupied with its pro-filmic arrangements—namely, the material and visual organization of objects in linear sequence. But in audibility, the sound, or rather its hearing, is what creates the leap. Because one's audibility can float free of spaces and occupy multiple times, a hodological field takes on a greater complexity than the few pages Deleuze dedicated to it, particularly when conceived as a *logos* relation rather than as limited to the mental engagement of the sensory-motor.

A hodological traversal *within the film logos* produces a simultaneity that gives rise to singularities of attentiveness in the now of the sensory-motor. A switch is flipped as pure memory informs an inferential association through the index. This takes us from a visually distant, montage-level holodology to one of attention and learning. This is difficult to do as *logos* because the hodological connection is both mental and audible, rather than spatial and visual. Yet the image that *results* can be, for the character, revealed in some manner through cinema and thereby for the spectator.

Coppola's The Conversation: *Simultaneity and Crystalline Audibility*

An example of this is found in *The Conversation* (Coppola, 1974). It begins with a wide, overhead shot of San Francisco's Union Square. Juxtaposed with this is the presumed natural sound of the setting: a jazz band playing in the square, a mime's shuffling feet, a dog bark, the low murmur of social activity. With the exception of the band, such sonic-events adhere to visual logic. Yet there is a strange sound: an unseen mechanical noise. The montage cuts to a particular man and woman as the sound field isolates their conversation. The mechanical distortion continues to reemerge and their dialogue occasionally breaks apart, moving from a question of what is sounding to *who* is listening. The audioviewer eventually sees that the spatial location of listening is at the headphones of character Stan (John Cazale) sitting inside a surveillance van; we hear as he does, including the distortion within the recording he makes. Normally in film there is a Euclidean match between the conventions of Renaissance perspective and that of sound perspective. But here the audible is displaced from the Euclidean.

This is known in film sound theory as a creative manipulation of "point of audition" (POA).[25] This concept is not about sound but, rather, an establishment of the location of listening, a correlation to the more known cinematic term: "point of view" (POV). Whereas POV requires a clear sightline from someone, POA does not need a straight line and indeed does not need to be in the same location as the image, nor even occupying the same time. It is removed from Euclidean space as visual. Occasionally such a move is done purely for effect, breaking a *logos* through reflexivity. In the opening scene just described, the sound that seemed to be occurring for the audience is revealed to be heard within. Audibility lives on a hodological duration that serves to break the dominant image of spatiality. If we were to view this scene strictly in visual terms, it would not fall into either of Deleuze's hodological or crystalline definitions. Taken visually, we are fully in the sensory-motor condition of a couple walking through Union Square while later we see a man listening to their conversation in a van nearby. Taken audibly however, we find a hodology that builds a tether between two Euclidean spaces. The hodological emerges in the *simultaneity* of a shared single time independent of space, where unseeing audibility is radically displaced from what is seen. Since Stan hears at the same time the camera shows, the two events share time but not space. Stan's audibility acts as the hodological circuit or tether that traverses the space by his conscious engagement. He creates the *hodos* through his engagement in listening. Of course, for an audioviewer to fully understand this, Coppola must move his Euclidean camera from the space of the square to the van without cutting, following Harry Caul (Gene Hackman) as he walks from space to space. Only then is it established for the audience that the one who hears is Stan. Audible simultaneity is not the same as hodology. In fact, what we find in this simultaneity is a partial hodology because it has not *made* the images from audibility. Rather, the two channels have gained

---

[25] POA is explained in complementary but slightly differing ways by Altman (1992) and Chion (1994).

independence through the *audiovisual* disjunction. In other words, we hear Stan's listening in a way that has broken Euclidean space, but we do not attend to the thinking or imagery that is within Stan himself.[26]

What pushes the film's audibility into the crystalline is that the conversation is being taped. The crystal-image, or here the audible process of crystallization, is the confusion caused by the distortion of the voices. Here we have broken both the Euclidean and the hodological; the virtual and its actual have converged into something that demands a listening to it as a new image of thought. It is not merely this moment, however. Through the course of the film, its recorded actuality draws Harry continuously back into the virtual. Through his own repetitions of playback, the recording follows Harry as he wanders the streets of San Francisco. Now in the crystalline, we have *coexistence*: rather than one time sharing multiple spaces, we have a multiplicity of times that share the same space. Harry has pulled the event outside of time and into his time through his objectification, subjecting it to deterritorialization by shaking the container of his own echoic repetitions and through repeatability and analysis. In fact, we never really "know" the time of any listening to the conversation owing to this ambiguity of simultaneity and coexistence, hodological and crystalline, actual and virtual. The state of causal indexicality is effaced and becomes reappropriated as an idea.

Perhaps, then, the opening sequence is not even Stan's listening, but is a precognition of Harry's later, more obsessive listening that continues throughout the film. These are indeed the running themes of the film, as the varying disclosures of the same event offer deterritorialization through difference in the repetition, leading to a reterritorialization in a new idea. Neither the object-event nor its sonic-event has changed; rather, Harry's *listening* changes. ("*He'd kill us if he had the chance.*") The recording's cycles continue, constituting his own breakdown until he comes to the tragic point of understanding. The singularity is not the event of the sonic but instead the event of the audible. But the overlap, the conjoined durations, and the variable repetitions under certain emotional states are what offer the chance for newness. The singularity of the audible-event has changed the entirety of what he previously considered as objectively, and even subjectively, truthful. In this, *logos* is transformed.

---

[26] Or have we? Perhaps what we see in the images is Stan's imagination. This is doubtful, however. To give thought and image to what is hodological, we have to turn to Malick. But for now this scene remains an introductory way of conceiving audible simultaneity, one that invites the possibilities of a rupture into thought.

This is done only rarely in film sound design because most filmmakers think of sound as Euclidean and audience-dependent—a *present* relation of image-events. But if we take the crystalline to the audible matrix, and if a filmmaker allows the space for time-events to multiply, it can certainly be done. In *The Conversation,* listening transformed the entirety of what has been. It was the clue not given but received, a call without a caller. It was there all along in his hearing, but it needed to be listened to from a certain shudder in the *logos.*

When taken to its highest levels of audible thinking, the hodological and the crystalline are able to fragment the indexicality of cause and effect and their assumed images and locations. Normally one audibly engages in Euclidean spatial relations, with a sonic-event that implies an associated object-event. Even though this process moves one along a future progression, the index functions unidirectionally. A hodological matrix opens to an arboreal rather than a strictly linear network of audible thinking. This omnidirectional process of audibility works with the physical omnidirectionality of the sonic. Mnemonically, the engagement provides a branching and leaping of thought that the frontality of unidirectional vision and its graspable objects tend to close. Cavell asks: "Is the difference between auditory and visual transcription a function of the fact that we are fully accustomed to hearing things that are invisible, not present to us, not present with us?" (1979, p. 18). We can scrutinize the presumption of what is "present," for what is unseen is just as present (sonically) as whatever is seen. But the question is a valid one. The answer is that the Euclidean and the hodological are why we are able to accept the audible world without needing to see it. Yet the crystalline involves a deeper relation, an invitation to seek within the *logos* of attention and branch out along the new. *The Conversation* offers a way in. To return to our example of the barking dog that creates the imagining of a dog that barks, we have not yet experienced the thinking *of the character* other than through the distance of audioviewer in Deleuze's affection-image. We *saw* Stan listening, but we did not see the thinking born from it. For this, we have to turn to Malick to fully explore the unseeing within that makes a new image of thought.

Terrence Malick's *Logos*

We can introduce Malick's *logos* by placing his work in relation to two filmmakers who share with him the tendency to use the cinematic form to open unseeing, mnemonic relations: Wenders and Tarkovsky. The three work similarly in embedding grand themes within their narrow regions of contact—marking points of relation to some larger scale—among the characters who inhabit them. Beginning with Wenders, his locus of connection is the voice within the *logos* that wishes to speak. Wenders is frequently concerned with seeking toward an intimacy of actual, present contact. The arc moves toward an act of speaking that has not yet come, requiring an opening to give oneself "voice." Throughout his work, but particularly in *Paris, Texas* (1984) and *Wings of Desire* (1987), we find confessions and thoughts that are restrained from within, and a moment of action comes in the unspoken becoming spoken. Such acts, whether painful or difficult, are often produced through a medium: a recorder, a telephone, or the membrane between life and afterlife. In both films, there is an unseeing relation—like a Pythagorean curtain or Catholic screen—that renders the reveal as hidden. Confessions come in an unseeing event, a visual concealment in the act of the unconcealment, or even more, a concealment that is necessary in order to unconceal. His characters' concealment manufactures a hodological audibility in the heard confession. Audible indices are well within the *logos* of now, emerging as character to character or character within character, whether externalized, offered to another, or kept hidden within the self. There is a reversal here: the unsaid is within the seeing. But the two fail to meet, the cinematic tension is never slackened, and the seeing and listening never quite fall into place. It is always in relation to this reveal, one that is audible, but as a relation to its visuality *in its lack* of seeing.

The early scenes of *Paris, Texas* open with a wandering protagonist, seemingly without history or name. Gradually he regathers his memory as family begins to reform into a sense of self. Travis (Harry Dean Stanton) frequently finds mnemonic points of connectivity through the assistance of media: a Super-8 film, a scrapbook of photos, a recording to his son, and finally the extraordinary scene of the confessional in the peepshow booth with its one-way mirror/window. To draw forth the courage to confess and make his presence known, he must turn his back on his wife Jane (Nastassja Kinski) as he speaks through the telephone line. This way neither can see the other and only voices build the conduit between them. In this unseeing, the hodology is entirely theirs; we see both of them, but *they* must traverse the mental space to arrive at a point of connection. Unlike his taped confession to his son, this unseeing is a co-present intimacy—the act unerasable in the presence of shared time. Jane is in actual simultaneity with Travis. Yet it is Travis's story that allows them to create together a virtual/actual coexistence that breaks the stagnation. Wenders's camera holds on Jane as she creates her hesitant reverie, bringing forth from memory her buried history, her storehouse of previously locked images, signs, feelings.[27] It is the sonic tether to memory, a recollection brought forth within the *logos* as audible. Finally, achingly, Wenders gives them the reveal as he gives it to us: Travis's turn. It is a turn from confessing to confronting, bodily and visually, in the hope that the present can offer forgiveness for the past. We might also find a resonance of the myth of Orpheus and Eurydice in this. Has she been listening, taking account? Has she been *following* behind him, with him at every step? As he turns, will she still be there? She is, but as he looks toward her, she is the one who cannot yet see him. She must turn out the light of her world in order to see. Only then does her mirror that maintains the past become a window to the new.

Wenders's audibility is a Euclidean co-presence that is complicated by an unseeing that sees along a series of hodological points. Tarkovsky's is crystalline—always pushing the margins, the borders of his *logos* in order to rupture and create. His use of sound may find a hearing somewhere and sometime, but it is expressed as an idea wandering free. It becomes its own commentary, a conflict that threatens to break down the membrane between *logos* and audience empathy. In this, his sonic-events are akin to Ingmar Bergman's shattered and foggy images, altered psychological states, and visual reflexivity in *Persona* (1966). We might think of Tarkovsky and Bergman as attempting to achieve the same effect, but with sound in the former and imagery in the latter. Particularly in *Nostalghia* (1983), Tarkovsky continually threatens to break apart the cohesiveness of his world through his reflexive application of sound. It seems his intent is for a film to find its artistry *as* a film—not only this film but also his whole *oeuvre*. Every one of his works repeats prior sonic motifs in variations: a dog barking, the sounds of water and fire, the overlaps of then and now, virtual hearings that have lost their home. In this he is like Malick in that there is a consistency of *logos* not only with a particular work but also across all his cinema. But Tarkovsky again is pushing his film *as film*, and therein lies the *sonic* difference. While Malick conjures the time of immanent experience that reaches along the horizons of possible transcendence, Tarkovsky builds a transcendent work of art. Because it is transcendent, its "sound" also transcends its *logos*, at least in the sense that his sound need not be heard by anyone within. His characters rarely respond to sounds,

---

[27] "Telephone. His voice makes him visible" (Bresson, 1977, p. 62).

but also do not seem to be in a state of audibility regardless of the sonic. This sound-as-art approach develops a sense of audible detachment in those who populate his visual worlds. Tarkovsky echoes Bresson when he writes: "As soon as the sounds of the visible world, reflected by the screen, are removed from it, or that world is filled, for the sake of the image, with extraneous sounds that don't exist literally, or if the real sounds are distorted so that they no longer correspond with the image—then the film acquires a resonance" (Tarkovsky, 1989, p. 162). But the question must be asked: for whom? The answer in Tarkovsky seems to be: the audience.

Wenders's *logos* establishes the intimate now of communicative relations between selves in a world; Tarkovsky's is the opposite, a nonrelational array of indefinable vectors building a transcendent work of art. Remembering that time is the enabler of audibility and its thinking, Tarkovsky and Malick approach it differently. The former is remarkable in how he places time not in montage but *within* his cinematic image. His elemental overlaps of fire and water are multiple durations that take hold in the single image-space, suggesting a *visual* coexistence that creates an observable crystal-image. His sound is a distinct manifestation of this same tendency, but one that has gained total separation from the film's inhabitants.

Malick's time, in contrast to both, is a coexistence that presents an inseparability of its *being expressed* in the independence of multiple durations. In other words, time is the means of creating an interplay of past seeings and hearings that share the same world, its same *real*, through *logos*. His unfoldings of time are expressions of experience within rather than Tarokovsky's transcendent collage of durations presented artistically for the audioviewer. And as distinct from Wenders, this experience of the present-actual is inextricably linked to the *was that now is*. Malick's *logos* is a relation of the long stretch of time that emerges through those who gather, recollect, and forget. It is a *logos* whose transcendence is an idea born within immanence. His *logos* is made of time, memory, and the unseeing threads that attempt to unify what has been lost. It is expressed within a natural world in its inconceivable reach of time and the individuals who momentarily pass through and think through connective points within, in an infinite array of signs and redemptive possibilities. We cannot simply think of this history as that which has escaped and is unavailable; on the contrary, it is time that is *made available* through the very acts of recollection and repetition that are given cinematically. Here we have a subjectivity not though a viewing of the screen but in the thought that emerges from one's hearings. We have penetrated the affection-image and turned it outward, the hodology and crystalline *within* rather than represented.

In this, Malick offers a hiddenness to Being in its disclosures, and the means through which one encounters any event is in the manner of its disclosure to Dasein. For Heidegger, *logos*—lying between φύσις and ἦθος, *phusis* and *ethos*, nature and ethics—is not a question of being (ontology) but logic. In his *Logic* and *Being and Time*, *logos* is specifically the making visible of any statement, which meets his phenomenology of any statement being *about something*. "The subject matter of logic is *speech* viewed with regard to its basic meaning, namely, allowing the world, human existence, and things in general to be seen" (2010a, p. 6). For him, truth is already in *logos*, ergo truth precedes the statement that reveals truth. "The proposition is determined by its reference to truth—not vice versa, as if truth were derived from the proposition" (p. 109). But a cinematic *logos* is not reserved to statements. It encompasses a wider relational engagement—neither being nor phenomenon but, rather, the very possibilities of relating to being in its becoming, its *being made*. Unseeing "reveals" through its audible faculty as a relation, brought forth as *logos*. This relation to what one has always been in the long reach of history constitutes one's being in the actuality of thought. In Malick, one threads an empathetic relation to such a cinematic *logos* that goes beyond what is visually presented as *world*.

Malick's Expressions of Nature

One might suggest that a Malick *logos* as itself "speaks" its own nonlinguistic form of expression. In cinema, as in literature, we often find a tendency to give voice to nature. In Socrates, the cicadas are not a sound; they are the unseen spies to the muses, the inventors of music. They sing to mortals who may—or may not—listen and find inspiration and perhaps a hint of madness.[28] Thus the tendency in poetic prose is to personify the sound of the natural world as a consciousness possessing hesitant caution in movement. Often it is expressed as a female uncertainty hidden behind the male ambition of objects and drives. Many of the writers already mentioned here—Nietzsche, Bachelard, Barthes, Benjamin, Balázs, Deleuze—express nature's sound as a voice without a mouth that speaks its consciousness in its own language through feminine expressions. By these accounts, nature's attributes shudder, whisper, voice, groan, and *tremble in their mother tongue*.[29] This points to a variety of problems in coming to

---

[28] See Plato (2002) for the singing of the cicadas in *Phaedrus*.
[29] See Bachelard, who quotes Pierre Reverdy: "'The poplars tremble gently in their mother tongue'" (Bachelard, 1960, p. 189).

terms with what is unseen in nature: (1) Embodying nature's unseen with human language and speaking is an anthropomorphic need to structure and objectify the chaos of hearing as statements, knowledge's other to visual objects; in short, it is an implied wish that nature come to accord with human rhetoric. (2) As Kierkegaard reminds us, nature has no moment because it does not live in time; it lives in eternity while man (and woman) lives in time and thinks historically. (3) The theme germane here is that while nature needs no language, in our hearing in time, nature *sounds to us*, even if we take no care to hear or listen. The sound of the world is its own expression, its own force. But it reveals to humankind as a power that harbors as much aggression and violence as quietude and order. One need not be told; we need no language to engage with its forces and its laws. *Logos* is not a consciousness but, rather, a relation of world and self that is in flux through the relation. One makes the choice to hear one's connection to its expressions.

Malick gives to nature its own expression, a suggestion—implied in Deleuze, Spinoza, and Leibniz as well—that not only people listen and hear. All of nature, humanity included, has its soul. But there is for Leibniz also its *realm* of soul. Nature's expressions need no language because there is no need to understand. Early in Deleuze's *The Fold* he writes of Leibniz's folding of matter and soul: the former, existing on a lower level with its windows seeing outward to appearances, constitutes the ground; soul resides in "the upper floor, blind and closed, but on the other hand resonating as if it were a musical salon translating the visible movements below into sound above" (1993, p. 4). Within the "mechanism of matter" is its "motivating force": spirit. Why is this force necessary for Leibniz? Bodies and souls are two expressions of the same world, or better stated, the same architecture. For him, souls are within bodies, constituting two inseparable levels. The upper level is necessary to force bodies up to a higher level. As Deleuze puts it, "there are souls on the lower floor, some of whom are chosen to become reasonable, thus to change their level" (p. 12). The reasonable look out of windows at appearances, and who at their best rise up to sing the spirit. But the souls residing in the natural already live in spirit; this aspect of nature resonates in such a way that nothing need be said.

No matter what or how nature shares or expresses, this much is true: its activity informs one's audibility. In Malick, it informs in a way that is often divine in its *account*—not that the *logos* includes God by necessity but, as with Bergman, a deity is often gathered in the relationship. This is the vastness of Malick's *logos*. While its relations are immanent, it endows his characters with the *thought* of possible transcendence. Malick's relations are a *logos* in the broadest connotation of the word because in the unspoken silences of his unfoldings, life must be attended to along these expressions. Because of this, *logos* is often ignored, which usually leads to violent confrontations. Malick is not asking his characters to obey (to "hear"), but he is at times *suggesting* and other times *forcing* the need to listen; and insofar as one does, there is an accounting of *logos*. This does not lead to one's salvation, but it does lead one to account for an awareness of one's time and present condition. If one does not listen, one does so at one's own peril.

Creating the New from the Past

The other vital element in Malick's *logos* is that which makes time meaningful: the interlacing of memory within presence, or to think in Bergson/Deleuze terms, the creative vitality of virtual and actual relations. This is expressed through everyday moments that are at times hodological and at other times crystalline. One's experience with the world is not only what is now and what has been. Audibility is seeded not only by nature's sounds but also by the life that continues to generate within oneself from the past. *Now* offers the ignition point. But what we have been and project forward gives the now its thought. The past is not merely gone; it also creates the impossibly vast, imprecise availability of Bergsonian pure memory that makes the audible world meaningful. This is Malick's unseeing cinema—it *expresses* the thought that makes the imagery. Its *logos* gathers from the entirety of the past as a projection forward. This is the pure memory, the transcendental earth and cosmos that comes through the one who gathers in her or his finitude.

Bachelard, responding to Bergson, writes that there is no date to this pure memory; rather, there are seasons. We draw forth the feeling of the sun, the wind, or the cold that resonates the experience within. Bachelard continues that the image of reverie *radiates*. This is his phenomenology, which for him turns toward the object or image of thought that radiates outward, as in the audioviewer's relation. In audibility, the image and its object are not enough. Reverie radiates the *event*, the experience that reflects images as it resonates all that has never been seen and felt, building from the chaos of a pure memory a field of echoic radiation gathered in signs. This is what is built from memory *as* reverie. This brings us closer to something like Virginia Woolf's everyday "moments of being." For Woolf, "picturing" is the wrong word for what takes hold in a meaningful recollection because its image is always mixed with the hearing of sound. "Instead of remembering here a scene and there a sound, I shall fit a plug into the wall; and listen in to the past" (1985, p. 67). She does this, she adds, so that she may live through the past as a means of beginning again. This is an apt description of Malick's films. They are not memories as such; rather, their process is of being made, not in the past but in the activity that imagines. Such a *logos* does not have to be either/or. The lines between living and recollecting, simultaneity and coexistence, are as thin as they are broad in reach. Past and future continually permeate and penetrate each other. One lives the moment through one's own remembrances, reveries, recollections, and repetitions—the various states of "again" that brings forgetting forward into action. Kierkegaard writes that *the moment* is the point of deciding, of rebirth—as Woolf writes as well, of entering into being.[30] Every audible account constitutes an entry, a rebirth of the past into a creative event. As sound's materiality dies, its presence remains to give life to the listener who continues to hear. The audible may conjure its own echoic event, but in that moment it resonates the whole experience of pure memory, even if it cannot be identified. It lives within us, unknowable, and becomes activated in decisiveness and creativity.

Finally, there is the return to the more active state of being in a relationship with the world: the imploring of Heraclitus to listen. He reminds us that what we live as the *everyday* is what we share as common to all; this is the everyday of *logos* that makes us deaf to its listening.[31] The common is the understanding that has already decided, which estranges one from one's world and one's time. In order to listen attentively, one cannot be told to obey its actuality. One instead has to open oneself to the *logos* as it is available in an apprenticeship with signs, an unconscious learning.[32] This is the important point in Malick's use of audibility that reflects Deleuze's transcendental empiricism: life, including that within cinema, is never given but, rather, is available and *made through* availability. Deleuze asks

---

[30] Kierkegaard (2009).

[31] See Heraclitus, Fragments 2 and 114, as well as numerous variations in other fragments. The "common" is the public, acceptance, understanding. See, as well, Kahn (1979), McKirahan (2010), and Brann (2011).

[32] On this apprenticeship with signs, see Deleuze (1994 and 2000).

for a rupture in the work of art, which Tarkovsky provides; Malick instead ruptures everyday experience—the sensory-motor, the common of the *logos*. This comes when one heeds the call to listen, the call to take flight. In the meantime, his characters live within the *common* as tiny collisions, the way a *logos* functions in its dormant state. Yet as his cinema evolves, the very questions of everyday or rupture, present or past, sounding or hearing, begin to overlap and dissipate. His cinema increasingly pulls the everyday of the external, the sensory-motor, into complications of thinking. The collisions of the everyday become pathways through which other times emerge into coexistence. Listening begins to take over, complicating images, as *logos* begins to form as itself in its making, the making of time-events and image-events through listening. There is nothing reflexive, for thought itself is making *logos*: the sensory motor swooped into the crystalline, forming its own overlaps of time. New sensations of the past or the future overlap with the sitting still of the moment.

With *The Tree of Life* we gain a better perspective of not only time but also the eternity that lives in time, constituting the binding of what began with *The Thin Red Line*. The *logos* that gathers coexistence becomes not only the virtual of the past that lives in the actual moment but also an opening to eternity that is a transcendental time. In Deleuze's Spinozism, while the body exists, "duration and eternity themselves 'coexist' in the soul as two elements different in nature" (1990a, p. 314). The soul "endures" in time, in the life of the body, but also *in the same life*, the soul has an intensive component that is its essence. "We should not imagine that the soul endures beyond the body: it endures while the body itself endures, and it is eternal insofar as it expresses the body's essence." There is, in other words, a coexistence of the intensive (eternal) and the extensive (duration) that is the soul of the living body. This is how one is able to experience the eternal within the finitude of life. This is only possible through the unseeing that hears what is other than the material or merely the past, an opening beyond that is inseparable from what is real.

Malick's cinema gives us the time of this complexity. His cinema is image-*making*, the process of thinking, a series of disruptions of thought, immanent movements toward a somewhere or sometime that lives. This is not sound; nor is it a command to obey. If the collisions within the common were amplified through cacophony and precision, if audibility was always *directed*, if listening was always *obeyed*, a character would have little reason to be open. But this is not nature, not the everyday. The everyday is unseen and nature loves to hide.[33] "For nature conceals herself beneath vague indications and dark hints" writes Philip Wheelwright about Heraclitus's *logos*. "There is a hidden attunement in nature, the discovery of which is far more deeply rewarding than the mere observation of surface patterns. Everything is interwoven with everything else; nothing stays fixed, and even at a given moment an event or situation can be seen in a number of aspects, some of them representing sharply antithetical and 'contradictory' points of view. Such a changing and problematical world cannot be known by easy or static conceptions. There must be an activity and resilience of the mind, corresponding to the ever fluctuating character of the world it seeks to know" (1959, p. 27). Within unseeing and its audibility, audibility in its unseeing, one cannot listen to what one is not hearing. Therefore, *this hearing*—an openness prior to one's engagement in listening—is key to a conception of Malick's unseeing cinema.

Cinema as *Logos*

Let us therefore consider cinema's unseeing, Malick's unseeing, as a *gathering* of repetitions. This expressive, experiential cinema cannot be reduced to a *diegesis* and its negation, nor a semiology and its "readings." Malick's unseeing cinema is *logos*, neither thing nor system but a field of event-relations that arises from finding oneself already within one's world, a world that has always been and as such is always being made.

Heraclitus was known in antiquity as "Heraclitus the Obscure," a moniker emphasized more recently by Nietzsche and Jaspers, among others. Deleuze, in *Nietzsche and Philosophy*, writes of this moniker: "Heraclitus is obscure because he leads us to the obscure" (1983, p. 24). Is he not then leading us to the unseen, much as Pythagoras lured his students to the veil, but for different reasons? Deleuze writes this in order to ask Plato's old question of what is the being in the becoming. In Deleuze's reading of Nietzsche, it is his *Return*—as Deleuze conceives it, the relation of play and art that overcomes *hubris*. Reflecting on Heraclitus's teachings, Nietzsche wrote:

> [T]hat past and future are as perishable as any dream... that the present is but the dimensionless and durationless borderline between the two. ...that space is just like time, and that everything which coexists in space and time

---

[33] Heraclitus, Fragment 123: "Nature loves to hide itself."

has but a relative existence, that each thing exists through and for another like it, which is to say through and for an equally relative one... [All this] is extremely difficult to reach by way of concept or reason. (1962, p. 53)

It can, however, be reached cinematically. Cinema expresses itself in its play in time, as Tarkovsky said. *Logos* is not being itself but, rather, the possibility to engage in a relationship with being through its becoming. Dasein, as Heidegger said, "must secure [its] own method" of passing *through* concealment" (2010b, p. 32). Cinema is a *logos* through which one passes and which passes through oneself, not *as passive* but in the activity of passing through, taking account, gathering. In such relations, one finds oneself through the finding of others within their relations. Any film holds its possibility for virtue within and outside of language in a world opened by the fire of projection, rendering such possibility in the distinctions of light and shadow, and resonating with the audible collisions within the common that *perhaps* become attended to in the continuance of hearing, and through which one listens to the *logos*.

References

Texts Cited

Agamben, G. (1999). Absolute Immanence. In G. Agamben (Ed.), *Potentialities: Collected Essays in Philosophy* (D. Heller-Roazen, Trans.) (pp. 220–302). Stanford: Stanford University Press.

Altman, R. (1992). Sound Space. In R. Altman (Ed.), *Sound Theory Sound Practice* (pp. 46–64). New York: Routledge.

Bachelard, G. (1960). *The Poetics of Reverie: Childhood, Language, and the Cosmos* (D. Russell, Trans.). Boston: Beacon Press.

Bergson, H. (1988). *Matter and Memory* (N. M. Paul & W. S. Palmer, Trans.). Brooklyn: Zone.

Brann, E. (2011). *The Logos of Heraclitus*. [E-book]. Philadelphia: Paul Dry Books.

Bresson, R. (1977). *Notes On Cinematography* (J. Griffin, Trans.). New York: Urizen Books.

Cavell, S. (1979). *The World Viewed: Reflections on the Ontology of Film*. Cambridge, MA: Harvard University Press.

Chion, M. (1983). *Guide Des Objets Sonores: Pierre Schaeffer et la recherche musicale* (J. Dack & C. North, Trans.). Paris: Institut National De L'Audiovisual &

Éditions Buchet/Chastel. Retrieved Online, January 24, 2014 at http://www.ears.dmu.ac.uk/spip.php?page=articleEars&id_article=3597
Chion, M. (1994). *Audio-Vision: Sound on Screen* (C. Gorbman, Trans.). New York: Columbia University Press.
Chion, M. (2009). *Film: A Sound Art* (C. Gorbman, Trans.). New York: Columbia University Press.
Deleuze, G. (1983). *Nietzsche and Philosophy* (H. Tomlinson, Trans.). New York: Columbia University Press.
Deleuze, G. (1984). *Kant's Critical Philosophy* (H. Tomlinson & B. Habberjam, Trans.). London: Athlone.
Deleuze, G. (1986). *Cinema 1* (H. Tomlinson & B. Habberjam, Trans.). London: Continuum.
Deleuze, G. (1988). *Foucault* (S. Hand, Trans.). Minneapolis: University of Minnesota Press.
Deleuze, G. (1989). *Cinema 2* (H. Tomlinson & R. Galeta, Trans.). Minneapolis: University of Minnesota Press.
Deleuze, G. (1990a). *Expressionism in Philosophy: Spinoza* (M. Joughin, Trans.). Brooklyn: Zone.
Deleuze, G. (1990b). *The Logic of Sense* (M. Lester & C. Stivale, Trans.). London: Athlone.
Deleuze, G. (1993). *The Fold: Leibniz and the Baroque* (S. Hand, Trans.). London: Athlone.
Deleuze, G. (1994). *Difference and Repetition* (P. Patton, Trans.). New York: Columbia University Press.
Deleuze, G. (2000). *Proust and Signs: The Complete Text* (R. Howard, Trans.). Minneapolis: University of Minnesota Press.
Deleuze, G. (2001). Immanence: A life…. In *Pure Immanence: Essays on a Life* (pp. 25–34). Cambridge: MIT Press.
Doane, M. A. (1985). The Voice in the Cinema: The Articulation of Body and Space. In E. Weis & J. Belton (Eds.), *Film Sound: Theory and Practice* (pp. 163–176). New York: Columbia University.
Heidegger, M. (1984). *Early Greek Thinking* (D. F. Krell & F. A. Capuzi, Trans.). San Francisco: Harper.
Heidegger, M. (2010a). *Logic: The Question of Truth* (T. Sheehan, Trans.). Bloomington: Indiana University Press.
Heidegger, M. (2010b). *Being and Time* (J. Stambaugh, Trans.). Albany: State University of New York Press.
James, W. (2002). *The Varieties of Religious Experience*. Mineola: Dover.
Kahn, C. H. (1979). *The Art and Thought of Heraclitus*. London: Cambridge University Press.
Kierkegaard, S. (1946). In R. Bretall (Ed.), *A Kierkegaard Anthology*. Princeton: Princeton University Press.

Kierkegaard, S. (2009). *Repetition and Philosophical Crumbs* (M. G. Piety, Trans.). Oxford: Oxford University Press.
Lewin, K. (1936). *Principles of Topological Psychology* (F. Heider & G. M. Heider, Trans.). New York: McGraw-Hill.
McKirahan, R. D. (2010). *Philosophy Before Socrates* (2nd ed.). Indianapolis: Hackett.
Metz, C. (1985). Aural Objects. In E. Weis & J. Belton (Eds.), *Film Sound: Theory and Practice* (pp. 154–161). New York: Columbia University Press.
Nietzsche, F. (1962). *Philosophy in the Tragic Age of the Greeks* (M. Cowan, Trans.). Washington, DC: Regnery.
Peirce, C. S. (1955). *Philosophical Writings of Peirce*. New York: Dover.
Plato. (2002). *Phaedrus* (R. Waterfield, Trans.). Oxford: Oxford University Press.
Smith, D. W. (2012). *Essays on Deleuze*. Edinburgh: Edinburgh University.
Tarkovsky, A. (1989). *Sculpting in Time* (K. Hunter-Blair, Trans.). Austin: University of Texas Press.
Wheelwright, P. (1959). *Heraclitus*. Princeton: Princeton University Press.
Woolf, V. (1985). A Sketch of the Past. In *Moments of Being* (pp. 61–160). San Diego: Harcourt Brace.

Films Cited

Bergman, I. (Director). (1966). *Persona*. [Motion Picture]. Sweden: AB Svensk Filmindustri.
Bresson, R. (Director). (1956). *Un condamné à mort s'est échappé ou Le vent souffle où il veut* (*A Man Escaped: or The Wind Bloweth Where It Listeth*). [Motion Picture]. France: Gaumont Film Company.
Coppola, F. F. (Director). (1974). *The Conversation*. [Motion Picture]. USA: Omni Zoetrope / United Artists.
Cronenberg, D. (Director). (2002). *Spider*. [Motion Picture]. Canada: Sony Pictures.
Park, C. W. (Director). (2013). *Stoker*. [Motion Picture]. USA, UK: Fox Searchlight Pictures.
Tarkovsky, A. (Director). (1979). *Stalker*. [Motion Picture]. Soviet Union: Mosfilm.
Tarkovsky, A. (Director). (1983). *Nostalghia*. [Motion Picture]. Italy, Soviet Union: Opera Film Produzione, et al. / SACIS, et al.
Wenders, W. (Director). (1984). *Paris, Texas*. [Motion Picture]. West Germany, et al.: Road Movies, et al. / Tobis, et al.
Wenders, W. (Director). (1987). *Der Himmel über Berlin* (*Wings of Desire*). [Motion Picture]. West Germany, France: Road Movies, et al. / Basis-Film-Verleih GmbH, et al.

CHAPTER 4

Days of Heaven and Hell

Terrence Malick released his first film *Badlands* in 1973 to tremendous critical acclaim. His next, *Days of Heaven* (*DoH*; 1978), is now regarded as one of the greatest films of the 1970s. Both are temporally linear films, with spoken narration that complements and in some respects defines the linear structure. Yet *Days of Heaven* is an audibly richer film. Its simplicity in narrative construction and drawn-out silences allows it to open to a wide array of audible signs, an opening that would become even more prominent in his work that followed.

Nature plays a significant role in both films. In the Greek sense of *phusis*, nature in *Days of Heaven* also expresses its *nomos*—a distributive order or law that develops through its activity. This *nomos* is not "knowable" in the abstract; it is only encountered through its "sentence and its execution" (Deleuze, 1984). While one might claim that Malick's characters are in a struggle with nature in the four films under discussion here, it is more that they are at their weakest trying to rationalize in a way that discounts *nomos*, and they are at their best accounting for it in hearing and listening to *logos*. When we think of nature in Malick, *phusis* is what is, *nomos* is what distributes, and *logos*, as the gathering and the account, is the means of discovery and creation. We often think of reason and passion as antithetical. But in a Malick film, problems arise when one finds oneself exclusively in either. Those who listen, revisit, and rejoin from a standpoint of openness build a way forward— a repetition that enfolds and projects the possibility of authenticity, grace, or redemption. One cannot overcome nature, for it is what continues.

© The Author(s) 2018
J. Batcho, *Terrence Malick's Unseeing Cinema*,
https://doi.org/10.1007/978-3-319-76421-4_4

The *logos* Malick develops for his characters through nature is never explicated to an audience in these two films. But in both, its principal characters are on a forward progression, caught within their own linearity of time. Kierkegaard calls this the "infinite succession," which is a thought of the present that is always segmenting the past and the future (1980). Kit in *Badlands* seems to have abandoned the ethics of succession and in this sense has discounted time; but Bill and the Farmer in *Days of Heaven* are always scheming time, counting time, awaiting time. There is neither recollection nor repetition in the central characters of these films. But in *DoH*, the time of nature *cycles* in its nomadic distribution, while for its characters time moves in succession. This disparity between the two—the failure of *logos* to account for *nomos*—is what produces the rupture and its conflicts. Caught as they are in time's succession, Bill and the Farmer offer us an expression of the present-actual of hearing, listening, and *nomos*, which will become fractured along virtual paths in Malick's films to follow.

Mixing: The Process of Differentiation

"There is no obligation on man to recognize the logos just because he is man. ... The same immanent lawful order and justice reveals itself in the highest and in the wrongest man. But if we press upon Heraclitus the question why fire is not always fire, why it is sometimes water and sometimes earth, he could only say, 'It is a game. Don't take it so pathetically and—above all—don't make morality of it!'" (Nietzsche, 1962, pp. 63–64). In Nietzsche's readings of Heraclitus, the *logos* of collisions and strife constitutes a grand cosmic game. *Logos* is not God; there is no harmony to appeal to in times of strife and its *phusis* does not determine any outcomes. *Nous* is the conscious element of *intelligence*, one that is determining and deterministic. *Logos* is not conscious and therefore does not *care*, certainly not for anything we might call ethics or any social construction of morality. Violence comes to everyone in its own way, and in the end, good and bad people all meet the same death. People are irrational in the face of Heraclitus's *logos* and in nature, humans have no favored position. In Malick, too, nature is inseparable from human; all entities, conscious or not, are wrapped within the same cycle of violence and rebirth.[1] One's reason brings one to follow a particular path, but in *logos*,

---

[1] Advocating for a conception that rings as Deleuzean and Spinozan, Simon Critchley writes that there is nothing "enchanting" to Malick's nature, rather that nature has its beings, which "continue on regardless of our strivings" (2005, p. 146).

one fails to account for its signs at one's peril. To listen to the *logos* is not only to engage with what is common to all but also to seek openly along the virtual resonances of any emergent signs or threads that actualize.

Nietzsche conceives of Heraclitus's strife of opposites as a mixed drink, a metaphor that calls to mind Bergson's conception of *duration* as waiting for sugar to dissolve in a glass of water before the activity of stirring can begin. Perhaps both are borrowing from not only Heraclitus but also themes that often arise in pre-Socratic and Stoic philosophy: that of the mixture. The Stoics concentrated on the *state of the mixture*, but audibility must account for its continuation—the flux and becoming that is a constant *activity of mixing*. In nature, mixing is the unseen micro-activity of life, conceived through philosophy in many ways—will, *élan vital*, chaos, etc. Mixing is also the vital element, the very constitution, of unseeing audibility. The interrelations of object-, sonic- and audible-events produce an infinite generative production—in their own activity but also as they overlap in engagements of time and the time of thinking.

Under the influence of the Stoics, Deleuze writes of *Aion* as incorporeal events, the time of resonating, the mixing that is not only unseen but also immaterial (1990b). He also writes of the "sound-effects" of noise as the *Aion* before it emerges to the surface in language. But Deleuze only listens to language or, in other writings, music. For him, there is nothing worth hearing in the mixing of incorporeal events because they have not yet risen to the surface. Yet this disregarded, deeper mixing is *matrix*, not *line*—the generation of events that have their own life and are given new life through their interaction. Living as it does outside of language, this matrixial mixing maintains its depth as it rises to the surface and, perhaps, extends into flight. However much this mixture resides on the surface depends not on language but on audibility, which widens to extend into earth and air. Each actual event maintains a mixture of infinite, virtual, unseen microevents of differentiation. An object-event has its kinesis born of this singular collision that resonates as a force or power. A sonic-event produces its own intangible materiality that is better conceived in its relation of tiny energies in infinite harmonics, subharmonics, and frequencies at variable intensities. The event moves through its natural medium and also resonates as a force. An audible-event is mind that is not independent of matter, resonating the fragmented thought of the other two. It is a kinetic relation that embodies the entirety of potential events that complicate the thought. Materiality and consciousness become indiscernible and only exist in the idea of the relation. But materiality is not the thought of audibility. Within all the complexity of energies, forces, matter, and consciousness at the micro and actual levels that constitutes the mixture, what becomes significant in audibility is what becomes made in the coexistence of memory, time, and unseeing. This is what one engages with constantly in hearings as they become active in audibility—the infinite repetitions of a complex matrix of newness. The collision, the sound, the thought in their mixing constitute the occurrence and its significance.

Logos-as-mixture brings us to the art that crafts it, and here we step outside for a moment to consider what is known in sound design as *mixing*. First, we must acknowledge the changes underway in film sound at the time *DoH* was released. Chion points to 1974 as the year cinema sound began to emerge from the artistic potential it always had (2009). For him, there are three aspects to the change: a wider frequency range (the breadth of sound), an increased dynamic range (the height, or volume relation of sound), and multi-channel surround (an increase in the number of speaker channels). Chion attributes such an advancement to Dolby technology and places the emphasis on surround; yet what is key to audible availability is clarity, which comes from frequency range, dynamics, and reduced noise. Sound has the capacity to present multiple perceptual layers of character audibility, whereas the visual montage can only present a single layer. Chion uses the musical term "polyphony": "While the filmic image always remains *one*… sound has always been *plural*" (2009, p. 119). Cinematic sound needed the sonic range (in frequency and dynamics) for such layering/polyphony to come through the speakers. The 1970s was an era of great artistic advancements in American cinema overall, not the least of which was the arrival of the "mix engineer," or "mixer." This was not simply a technological advancement but, rather, the emergence of sonic artistry that aimed specifically at opening new audible possibilities.

Mixing as an art is delivered outward to encompass the audioviewer in his or her own gathering. As a craft it manages the chaos for an audience in a way that the characters must do for themselves. It accomplishes this by creating threads of hearing and listening within the whole, in time. Mixing establishes everyday generalities while emphasizing emerging particularities. In one sense, it manages sound for the audience. But it can also be thought of as the artful interplay of the general and the particular, the common and its collisions, habit and its ruptures. As with the everyday capacity of audibility, mixing also opens to metaphysical questions. For an audioviewer, film mixing establishes singularities through which the mixer offers an account of audibility. It opens to what is ignored or noticed, what is forced and what is gathered, within the audibility of its characters. But in an artful "mix," the gathering is more question than answer. Mixing as art is the mixing that one *does*, opening such metaphysical questions—the audible consciousness and unconsciousness, the continuous and fragmented hearings and listenings—that a character is involved with. For the audioviewer, a mix builds empathetic circuits, as an assumed audience comes to inhabit the *logos* within. The sonic matrix rises, falls, evolves, maintains, presumes, and complicates in varying degrees of hearings within unhearings and listenings within unlistenables. Such artistry, such a *metaphysics*, is only possible if these layers are conceived creatively. *Days of Heaven* has this layering and selectivity in ways that *Badlands* does not, widening our availability to the characters' horizon of audible access. It offers singular moments as unspoken expressions of the totality of the world his characters inhabit. Its events are signs: signals more than significations. They are often ignorable and must be audibly *gathered* by those who live the reality.

Audible Differentiation in Malick

Let us return again to the *logos* of immanent relations within itself, its hearings and listenings. Even more pronounced in Malick's later films, a "mix" offers points of differentiation and detachment from generality or universality. It gains its own time and floats within multiple relations, giving its array of audible tethers their invisible thickness, length, and resolution independent of the linear progression of images. Any index may then become stronger and form an inferential relation, or lose its friction and become audibly translucent, thereby lessening the possibilities of attention. The opposite of friction is harmony, which thins the audible relation, dissolves the index, and pulls the sonic-event back into the common where it undifferentiates, not from world but from thought. In this way, hearing dissociates from listening and becomes acceptance. This is a key difference between audibility and sound: synthesis and distinction lie within oneself as a folding of the world to subjectivity. In harmony, movements along the course of reason and judgment often take the form of a listening that discounts other listenings; and acts of ignorance amount to an abandonment of hearing as a multiplicity. Both are manifestations of harmony that amount to the same end: they close the question.

Mixing, as variable overlaps of the sonic world and the audible self, is never complete. A film maintains its constant and immeasurable repetitions of becoming and fading. One's attention gathers in the same moment of disregard, remembers in the same moment of forgetting, as life continues. Nothing enters a state of being soluble in its combining, never achieves a oneness, a *solution*. It might be better to call the process "differentiation," because this is what the activity of mixing produces. The mixing of the sonic world gives rise to understandings and beliefs, but captures no object and achieves no *telos*; its idea comes from the fact that the *logos* has no beginning and no end and must continually be reengaged, regathered. The mixing of a matrix of sonic-events is offered as repetitions in the audible-event, born of recurring, mnemonic interjections that resonate one's entire life, even to life's ultimate limits, reaching out to eternity. It bears repeating that the *haecceity* of any event is only *this* particular emergence and fading in *this* revisitation of layers that has always sounded. But it has the capacity, as Kierkegaard longed for, to become "a moment" in which eternity enfolds within the instant.

In the everyday, one is always already in the middle of whatever is audible. In my daily life, I pick up what is already occurring. I can choose to listen to the woman at the table across the room or the man sitting in front of me. I can listen and hear, listen or hear, hear or listen. I can open my hearing wider and choose to shift my listening to low-frequency rumble, the ambience of the air-conditioning unit above me. I can hear the din of conversation while listening to a song playing over the restaurant loudspeaker. Audibility engages in a continually shifting simultaneity of logic and spirit, conscious attention and unconscious envelopment. It is not always a choice but often is a compulsion or forced engagement. This is what is so exceptional about a film such as Lynch's *Eraserhead* (1977)—the offering of events that the film's protagonist Henry (Jack Nance) cannot help but attune himself to.

This hearing-plus-listening is done in all aspects of sound, but usually those that adhere to some structural system such as music, as lyrics *plus* melody and instrumentation; or as language and its conventional structuring *plus* the tonalities of the speaking person. What one cannot do is *listen* to two complete presentations of systemic sound. I cannot listen to and form an understanding from two speaking persons, nor someone speaking as I listen to a piece of music. I can hear one or many as I listen to another, but I can only listen to one. This is how listening plays the dual role of faith and/or ideology, because it must suspend all other possibilities. Time's hearing is layered and matrixial, but its listening is linear, which is why one line of dialogue, if it is to achieve clarity, is presented above that of any other dialogue or music that carries an intention toward listening. The overlapping dialogue of a director such as Robert Altman is described as having "energy" for this reason; one must involve oneself in a choice of listening. For Malick, it is different: a voice or a melody has the ability to stop time, to silence the dominant strain of listening that falls back to identity. Such moments of crystalline eternity, moments of "being," as Virginia Woolf called them, are often found in acts *toward* love or toward faith that suspend linear progression and invite eternity. This is always possible in the everyday, which Malick unfolds in such overlapping durations. This is why he takes great care with his silences, which break the language of dictation—as both dictating and dictatorial—in order to allow another thought, idea, or reverie to enter. Hearing, as distinct from listening, maintains simultaneity through its matrix of availability, allowing other listenings. To be truly open, hearing must invite another time of listening.

There are two points of emphasis here, both regarding systemic hearing but language in particular. As Wittgenstein writes, language implores, placing one under constant influence and pulling one toward its "fibres" of thought that are already knowable (2009). Therefore, to *hear* in its deepest, most primal mode of being present, one must eliminate language from one's attention. Similarly, to *listen* to that which is not language one must eliminate language, including the inner dialogue of thinking. Both channels free hearing to its own openness, which is vital to any opportunity of listening that the matrix may offer. "Understanding"—in other words, one's private knowledge—must be upset or overturned by the continuance of hearing that allows a new listening. To hear as one listens one must not fall back to what is known but continue to take account within the *logos*—to pay *attention*.

Compared to the lived world, one's ability to discern in cinematic audibility from the distance of audience requires direction; no matter how many loudspeakers are present, cinema is a flatter world. In any film the mixer must direct the experience of the matrix of sonic-events, anticipating the event of audibility on behalf of an imagined universal yet discerning audience. The individual is the one who listens and ignores, who gathers in the moment of forgetting. The mixer can only offer *anticipated* tendencies, indications toward listening—the implicit suggestions of possible audibility within. Among such anticipations is that of openness itself, which is often incorrectly referred to as space. Openness is the negation of audible direction, a suspension of sonic-events in time, which in Malick allows thought and reverie to enter and breathe. Mixing is therefore pedagogical, Pythagoras's delivery of unseen knowledge for the unseeing learner. A mixer can only give the audience a choice to learn the dynamics of character and condition along its various means: direction, suggestion, dictation, openness, closure. One may decide to be selective, to invite a particular listening to only the most attentive hearer. This is the sonic-event that does not *deliver* a lesson, but offers a nontextual *lection*, the Latin predecessor to "lesson," which is an act of *choosing*. Such sound is designed to be discovered, to perhaps, but not necessarily, be noticed.

A Heraclitean Lesson

Music is mixed in a Pythagorean harmony. A film is mixed in a Heraclitean harmony, with its fluid differentiations and recurrences through time. In this distinction we find the audible subtext of Malick's *Days of Heaven*. The film is aptly named, because the "heaven" is religious, spiritual—an ephemeral achievement of an almost Platonic ideal, or at least the idea of the eternal and the transcendent. But the "days" embed life within the temporal, the immanent, marking the time of succession. This is Malick's unstated thesis, a concept that returns often in his work. Eternity comes to live within the time of struggle and anxiety. One lives the unseen resonances of hell and heaven on earth. In *DoH*, hell is that which returns, while heaven is the time of the interlude. This is expressed in the expression, the Deleuzian affection-image, of Bill's (Richard Gere) face as he arrives in the fields, an impression of *eidullion perfectus*:[2] a stem of wheat in his mouth, a simple smile and bright eyes. It is as if, in emerging from the audible and tactile nightmare of the coal furnaces and the punishing, undifferentiated repetitions of industrialization, he has finally found his way out of the cave and emerged into Plato's forms. Yet whereas Plato's prisoners live in blissful ignorance, Bill is continually reminded of his own knowledge of his confinement, as he repeatedly cycles toward the fire, to always confront and contribute to his hell with each shovelful of coal. Outside in the wheat fields, the fire no longer burns, pounds, and hisses in its proximity. In its distance, the fire of the sun is silent and its light is diffused; it bathes him in a state of reflection and occasionally streams through

---

[2] Lifting from both Greek and Latin to mean "the completed form" or "the perfect image."

the clouds as divine revelation. Around him the imperceptible hum of locusts and the whisper of the breeze provide an audible embrace that is easily accepted—and ignored. But this seeming arrival of transcendence hides an imperceptible chaos, an unseen immanent activity of change and differentiation. What its characters will come to learn is that heaven and hell are not separate transcendent places, but immanent emergences arising within the same world. The *difference* is not of worlds or realms but of *logos* and *nomos*.

In Book X of the *Republic* is Socrates's story known as the "Myth of Er." In it he mentions four passageways of Tartarus, two in the earth and two in the sky, one each, coming and going. Judges preside over these entry and departure points. Those coming from the heavens are blissful, those from the earth sorrowful. The most lamentable of the souls waiting to come up to judgment (such as murderers) would not be allowed out of Tartarus. Each soul approaches the opening to ascension and if refused, the mouth roars, while those granted the right to rise hear only silence. At the moment of the roar, fiery figures take away such unfortunate souls or beat them. Er says that hearing the roar was every soul's greatest fear. Socrates narrates Er's story: "He said that of the many and multifarious fears they experienced there, the greatest each of them had was that the sound would be heard as he came up, and that each was very pleased when it was silent as he went up" (Plato, 2004, p. 321). Socrates then explains that salvation comes in the light that binds the universe together. It comes in a great meadow, through which those spared wander for seven days. Finally they witness a single shaft of light through the clouds, the Spindle of Necessity, whose sirens sing a single note in perfect eight-part harmony.

In Bill's hell of the factory, the only sonic presence is the roar of oppression itself, in cycles of unchanging succession, disallowing conversation and silencing reason—their means of connecting with one another. In the wheat fields all is quiet and bathed in sunlight, a single note of harmony produced by the ambient multitude of soft locusts, humming in unison. In this moment of Bill standing alone in the open, the machinery has stopped and the wind breathes over the wheat in a sonic-event that feels tactile. In this place, the *logos* is the common, the open breadth of "silence" that signals no need for attention. Over the next hour of story time, the film reveals in other susurrations; there is little dialogue, being as it is unnecessary in heaven. Silence, vital in Malick's *logos*, offers the opportunity to forget and to allow the opening of the new. But silence is not a total absence. Something hides in this tranquility, a presence that is audible yet *undifferentiated*.[3] This place has a singular ambience, an immanent harmony: the murmur of harmless locusts. It is a sign to which no one is attending.

First: Hearing

Hearing is passive when *logos* is not active. In the everyday, this openness cannot be bothered to close. This is because hearing is unmediated audible experience, the "immediacy" of unseeing in both uses of that word: the now and the not yet made. This is audibility in its primal state, the readiness of the unconscious, the always arriving that waits, the activity of life and the persistence of death. *Hearing comes first*, and here we can borrow from Charles S. Peirce's trichotomy of signs and apply it directly to the presence of audibility.

For Peirce, Deleuze's source of semiotic inspiration, everything is a sign, including sound. "Firstness" is his term for total freedom in experience because here signs possess no determining quality. It is the uncontrolled "measureless variety and multiplicity," Kant's manifold of sense without the unity of synthesis (Peirce, 1955, p. 79). Peirce states outright that *sound* is in the faculty of firstness, although he places the sign in the world rather than the audible relation ("sound of a railway whistle") (p. 80). We can think here of James's radical empiricism, which accepts a nonmonistic (pluralistic) simultaneity of experience. Not only does experience include extension but it also manifests in singularities—elements rather than principles or universals (James, 2003). What James describes as a "mosaic" experience, similar to Hume, is in Peirce a network of signs.

Deleuze writes that firstness "is felt, rather than conceived" (1986, p. 100). He continues that it is "what is new in experience…fleeting and nevertheless eternal." It comprises the signs that emerge "independently of any question of their actualization." Firstness, he adds is for itself and in itself, the undifferentiated, and a quality of possibility. This applies well to Deleuze's affection-image. He calls "affect" the prior of consciousness that becomes disruption. As with the *possible*, affection is that which enables what is to come but does not itself become—the interval that never fills the gap. In cinema, affection is the aspect of the movement-image that lies

---

[3] For ease of readership I will maintain the use of "differentiation" rather than Deleuze's "differenciation," the latter of which would be more appropriate in this case. On the distinction of the two terms, see Deleuze (1994).

between sensation and action. Deleuze thinks of an affection-image as a singularity—one undifferentiated but which doesn't blend into indifference. "Affects...have singularities which enter into virtual conjunction and each time constitute a complex entity" (1986, p. 106). Usually constructed visually by Peirce and Deleuze, firstness appropriately describes hearing prior to and within listening. But this *first-order hearing* is inclusive, both openness *and* sensation as a present availability prior to perception. This aspect of audibility waits without expectation. As mentioned in the previous chapter, hearing is always already providing some level of audibility, whether one is asleep or awake, eyes closed or open. Whereas vision is always forward-oriented, the openness of hearing is within what is *already* audible, prior to perception, an overlap of the possibility of the actual with its potentialities as virtual, the "may-be" of Peirce.

In *Days of Heaven* we take note of two variations of firstness: the hellfire of the factory and the quiet of the wheat fields. The factory churns in its linear, plodding, steaming rhythm. Its continuity is so loud and so psychologically punishing that its continuous density drowns out any possibility of a rational discourse (secondness) toward an appeal to law or *nomos* (thirdness). Such first-order hearing is audibility that maintains its own total *closure* in acceptance. Its volume and lack of difference or plurality make it unlistenable, establishing an audible fascism, a master–slave relation of unconscious passivity where no questions can be asked. On the farm, by contrast, there is the openness of preconscious hearing that allows the possibility of listening. The ambience of the locusts upon the arrival of the "sackers" early in the film is the firstness of "ambient sound"—one's pervasive audible connection to place and time. Narratively, ambience is the sonic/audible relation with one's *condition*, an audible "signature" that connects self and world. Its relation is a temporal one. The unique quality of ambience signals history or timelessness—the age of an environment or setting. The ambience of a city is relatively recent compared with that of a meadow or seaside. The latter, "natural," ambience is the time of now that is inseparable from nature's timelessness.

Is it any wonder, then, that Malick often juxtaposes such ambiences—the timeless earth and the temporal world of men? In both, *this* ambience—for ambience can only be particular—situates one within a place's time in a common, predictable, shared continuity that is knowable by being ignorable. It carries the sense of an audible *ground*, an unconscious, ungathered state of one's connection within the place's past. Ambience is a persistence of the past through a connection to the world, to what has always been, what is reliable and unchanging. It is the closest we have to an immanent eternity, a history whose perfection lies in transcending the activities of women and men.[4] Narratively, we can think of it as audible *setting*, not in its things but in how one feels in this world. It is, by nature and in audibility, indistinct.

In *DoH*, the ambience of the wheat field and its lack of difference give it a kinship to the factory in this one sense: nothing is listenable in itself.[5] The ambience has no discernment as itself. Yet in the fields, the *quantity* of sound is so low density that *audibility* allows for other pluralities within ambience. It lays fertile ground for moments of distinction, the emergence of a secondness of thought. Here, unlike the factory, ambience takes on the character of silence. Even as it invites the openness of hearing, it is not attended to unless one were forced or compelled to make the choice of attending to it. The four principal characters in *DoH* give themselves no reason to attend, to notice. Its hearing is forgotten as it dips into the eternity of its own past and future, like an eternal and shared unconsciousness. In this way it is a virtual tether that lies slack.

This ever-present ambience can be carried to an existential level though Kierkegaard's objective and subjective anxiety. Because Adam brought sin into the world, the world one conceives as created by God is and always has been in sin. As one is born into the world, he is born into history. In other words, the self does not just begin at birth but is in the midst of the long stretch of history beyond the self. Anxiety is in relation to sin in that one is always in a *condition* of being within the time that exceeds oneself. Kierkegaard describes this midst as a "more" that one must rise above.[6] We can think of the soft locusts in the wheatfield as the continual and ignorable murmuring of sin, the anxiety that is unattended. For Kierkegaard, anxiety is not a negative state to be overcome but, rather, an

---

[4] "Nature's imperfection is that it has no history in any other sense, and its perfection is that it has the intimation of a history (namely, it has come to be, which is the past; and that it is, the present). But it is the perfection of the eternal not to have a history, to be the only thing that is and yet absolutely without a history" (Kierkegaard, 2009, p. 143).

[5] Could we not say the same about God and the Devil? The hearing of either comes from within the everyday of the indiscernible.

[6] "Christianity has never assented to giving each particular individual the privilege of starting from the beginning in an external sense. Each individual begins in an historical nexus, and the consequences of nature still hold true. The difference, however, consists in that Christianity teaches him to lift himself above this 'more,' and it judges him who does not do so as being unwilling" (Kierkegaard, 1980, p. 73).

acknowledgment of one's condition. In this, it "is altogether different from fear and similar concepts that refer to something definite, whereas anxiety is freedom's actuality as the possibility of possibility" (1980, p. 42). As ambience is the continuation that houses a possibility of hearing the long draw of time, anxiety is the condition of sin from which one may draw a sense of action through choice. Ambience and sin are the possibility of hearing and anxiety, which themselves lie in wait. They become subjective through a new listening and a new choice, as both share the same *logos*. Bill and the Farmer attend to neither ambience nor sin, and *logos* never gains its chance to offer them more.

The presence of the locusts is first heard, unseen and unattended, upon arrival in the wide shot of the landscape and the Farmer's (Sam Shepard, unnamed) house in the distance. It is, in the sense of cinematic composition, the familiar natural sound of the setting. All within the film can hear it but do not listen because there is no need, no difference, no threat. Yet "nature," in the naturalistic sense, does not entirely supplant the infant, squealing industrialization that Bill left behind. The churn of the factory returns intermittently in the film in the form of machines. It is a revisitation of industry in its manufactured rhythms heard in the swishing, slicing violence of the automated thrashing machine, so dominant and threatening in the mix; it is in the heft of the coal-fired train cars pulsing their way through the fields. In their simultaneous soundings there is not one rhythm but two, a continual polymeter that strays and rejoins in its maddening, artificial entrainment. It calls back in suggestions to Bill's prior hell in the factory, in echoes of the noise of confinement and incomprehensibility. Hell not only cycles back to him but it also returns *in its cycles*, the unthought memory of the cycle he left behind.

As with the characters in *DoH*, one in daily life always hears but is not always open to the open, unless one allows oneself to be. Hearing is what one has in the moment prior to an *apocalypse*, in the Greek sense of the reveal. One hears what is present before the uncovering, a disclosure of what was previously hidden. The locusts are always there in the soundtrack, submerged in their mix, waiting. Prior to the *vision* that is the reveal and the attainment of what one takes to be knowledge, the voice of God always whispers, the presence of spirits is hushed, and nature continues.

First-order hearing then involves a *parouisa*, another Greek word that suggests not only presence but also an arrival or visit—a *potential* presence as openness to that which has not yet arrived. When the apocalypse of *DoH* comes, it is in this Greek sense of the word, a visual reveal: the locusts that now threaten all of them. In hearing, one is in the world as a sensorial being. There is no need to *call forth* from one's hearing unless—whether through the violence, suggestion, or choice of differentiation—one engages within continuance, and one's involvement calls forth the virtual array of prior experience in the moment. As a choice, an acceptance of hearing becomes an availability within what is gathered as present and actual, a gathering of difference. I can at any moment open up my hearing that already exists to take account of whatever I may gather through an engagement of listening. As an engaged individual, a sensitive individual, I can choose to dig inside the matrix and pull out what is otherwise ignored. Rather than the birds of my neighborhood, I isolate a particular bird, or anything else in the common, as an attempt to unfold the difference in this event and carry it forward. It is not merely a phenomenon but also an isolation of what *concerns me* as Dasein. A turn from hearing to listening can also be forced upon me, as Deleuze's signs do. I might, against my will, encounter a collision in the *logos* that differentiates within the matrix. This brings a jolt of attentiveness in which I do not actively bring forth my history. My history, my experience, is thrust upon the moment, and memory narrows the event to a single point of significance that is instinctual rather than reflective, but one that allows me to then enter into new thinking and feeling. An arrival of this variety turns toward a different kind of presence, a question of actuality, because it has turned toward listening and thought. The question in Malick's later films is whether or not this turn toward another time is *immanent*. In either case—by choice or by force—such encounters as disclosures or singularities necessarily disrupt hearing and move cognition forward into the realm of listening.

Second: Listening

As the collective *pathos* becomes more tense, the principal characters in *DoH* find themselves consumed by their attachments of jealousy, guilt, and distrust. Stewart Kendall writes that after the circus performers leave, it "becomes more persistently a film about watching. Much of the film consists of characters watching either things or other people" (2011, p. 151). In such fixed, furtive gazes and hiddenness the characters also find themselves in states of unseeing, but incapable of hearing. Each carries an inaudible noise of thought—an inner listening devoid of hearing—that further masks the unseen threats. Bill throughout is locked up in maintaining his deception, which along the way also morphs into regret and jealousy. Abbey's (Brooke Adams) complicit role merges into a sustained guilt. The Farmer is not only blinded by his cycle of love and suspicion but also muted to all else in the process.

The two reveals of what was always unseen come one after another: first, the Farmer comes to understand the romantic deception; and second, everyone comes to understand the existent threat of the locusts. Both disclosures reveal visually what has always been present to hearing yet unattended in listening. The first reveal comes as the Farmer stands next to his weathervane. The placement of the weathervane is interesting in the position it occupies in relation to the Farmer. The first time we hear its sonic-event (object-event out-of-frame) is when we first see him in the film. This gives us an audible association of the two elements, weathervane and farmer, to the audioviewer. The next time they are connected is when he stands watching Bill and Abbey from a distance, and Malick dissolves to the weathervane as it whirs loudly behind him, marking the first time he becomes suspicious of the affair. The final connection is its reveal: the Farmer had previously suspected their deception but only in a shadow on a curtain. This time, he sees them kiss in the full light of day, as he stands next to the weathervane. Taken in material or rational terms, the weathervane here is not an audible index because it is seen and therefore known. It is instead a rare case of Malick creating an *audiovisual symbol*. Visually it indicates beyond what it is, that there is some direction that he should follow to find the truth, while audibly it is that which symbolizes his inattention to his hearing. He could have listened to the footsteps of their departure from the house in the middle of the night; he could have listened to the conversations in other rooms, or the audible inflections in their voices; he could have listened for the noise of the locusts. But the noise of the weathervane constitutes an audible mask,[7] just as the factory masked Bill's ability to reason his way out of a deadly confrontation with his boss. The Farmer only becomes aware of the deception as he stands next to his weathervane, as its cyclical repetitions noisily point in Bill and Abbey's direction, indicating what has always been available but never seen.

The second reveal comes in the seeing of the locusts, now so prominent in visual and audible *actuality* that the threat becomes knowable. Within this *parouisa* (arrival, *apocalypse*) comes the *anagnorisis* (discovery), which

---

[7] "Masking" is a sound-engineering term for one sound that covers another, which is normally unwanted.

unfolds as a *paripeteia* (a reversal).[8] *Anagnorisis* is the key element here because the discovery in Aristotle is associated with knowledge. The visual reveal of the locusts is the knowledge of what was available to audibility but inaccessible to visuality. Were the first reveal to be the only one, the Farmer could confront his deceivers and deal with them rationally by banishing them from his home. This can be considered therefore as a narrow reveal, not in a lesser import, for it is the important turn in the story among the three characters; rather, it is the one with a narrower scope in terms of the weight of the *logos* relation. The wider reveal is the locust swarm, the full brunt of nature, the *logos* screaming beyond cohesion. This *paripeteia* is first seen by the film's only innocent, its storyteller Linda (Linda Manz). We see it in her eyes, but it is an understanding brought forward in the fullness of sense: The prior hearing-virtuality meets the triple-actuality of thought, sight, and sound. Knowledge is now given to total consciousness: sonic-event meeting audible-event meeting object-event, forming understanding. This is the overlapping *anagnorisis* that, owing to its width and impact, subjects the players in the unraveling action to the impossibility of reason. The unattended *logos* has taken over, passing no judgment and erasing the possibility of discourse as it whisks everyone along to their fate.

If we think of this in sonic or audible terms, the first of the two reveals could have been heard and understanding could have been born from it. In this sense, we empathize with the Farmer's inability to listen. Like the celestial bodies of the cosmos in Aristotle's *De Caelo,* all is heard but unlistened, taken as a Pythagorean harmony in which everything is normal.[9] Yet the weathervane symbolically masks his openness. When the reveal finally comes, it must be seen; he must see, like the turning toward the fire in Plato's cave. The betrayal was always there, always presenting the possibility of knowing. But he didn't hear it. This is the silencing of openness in oneself, the hearing prior to listening, that never allowed him to listen.

At this point, the actuality of this common ambience, its ceaseless collision of micro-events, has emerged from its immanent virtuality. But in audible attention, this actual now reaches out to its virtual significance. All this evades causality because sound, hearing, actuality, and virtuality have

---

[8] All three terms are attributed here to Aristotle's *Poetics* (2005).
[9] Aristotle is responding to the Pythagorean *music of the spheres* in *de Caelo,* that its sound would not be audible since it has always been with us. See Allen (1991).

conjoined into simultaneity at every instant, with no beginning and no end. As virtual it maintained its secret, but out in the open it is a reminder that this force, this power, has always been secretive. Its ambience, a ceaseless murmuring of *logos*, now emerges into thought from within itself. In *DoH*, this is the moment of a forced engagement with signs; what was always heard but never listened to emerges in a seeing that is knowable. But once visible it is too late.[10] When Linda finally sees, the sonic-event comes forth to audibility violently. We are given the full fury of *their attentive hearing* of nature in its buzzing, chewing, rattling, and hissing. The sounds of Hell arrive from within nature, rather than an imposition of industry, to literally consume Heaven. This is followed by the return of industry in full force as technology churns in metallic rhythms. Even Ennio Morricone's organic orchestra cycles now in mechanical patterns, its strings and woodwinds taking on a synthesized quality.

Audibility now closes on secondness through its prior denial. As with the beginning of the film, hearing becomes noise as characters confront each other openly; the two streams of *parouisa* now exposed converge and become one in a blaze of fire. "*Let it burn!*" the Farmer yells, speaking not only of his farm but also his entire world and all within it, including himself. In Deleuze's secondness "Everything is individuated…determining and determinate" (1986, p. 146). Secondness in Peirce is the state of indexicality and what I (not Deleuze, and only intimated in Peirce) name as listening. This listening never had the chance to occur in hearing and therefore never turned over to a relation that might lead to some understanding. Now the noise of Hell has found them all and they are helpless as the world burns.

Third: Nomos

We now come to "thirdness" in Peirce—the association of law. I situate it here with the Greek law of *nomos* (νόμος) because *nomos*-thirdness is the element of thinking or reasoning that falls outside of the audible engagement without fully abandoning it. In this sense, *logos* is an engagement that encompasses *nomos* into the relation. Considered within Malick's

---

[10] "The aspects of things that are most important for us are hidden because of their simplicity and familiarity. (One is unable to notice something—because it is always before one's eyes.) …we fail to be struck by what, once seen, is most striking and most powerful" (Wittgenstein, 2009, s129, p. 56).

cinema, *logos* opens an *existential* field of closure and openness in a conscious negotiation with a *nomos* of *phusis*, a Greek relation of natural law. The *phusis–nomos* relation works through how things are versus how they ought to be, as well as that of reality versus appearance (McKirahan, 2010). The problem with early Greek notions of this relation is an emphasis on externality more than an engagement. But for Heraclitus, "there is no split in principle between *nomos* and nature. As an institution, law is neither man-made nor conventional: it is the expression in social terms of the cosmic order for which another name is Justice (*Dike*)" (Kahn, 1979, p. 15). Nature is the totality,[11] but *nomos* is an inseparable human expression, while *logos* is that which activates *nomos* in its distribution—a seeking along the open of nature that precedes any division and which thereby changes the whole.

We can think as well of Deleuze's writings on Spinoza, but applied to the audible dimension. Laws are not made of essences. Sound and hearing do not come from any prior order; rather their relations manifest within laws of composition and decomposition. If there is understanding to be had, it lies within this ongoing movement and ephemerality of object/sonic/audible-events, which find themselves working through a particular condition that we can consider as *nomos* in its becoming. In other words, *nomos composes audible law.* But this "law" is continually in flux and not determined prior to the audible engagement. The law that finds itself as a *logos* relation, therefore, is one of emergence in experience via the immanent, mobile relation—no entity beyond, nothing predetermined. It is an availability to distributive individuations as manifestations of natural law, which stretches along the entirety of its duration. This durational composition, or if you will, a compositional duration, is the rational accounting of *logos* that does not accept, but continues seeking. A *logos* relation of *nomos* is a signifying network that seeks along a field of law as a gathering, rather than an *a priori*, divine determinant of understanding (*nous*).

Whatever we consider as laws of nature require nothing previously and objectively established. Rather, the relation is the field of experience, a continual creation taken in its action and development. The important aspect of *nomos* that differentiates conceptually from *logos* is that *nomos* is

---

[11] "For the Greeks, φύσις takes in the entire realm of the world in the sense of what's out there—the totality of stars, earth, plants, animals, humans, and gods" (Heidegger, 1969, p. 1).

territorial. It seeds itself along a territory even though its limits are not established. It is not fixed; rather, it is in constant redistribution through *logos, ethos*, and nature. One's audibility stops when thought references a universal, but it remains creative in the thinking that *passes through* a continuing state of composition and decomposition.[12] The *nomos–logos* relation remains alive so long as it keeps moving, or so long as time is given to thinking. In this constant flux of change and becoming, we can think of the relation metaphorically as a Heraclitean fire that continues to burn. This fire is here, it has a territory and its natural law; but it only continues as kindling becomes ash, as each individual element or thought ignites, burns, and dies out in the collective, eternal fire. As Witt narrates in *The Thin Red Line* (1998), expressing the whole as faces of the same man: "*Everyone looking for salvation by himself. Each like a coal drawn from the fire.*" The crackling of this fire is not outside, a deity beyond, but a multiplicity within. *Logos* defies capture and continues on undocumented, uncategorized, undefined. There is only *logos* to the extent that one's relation makes it so, and only then is its immanence open to the transcendental field, in the sense of the whole that is changed by one's engagement. An unrelated *logos* is meaningless, since *logos* ignored has no relation. We can think of *logos*, therefore, as the *element that differentiates* in the actualization of thought and appearance within the distributional field of *nomos*. *Nomos* is a *permeable law of inseparability* that is one's arrangement of thought, rising to the *surface*, carrying and contouring mnemonic associations—the network of lived sounds, sensations, and the language of and through its inhabitants.

At this point we bring *nomos* together with Peirce's *thirdness* to express the working-through of listening that finds its interpretive, rational disclosure as different from a lexical-visual knowledge. Thirdness is the act of deciding, an earthly, ethical "because" based on logical, causal references. Yet an *audible* thirdness requires a modification in its thinking as *because*—not a because that refers, but one that again *infers*. Consider that Peirce's trichotomy, as Deleuze explains, is a cardinal rather than ordinal law of exchange that need not abandon its other, prior modes (Deleuze, 1986). In other words, there is a direction to the process that maintains what comes before. Secondness may maintain its firstness and thirdness may maintain all three. This is important for audibility in two connected ways: (1) in unseeing, each successive state threatens to lose its prior one; and (2) any state on its own is ideological. A listening without hearing is a divided audibility, searching for a predetermined identity. A thirdness that

---

[12] See Deleuze (1990a), "Spinoza Against Descartes."

works through *nomos* without hearing or listening has already decided; it refuses not only listening but also its vital component of continual openness because its territory is fixed. But a *nomos* of reasoning that maintains its hearing and listening nurtures what is distributed into decisiveness. We infer natural law through our incorporation of what is relational in secondness. For this reason, thirdness threatens to *abandon audibility* if inferentiality is abandoned, even when one may continue to be engaged with the sonic-event.

Nomos and thirdness are not audibility, but what audibility gives way to in the negotiations of rational thought—what we name as understanding and believing. Once one reaches the state of *because*, reason seeks to terminate audibility—to terminate all resonances and answer the question or solve the problem. At this point of "understanding," *nomos* has doled out its fixed properties—its laws or conclusions. Yet audibility can also remain within this territory, as the undetermined thought that allows one to continue to question or problematize against one's ethical fixity and to potentially deterritorialize the distribution that is made. For audibility to remain in its state of attention, it *cannot decide*; it must continue to work through problems as a chance to break one's gathered *nomos* and find something new. This is the existential *and* ethical aspect of a *logos–nomos* relation: the question of what a character will do. For Kierkegaard, faith decides, leaving behind universals of ethics and reason. In faith, *nomos* is transcended. But this is not the dilemma in *DoH*, which is grounded quite literally in the earth and the flat plane of available, present signs. The problem for its four main characters is the need to continue gathering what is unapparent within the immediate. Such audible gatherings gather not only signs but also all that one has ever been that makes the sign, leading one along threads of acceptance, disavowals, ruptures, creative pathways, and terrors that *find nomos*. *Logos* is one's capacity for seeking, but *nomos* is *finding*. An ethical openness is the continued resonance of both: the finding that continues to seek. As its Greek origins suggest, *nomos* is a not a dictate but, rather, a *melody that sings*—an accountable, *uncountable* law of "spirit." As it sings, we create new harmonies or new dissonances.

With this, we continue to engage what comes *first* in a movement forward, opening to a possibility of new thinking. What is relational begins with and carries what is available in an openness. This is the lesson unlearned in *DoH*, the unhearings that are muted by other acts of listening. Maintaining firstness opens to another possibility of secondness, which may then alter the territory of *nomos*. Malick's characters have not yet learned this, and in *DoH* his characters unwittingly ignore or close their own hearing. In this case, the Farmer is incapable of taking account from what he can neither see nor hear in his seeings and listenings. Such a listening rides the dogmatic thought that fails to find other listenings. This is how we as auditors of the film gain a path that is empathetic—we hear these characters' failings as well. In the case of Bill, we feel without needing to recollect the heard-seen hell of the factory, the machinery, and the fires; we feel the devil's presence in the sonic-events of the machinery that follows him to heaven, waiting for the moment to drag him back. We feel it because Bill feels it, too, with every recurrence, but he is stuck in his linearity. Kierkegaard reminds us that *"anxiety about sin produces sin"* (1980). Bill cannot escape time, which means he cannot escape himself and his past, and he is doomed to repeat his sin in the future. He fails to account for the *logos* in a different way than does the Farmer, involved as they are in different struggles. His unlearned lesson is only found in retrospect through the subtexts of Linda's retelling of the story: Instead of living in Platonic virtue on the farm, in relation with the *logos* as common, Bill chose deception. Bill's decisiveness (in the Kierkegaardian sense) could have produced *a repetition*, a creation of the new from anxiety by reaching out to his higher state. Instead, he revisited his sin that never left and repopulated it in heaven. Whereas the Farmer never gathered his necessary problem, Bill created his problem from the harmony of collisions. As Linda says early in the film "*See, the people that have been good, they're gonna go to heaven and escape all that fire. But if you've been bad, God don't even hear ya, he don't even hear ya talkin'.*" And later, she recounts a turn when the circus performers arrive. Bill and Abbey lose their inhibitions, but the Farmer can only see shadows of them behind the curtain; he cannot see-to-know and is unwilling to hear their signs. "*The devil just sittin' there laughin'. He's glad when people does bad. Then he sends 'em to the snake house. ... I think the devil was on the farm.*"

To put this in a Heideggarian framework, Bill was never *waiting* and, rather, was *waiting for* the attainment of his objective. As Heidegger's scholar on a country path says, "as soon as we re-present to ourselves and fix upon that for which we wait, we really wait no longer" (1966, p. 68). Whereas in the openness of *Gelassenheit*, as the teacher replies, "In waiting we leave open what we are waiting for." At the end we can feel, on an unthought level: because hearing was closed, because it *remained* passive, thirdness lay barren and *nomos* was fixed, leaving *logos* abandoned as judgment constructed hollow determinations. There was no engagement, no *logos*, only *listening toward nomos*, a dialectic of inner conflict based on presumptive external causes and the desire to attain an end.

Without *logos*, *nomos* dies under the weight of preconceptions. One then conceives law within a mesh of private ideas.[13] To relate as *logos* is to seek along the openness of hearing that invites an authentic listening within movement and activity of law: the locusts as conceivable, as actionable. Additionally and conversely, to listen to one's private preoccupation masks the possibility of listening to what is new, the *inconceivable* law: the footsteps of Abbey in the middle of the night, the whispers between her and Bill. Whereas the former reveal is the everyday that can be found with attentive audibility, the latter is the audible version of a new thought that must be sought out in sensation rather than one's closure of presumptions. The Farmer is closed to the former, but in the arc of deception he seeks the latter in his *seeing*, a narrowing effort toward visual verification that is always masked to him. To find understanding, both require an openness to what is unseen within one's seeing, an imagining of difference, an engagement with the creative mind that does not dwell on dominant streams of the material, the objective, the linguistic, the expected, and moves instead along new threads of learning.

The unlearned is a Heraclitean lesson. To return again to Bill's moment in the fields, his arrival there feels like a liberation of the spirit: a Pythagorean–Platonic harmony of nature, the single chord of the whirling spindle described by Er. He does not gather in a Heraclitean harmony of collisions buried unseen all around him. When his hell reemerges, it is born of the *logos* unlistened, not *nomos* but *nature* that *forces its own* distribution, which from time to time must bring forth from the fire that illuminates a need to burn in a roar of destruction.

The *logos* ripples in sound and hearing. The *apocalypse* is unseen and unforeseen, announcing itself always even if it does not yet actualize. Anxiety, perhaps caught up in jealousy, brought Bill back to his nature. For Kierkegaard, and Malick as well, anxiety carries with it as much opportunity for freedom as it does for dwelling in sinful acts. But this freedom requires a repetition that is a step outside of time in the same instant it is a gathering of lost time—a reaching out within the virtual, the eternal, which breaks the habit of time. If our present seeing and listening are dominated by habit, thought becomes fixed to indices of representation and causal determinacy. Here, Kierkegaard and Deleuze share the same

---

[13] See again, Heraclitus, Fragment 2. (McKirahan, 2010).

problem: the paradox of thinking is to discover what has not been thought. To think the new, one must break habit and enter the unthought. This is the challenge Malick's characters often face: the need to break the straight lines of seeing and listening without falling back into a return of sameness or identity that leads to despair. Perhaps then one's "nature" need not have the last say; perhaps what breaks through into the becoming of the new is something larger, something like grace.

REFERENCES

Texts Cited

Allen, R. E. (1991). *Greek Philosophy: Thales to Aristotle*. New York: The Free Press.
Aristotle. (2005). *Poetics* (J. Sachs, Trans.). Newburyport: Focus Publishing.
Chion, M. (2009). *Film: A Sound Art* (C. Gorbman, Trans.). New York: Columbia University Press.
Critchley, S. (2005). Calm: On Terrence Malick's *The Thin Red Line*. In R. Reed & J. Goodenough (Eds.), *Film as Philosophy: Essays in Cinema After Wittgenstein and Cavell* (pp. 133–148). New York: Palgrave Macmillan.
Deleuze, G. (1984). *Kant's Critical Philosophy* (H. Tomlinson & B. Habberjam, Trans.). London: Athlone.
Deleuze, G. (1986). *Cinema 1* (H. Tomlinson & B. Habberjam, Trans.). London: Continuum.
Deleuze, G. (1990a). *Expressionism in Philosophy: Spinoza* (M. Joughin, Trans.) Brooklyn: Zone.
Deleuze, G. (1990b). *The Logic of Sense* (M. Lester & C. Stivale, Trans.) London: Athlone.
Deleuze, G. (1994). *Difference and Repetition* (P. Patton, Trans.). New York: Columbia University Press.
Heidegger, M. (1966). *Discourse on Thinking: A Translation of Glassenheit* (J. M. Anderson & E. H. Freund, Trans.). New York: Harper & Row.
Heidegger, M. (1969). *Identity and Difference* (J. Stambaugh, Trans.). New York: Harper & Row.
James, W. (2003). *Essays in Radical Empiricism*. Mineola: Dover.
Kahn, C. H. (1979). *The Art and Thought of Heraclitus*. Cambridge University Press: London.
Kendall, S. (2011). The Tragic Indiscernibility in *Days of Heaven*. In S. Kendall & T. D. Tucker (Eds.), *Terrence Malick: Film and Philosophy* (pp. 148–164). New York: Continuum.

Kierkegaard, S. (1980). *The Concept of Anxiety* (R. Thomte, Trans.). Princeton: Princeton University Press.
Kierkegaard, S. (2009). *Repetition and Philosophical Crumbs* (M. G. Piety, Trans.). Oxford: Oxford University Press.
McKirahan, R. D. (2010). *Philosophy Before Socrates* (2nd ed.). Indianapolis: Hackett.
Nietzsche, F. (1962). *Philosophy in the Tragic Age of the Greeks* (M. Cowan, Trans.). Washington, DC: Regnery.
Peirce, C. S. (1955). *Philosophical Writings of Peirce*. New York: Dover.
Plato. (2004). *Republic* (C. D. C. Reeve, Trans.). Indianapolis: Hackett.
Wittgenstein, L. (2009). *Philosophical Investigations*. Malden: Blackwell.

Films Cited

Lynch, D. (Director). (1977). *Eraserhead* [Motion Picture]. USA: AFI / Libra Films International.
Malick, T. (Director). (1973). *Badlands* [Motion Picture]. USA: Warner Bros.
Malick, T. (Director). (1978). *Days of Heaven* [Motion Picture]. USA: Paramount Pictures.
Malick, T. (Director). (1998). *The Thin Red Line* [Motion Picture]. USA: Geisler-Roberdeau, Phoenix Pictures / 20th Century Fox.

CHAPTER 5

Malick's Temporal Shift

Audibility, *hearing with listening*, is grounded on repetition. It works not through any language but through memory in its recurrences and reconstructions. It manifests and is made through repetitions of signs, indices, and inferences that cannot be written or notated. One gathers, learns, and makes from audibility because one has lived. Cinema is an audible expression because it, too, is learned in experience, in time and memory, not through any language. One comes to know cinema through repetitions of cinematic experience, itself an aspect of experience. Cinema at its most evocative makes this connection, not by repeating the same but by creating in new repetitions, by growing experience, drawing memory forward into new expressions of thinking.

For both Kierkegaard and Deleuze, repetition is the creation of the new as an expression of time. As mentioned in the introduction, Kierkegaard makes the point that recollection and repetition are the same condition, with the former arcing toward the past and the latter toward the future. The act of gathering is the same, but only repetition creates the new. Recollection for Socrates is inherent within us, a means of attaining answers within a great paradox of epistemology: How can one know what one has not yet known? His answer was that the search, and the process of learning, is recollection (Plato, 2005). In Plato this is known as *anamnesis*, the recollection of past lives. Knowledge is then the cycle of gathering not only one's immanent past but also one's transcendent past—the other lives that have known what this life, this current life, does not yet know. Kierkegaard's response to Plato is that recollection gathers in a manner that is sorrowful, whereas repetition "has instead the blissful security of the moment" (2009, p. 3).[1] Recollection is a youthful indulgence, but repetition is a willful act of courage, the courage to gather within the moment and move forward. He suggests that God himself willed repetition, and this is why the world was created.[2] Repetition in the individual life is similarly creative because it makes actual from the gathering of thought. We can think as well of Nietzsche's concept of the eternal return (recurrence), which to Deleuze is a positive, active engagement in creative repetition.[3] Agamben picks up from Kierkegaard, Nietzsche, Heidegger, and Deleuze in writing that the novelty of repetition comes from its "force" and its "grace" (2002). It is the transformational element of memory, in which the real and the possible are in constant exchange. In this, he adds, repetition is like cinema. It is the *transcendental* element in which everything is possible.

At play here is time, which opens audibility to its relations. The distinction being made philosophically is one of time and eternity. The former is finite and closed while the latter is infinite and open. As Kierkegaard phrases it, one lives in a relation with the wholeness of time; but the future is eternal while the past is only its fragments.[4] Yet the point of emphasis that leads us through Kierkegaard and Deleuze and into Malick's unseeing cinema is that one lives time in its sequence while having the power to enfold eternity.[5] Both existentially and cinematically, the experience of time becomes a question of what one resonates. One gathers the past as closure, sorrow, recollection or the future as open, joyful, repetition.

Eternity for Kierkegaard is entered in a forward movement, a forward recollection that he names as repetition. Repetition is "the originality of disposition," which marks the eternal in earnestness. This originality and

---

[1] "While Greek pathos is concentrated on recollection, the pathos of our project is concentrated on the moment, and no wonder, or is it not a highly pathos-filled thing, to come to be from not having been?" (Kierkegaard, 2009, p. 98).

[2] "If God Himself had not willed repetition, there would never have been a world. He would either have followed the easy plans of hope, or recalled everything and preserved it in recollection. He did not do this. This is the reason there is a world. The world consists of repetition. Repetition is actuality and the earnestness of existence" (Kierkegaard, 2009, p. 4).

[3] See Deleuze's writings on Kierkegaard's return alongside Nietzsche's recurrence in the introduction to his *Difference and Repetition* (1994). And of course, see as well Deleuze's *Nietzsche and Philosophy* (1983).

[4] See Kierkegaard (1980).

[5] We find this expressed in many writers and thinkers, among them, Plotinus, Kierkegaard, Borges, and Woolf.

eternity go together in breaking time's habitual line. He writes that "habit arises as soon as the eternal disappears from repetition. When the originality in earnestness is acquired and preserved, then there is succession and repetition, but as soon as originality is lacking in repetition, there is habit. The earnest person is earnest precisely through the originality with which he returns in repetition" (1980, p. 148).[6] It is informed by his passionate Christianity, and perhaps Malick picks up from here as well—eternity as the fullness of time. Malick grants action and mobility to Kierkegaard's concept through his characters who think and who reach out along eternity through their rupturing of habit, either by thought or by force. Repetition is an ethics of unseeing, in which audibility is involved with the seeking of a new time, a new territory, the fullness of eternity in the immanence of time.

Repetition and Coexistence: Malick's Expressions of Immanence

Between the release of *Days of Heaven* (1978) and his next film *The Thin Red Line* (1998), Malick's *logos* opened to such a coexistence of time, a verticality of expression. Here, in this temporal shift, unseeing takes on a wider scope. It is not only a matter of one's faculty of audibility aiming toward an understanding. Unseeing becomes a question of the actuality of the transcendental and the maybe of the transcendent within immanence. How far does *logos* reach in Malick? Is the condition of unseeing another opening *within* existence or *to* something beyond it? Such questions help to shape the world that Malick builds through his characters. As Wahl writes about Jaspers and Kierkegaard, transcendence as a question of freedom and choice is veiled, unknowable.[7] It "refrains from revealing itself save indirectly so as to put our freedom to the test" (1969, p. 60). Because of this, freedom "appears only in flashes" (p. 63). Recollection and repetition work along this very question: the uncertainty, the *work* of choosing within the vastness of one's unseeing possibility. For Kierkegaard, the

---

[6] Here, in an amusing move, Kierkegaard's writers reference each other. *The Concept of Anxiety*'s Vigilius Haufniensis footnotes *Repetition*'s Constantin Constantius, who wrote that only the eternal is the true repetition.

[7] It bears repeating that there are different definitions of *transcendence* in philosophy. Kierkegaard's and Deleuze's are different from Sartre's and de Beauvoir's, for example. The latter use the concept as a capacity within freedom.

question of immanence and transcendence is one of faith in God. For Deleuze, there is no God beyond; rather, there is the indefinite transcendental infinite. For Spinoza, God is immanent, and each expression is a manifestation of God's totality. All such conceptions are various openings, aspects of availability toward movement within unseeing. One might say that at least in his unfolding, through the gatherings of his characters, Malick does not close explicitly on God or lack thereof. Perhaps faith in God is his personal *ethos* and *pathos*, but in his characters this is kept open and unsaid. The seeking along the question is what unfolds.

Recollection and repetition are both a gathering in accordance with one's present, unseeing condition—the audibility that moves away from seeing to see another time. Recollection and repetition therefore fall within the same *logos*; without either, one falls into meaningless noise, as Kierkegaard wrote. They are not necessarily in conflict, but are moving in different directions, speeds, and magnitudes, widening the tethers of multiplicity and complicating any engagement. Indeed, Kierkegaard writes that "intensified" recollection is "the eternal expression for the beginning of romantic love, is a sign of genuine romantic love.... At the dawn of love, the present and the future battle for eternal expression. This recollection is precisely the reflux of eternity into the present, when, in any case, it is healthy recollection" (2009, p. 8). This intensification stands beside repetition and is described by Kierkegaard as a Heraclitean relation rather than a Hegelian mediation. The two types of love are not in opposition but, rather, are two circuits in the organization of noise as a condition of despair.[8] Therefore, when audible simultaneity gives rise to coexistence, repetition and recollection find themselves in strife, an immaterial collision of habit, desire, will, and choice.

The "Malick effect," if one wishes to use such a term, is this coexistence. Malick is indeed the inventor of cinematic coexistence. No other filmmaker has created sustained repetitions built upon the recollections and thoughts of imagery born from unseeing. This tendency is particularly strong in *The New World* (*TNW*; 2005) and *The Tree of Life* (*TToL*; 2010). The audible gatherings of *logos* deterritorialize and reterritorialize time in fragments, giving flight to a multiplicity of durations. These two films express his temporal shift that started with *The Thin Red Line* (*TTRL*). His formulation of

---

[8] See also Melberg, who writes of the auditive in repetition. Constantin's Young Man is Orphic; he "escapes seeing his nameless Eurydice, and his final fantasy of a sublime presence is beyond the eye and its glance in the sense that his fantasy is auditive" (1990, p. 78).

time became broader by turning inward, taking on more dimensions and complicating the lines between the sonic and the audible. In other words, his *logos* began to mutate and express *itself*.

In *Days of Heaven* (*DoH*), Malick's *logos* unfolds a linear activity—a causal indexicality, even in its unseeing, among present object-, sonic- and audible-events. After *DoH*, his *logos* shifts in time and dissociates from the present. *Logos* occurs this way in any event, but *cinematically* this is typically only expressed through the surface and distance of the affection-image, the thinking of the character from the outside. Deleuze's affection-image discloses affection as the condition of the character, but does so as felt by an audience. What changes in Malick is the turn from faces that express outward for an audience to the expressions inward, the lines of flight that are *their hearing and listening* that make *logos*, make the imagery, make the thought that *becomes* Malick's cinema. Starting with *TTRL*, thought and imagery unfold themselves, a becoming of relations—memory, recollection, repetition. His cinema in this period expresses the relations that were not visible in his first two films. It is a shift from the transcendent "outside" of audioviewer to the *inside that folds* the outside of *itself*, the thought that imagines the audible within the self and which in turn creates the repetition, the new image of thought.

The examples of the hodological and crystalline discussed in Chap. 3 become fully realized after *DoH*. From *TTRL* to *TToL* the virtual begins to express its own actual, the actual of thought. He shifts from making images to making thought as imagery, bringing him to a more deeply Kierkegaardian unfolding of anxiety that shifts between recollection and repetition, opening the realm of faith through various expressions of love and redemption. *TNW* and *TTRL* express not only a memory-recollection-imagining coming forth but also its coming forth as what is outside within oneself. This is Malick's *poiesis* in a wide meaning of the word: the making of cinema in the expression as the making of *logos* in the gathering. Malick's (and his characters') *made coexistence, made leaps into regions,* allows the audioviewer to imagine this gathering. Cinematic audibility, as designed sound, establishes a means of anchoring or rupturing these overlapping durations. Malick maintains his organic sound while he sends other audible channels free from Euclidean coordinates onto unseeing holodogical paths and into crystalline suspensions. These multilayered durations of seeking, finding, and losing enable thinking to express its time, while the film's soundtrack produces a floating multiplicity of time independent of, yet not inseparable from, the demands of objective time.

Cinematic Leaps in Time

The Thin Red Line introduces a shift from linear events to the coexistence of thinking within moments. The "unseeing" story is a gathering of thinking that seeks out unity through fragmentation. Unity, lost in the past, desires a rehabilitation in the future. Lou Andreas-Salomé writes of the manly brotherhood of war: "It was 'comradeship,' a fellowship in shared experience that went far beyond friendship or family, uniting them in a totality, a self-same being, as if a time once more existed in which mankind was unified and strong, prior to its separation into individual consciousness" (1990, p. 114). Malick's new time is perhaps this very effort: gathering together the threads of time into an ideal unity. The bringing together of family, in all its connotations, is a wish to bind lost time. This may remind one as well of the opening lines of Andreas-Salomé's essay "The God Experience": "Our first experience, remarkably enough, is that of loss. A moment before, we were everything, undifferentiated, indivisibly part of some kind of being—only to be pressed into birth" (1990, p. 1). She continues that the tiny aspect that remains with us, constantly and unconsciously informing, is a "residue of the whole," which stands before the world that rises, a world into which we have fallen, from fullness into a void that deprives.

Kaja Silverman, who wrote about Malick and Andreas-Salomé in *Flesh of My Flesh*, describes *TTRL* as a film that "defies localization, because all beings are 'features of the same face'" (2009, p. 12). It is Heideggerian in the sense of a wholeness that she describes, yet also Deleuzean in that the features are what express the imagined whole.[9] Bergson writes that one is both unity and multiplicity, and that what matters is how one intuitively grasps the unity and multiplicity of oneself (1999). The whole becomes not the identifiable, changeless entity but the work of repetition.[10] Through his multiplicity of voices, each unfolding its own time, Malick expresses many aspects of these philosophical problems—both the psychological and

---

[9] According to Badiou, Deleuze's univocity is not a numerical One nor identity to One; rather, univocity is about multiple *forms* of being (2000).

[10] Again, Badiou argues that "the One" is Deleuze's metaphysical effort, not as a general or numerical identity, but through the simulacra that actualize its power. "Conceived as the immanent production of the One, the world is thus, in the same way as for Plato, a work and not a state. It is demiurgic" (2000, p. 26). Perhaps, however, he should have stopped before invoking the demiurge, which is conceptually contrary to Deleuze's immanence in that it orders from beyond.

the metaphysical. Cinematically, his use of voices evades the ideological falsehood of cinema's need to attribute any speaking or hearing in a unified body. They are neither a voice-on-high nor a hero-subject, both of which are common in popular film. By decoupling the words from any single voice of authority, Malick shatters both technological and ontological unification. Existential unification is what his characters seek—a *reaching out* to the whole from this loss that Andreas-Salomé writes of. In a Malick film, memory does not reside for long in any individual but, instead, becomes a cinema of memory itself as experienced, a gathering of others through the gatherings of time. It is only in *The Tree of Life* (2010) that the experience comes down to a single consciousness; but even here, subjectivity matters less than the resonance and co-emergence that all within feel, the signs that all share in the projection forward.[11] In the "end," the multiplicity meets as the whole—all durations sharing the walk along eternity—which is the ideal that Jack projects. *TToL* is the movement on the part of the adult Jack (Sean Penn) to share his revelatory rupture in his fallenness, to be able to express in experience what could not be put into idle talk, embodying the dream of togetherness at the end. Whatever becomes, he is the becoming, the opening *to all*.

Malick's films do not have memory, time, coexistence, or dreams explicit in the plot. Rather, it is his *logos*, his seeking of unseeing connections within seeing, that cannot be found through language. Memory is engaged in the act of gathering as (and from) experience into recollection and repetition.[12] Again channeling Bergson, Deleuze writes that the past is that which we leap into. When we search for a recollection, "we jump into one of its circles in order to form images which correspond to the actual quest" (1989, p. 100).[13] Malick's leap is in constant motion, not always backward but ideally projecting into the future. Deleuze quotes Fellini in his *Cinema 2*,

---

[11] Deleuze might call this an expression of "world-memory." He mentions that Resnais would sometimes give memory to one character (*Je t'aime je t'aime*, 1968), two characters (*Last Year at Marienbad*, 1961), or more. (See Deleuze, 1989, pp. 116–120.)

[12] "For memory is clearly no longer the faculty of having recollections: it is the membrane which, in the most varied ways (continuity, but also discontinuity, envelopment, etc.), makes sheets of past and layers of reality correspond, the first emanating from an inside which is always already there, the second arriving from an outside always to come, the two gnawing at the present which is now only their encounter. ...[T]he cinema of the brain develops ... the order of time according to the coexistence of its own relations" (Deleuze, 1989, p. 206).

[13] Or as Elsaesser and Hagener write of Deleuze's Bergsonism as it pertains to cinema, "time is an indivisible continuum that splits in the present moment" (2010, p. 159).

but the statement echoes Kierkegaard as well: "We are constructed in memory; we are simultaneously childhood, adolescence, old age and maturity" (1989, p. 99). The construction, the composition, of childhood is both leap and gathering. Childhood is a time of chance encounters and mostly sad passions; a time of being cut off from one's power to act.[14] The leap is an act of creation from this virtuality of time, inclusive of the past, into the actualization and activation of something new, a new plane extending forward in time. This distinctly cinematic entanglement of recollection toward repetition is a deployment of creative forces within the process of unfolding and layering time through listening and memory. These zones, betweens, regions, sheets, and circles are conceptualized most dramatically in crystalline durations of audibility and imagery, in which the two gain separation from each other and follow along movements enabled by their various threads of time, all in a hope of regaining unity. The sensory-motor and its common signs of sensation (object-event, sonic-event) become severed as one's audibility pushes into the "large circuit" of recollection-images, dream-images, and world-images. This is how audibility creates its own unfolding from memory. The virtual timelessness of memory makes time through a gathering in unseeing.

These gatherings and leaps into regions are what Jack's character does throughout *The Tree of Life*. Except for the initial sequences, the "space" or sensory-motor of the film only occurs in two physical locations: Jack's adult home and his workplace. Everything depicted after his ritual lighting of the candle is Jack leaping into imagined regions of the past and future. It is not a filmic depiction, nor a narration (*diegesis*), but a leaping-into that is the sensorial and emotional fragmentation of childhood remembrance and forgetting, imagined into the new.[15] Malick's *logos* allows us to cinematically live within Jack's memory-recollection-imaginings, his struggles to gather within his heightened unseeing. Heidegger has his own conception of such a shift; rather than the leap, it is the "spring" into Being, which he calls "the event of appropriation" (1969). This is the mode that "speaks to us directly from the very nearness of that neighborhood in which we already reside. For what could be closer to us than what brings us nearer to where we belong, to where we are belongers, to the

---

[14] See Deleuze (1990), on Spinoza's "Ethical Vision of the World."

[15] "In the sphere of historical freedom, transition is a state. However, in order to understand this correctly, one must not forget that the new is brought about through the leap" (Kierkegaard, 1980, p. 85).

event of appropriation?" (p. 37). In this regained relation, one contributes to the "self-vibrating realm" of man and Being. One thinks away from calculation and technology toward another thinking that is a new relation to time.[16]

The leap and the spring also lead us to a better notion of what film language calls "the flashback"—cinema's method of visually dividing time to clearly delineate past from present. For Deleuze, the flashback is a closed circuit that "only confirms the progression of a linear narration" (1989, p. 48). It is not memory but representation, a "then" *of the past* lifted into the apparatus. The flashback reifies the past that is gone, rather than the coexistence of memory that persists. We might think of the flashback in a linear-montage conception as that which is reserved to what is no longer—an expository correction. Cinema usually falls into cliché by making the lines between a then and a now too sharply rendered, which freezes the past into a *rigor mortis*, which Heidegger critiques in fixed conceptions of the past as *passed* (1968).

A crystalline audibility offers a coexistence rather than a flashback—for one is never fully "back" in the past, nor the present.[17] Here audibility functions as the binding energy that maintains the life of the past within the present. Bergson seems to describe Malick's cinema when he writes that any perception is loaded with memory, and in most cases "these memories supplant our actual perceptions, of which we then retain only a few hints, thus using them merely as 'signs' that recall to us former images" (1988, p. 33). This is quite different from Heidegger's *logos*—the spoken word that reveals the image of truth. Rather, this hearing and listening to time unfolds not only images but also all of time's resonances of thought and feeling in their fragmented attempts to take account of the past and carry it into the future. Contemporary directors such as Steven Soderbergh

---

[16] Although for Heidegger this is a *return* to Being, rather than a creation of the new. In many respects, this is how Heidegger is different from both Kierkegaard and Deleuze.

[17] Heidegger and Deleuze are somewhat different here. Deleuze in one regard advocates the necessity of distance in *The Logic of Sense*. But in his cinema, his effort (and Kierkegaard's as well) is one of overcoming such distances of "back" toward a movement of bringing time into nearness, closeness and coexistence. For Heidegger, distance is necessary to regain the nearness that has been lost. "Only as this step gains for us greater distance does what is near give itself as such, does nearness achieve its first radiance. By the step back, we set the matter of thinking, Being as difference, free to enter a position face to face, which may well remain wholly without an object" (1969, p. 64).

seem to have taken Malick as inspiration in this regard,[18] but only in brief moments and because it is written into the story. Malick brings forth an extended sense of such coexisting durations: the making-present of simultaneity with the coexistence of actual and virtual. This is because his films are not *about* memory; they are themselves the reimagining of memory—a gathering and preserving of memory within the life of the character.

Dreaming and the In-Between

Bergson writes that the dreaming state is one of openness while consciousness is a state of closure. Deleuze adds that "*the dream represents the largest visible circuit or 'the outermost envelope' of all the circuits*" (1989, p. 56). Remembering again Jack's shift in *TToL*, Bergson's dream state suggests to the awake state "I… am the totality of your past" (Bergson, 1920, p. 126). The dream state further informs the individual that his awake state as rational wanders around from contraction to contraction in order to close him inside a present action. Being awake consists of striving and willing, a constant transition from closed experience to closed experience. The enclosing is a field of attention, a willful narrowing of perception and the intellect. "[T]he same faculties are being exercised whether we are awake or dreaming, but they are in tension in the one case, and relaxed in the other. The dream is the entire mental life, minus the effort of concentration" (p. 127).

In one's audible condition, hearing is an openness while listening is the attention on its act, an emphasis that is attuned to this contraction, to the thinking event of interpretation. In a dream state, to think in a Bergsonian manner, one's listening fragments not by choice but by shifts and distortions in time. This fragmentation is a pure condition of unseeing, in which audible-image relations have no connection to the present-actual. This is what creates the fragmentation of disunity, a continuous multidurational unfolding of memory lifting from various contractions of the past. We find this disunity in *TToL* often, but most pronounced in the scene in which young Jack witnesses a man being taken away by police. Rather

---

[18] I am thinking here of Soderbergh's *Solaris* (2002) but there are many examples. Malick's influence can be seen/heard in newer films such as Spike Jonze's *Her* (2013), Jean-Marc Vallée's *Wild* (2014), and Denis Villeneuve's *Arrival* (2016), all of which feature multiple scenes of crystalline coexistence. Such audible elements unfold the *logos*-as-coexistence rather than depiction-as-flashback.

than synchronizing and thereby unifying the audiovisual recollection, older Jack distorts the memory in imagination by having forgotten the sound of voices (muted in the mix). Instead, his account imagines what was gathered, shaping and creating the new gathering: the unspoken audible-events of shuffling feet, handcuffs, birds, a plaintive moan, a silent outburst. The dream state is memory relaxed, opening up hearing to what was previously listened to, a reversal of the awake state.

Cinema shares with dreaming these contractions within total openness wherein, as Bergson said, one releases one's will. Nietzsche wrote something similar, that "the dream is a relaxation for the brain, which has had enough of the strenuous demands in the way of thinking such as are imposed by our higher culture during the day" (1996, p. 18). Nietzsche also contends that dreaming "brings us back again to remote stages of human culture." This "dream-thinking" is a different kind of understanding, a relation to the past in a way that could never be consciously recalled or remembered. Both Nietzsche and Bergson spoke of the *audible* component of dreaming as well. For Bergson, hearing is the overlap between the two realms during the dream state. Here the sonic-events of the world can invade the dream state and alter it. In such a state, the audible and visual sometimes flip: an event incorporated as audible is rather something visual that one takes to be audible. "Often, indeed, we are only seeing, when we believe ourselves to be also hearing," (Bergson, 1920, p. 108). Such associations are not determined by sound, but made through a shifting deterritorialization of echoic memory.

In *The New World*, Capt. Smith (Colin Farrell) is stripped of his presidency and the film suggests that he undergoes some torture. We see the insane ramblings of his captor who throws his arms down in a violent gesture to the sounds of a loud, cracking whip. Yet in his hand he holds what seems to be a piece of bark, not a whip. While such an object of torture is not seen, the association of this hearing to his despair and dehumanization creates a more powerful hearing. Here Smith creates an "identity" with nothing material or representational; rather, it suggests an association that is significant as an indiscernible recollection/dream state. Both are populated with and made meaningful by such associations, in which the events of one's life become rendered metaphorically, just as one's hearing of the extended world becomes metaphorical in unconscious transference. All this involves various aspects of the in-between, the overlay, the coexistence and ambiguity of maybes. The between is not a division but a *within*—sound with audibility, sleeping with waking, seeing with unseeing, believing with knowing, virtual with actual. It is not a set matter of residing in sleep, belief, or waiting. Time runs its course, and one lives within the course of what comes. The between is the suspension that allows the crystalline event to formulate, however briefly.

We continually make similar connections in experiential cinema, but in ways that are different from the lived world, and therein it takes on its oneiric quality. When dreaming, one has faith in its world; otherwise, it would have no effect. Bachelard writes that dreaming takes on an aerial quality, one in which the dreamer lifts off and levitates, knowing he is dreaming and convinced he can also accomplish the task in waking life (1988). One lives, moves, and changes within the laws of its world, its *nomos*. But if dreaming releases one from the bounds of gravity, it is not all release; a cinematic dreaming also has its gravitas. Bergson notes that in dreams one is essentially dealing with oneself. He cites an example of a conversation in which nothing has been spoken. These overlapping relationships of world and self, self as self, even sound and nonsound function also in cinema. Malick's films embody this dreamlike aspect but in a different way. If the cinematic carries some quality of dreaming within it, it is again because the audioviewer is engulfed in the real *logos* of another, constituting an extended reverie. But if the reality is itself a reverie, an audioviewer also shares some relation to its building, making, and imagining of memory, which Bachelard notes are the constructive aspects of reverie. If Malick's cinema is the cinema of thinking, one is invited to think the thought that gathers and makes. One imagines as well Jack's mother, who embodies grace by levitating into an aerial dance, as in *TToL*. For *TNW*'s Smith and Pocahontas in the forest, barely a word is spoken, sequences are clipped, music and ambience emerge and dissipate in time. In an idyllic imagining of memory through the creative gathering of recollections, one *imagines the reimagining* of events of sensation and feeling. One remembers in fragments, short scenes, snippets of spoken phrases, brief interludes. It is again the overlay of the in-between, but in this case the now that brings forth the imagined then can only be given life in the effort of recollecting what has been gathered.

For Kierkegaard, dreaming is aligned with an artist who is capable of drawing the eternal into coexistence with time. "Some bend eternity into time for the imagination. Conceived in this way, eternity produces an enchanting effect. One does not know whether it is dream or actuality. As the beams of the moon glimmer in an illuminated forest or a hall, so the eternal peeps wistfully, dreamily, and roguishly into the moment. Thought of the eternal becomes a fanciful pottering around, and the mood is always the same: Am I dreaming, or is it eternity that is dreaming of me?" (1980, p. 152). Many wondered what Sean Penn's role in *TToL* was supposed to be, including Penn himself.[19] It is exactly this, that he is Kierkegaard and Malick's knight, struggling between resignation and faith, striving to draw the eternal into temporality. He is our storyteller, our Bergsonian dreamer, but an active one engaged in his own Dasein. He builds a poetic reverie for us by breaking from the sensory-motor and the fallenness in which he is otherwise engaged. He does this by abandoning his familiar associations: the banal and the mundane, with its unceasing dialogue and constant demand to listen. As Bachelard writes, "reverie liberates any dreamer, man or woman, from the world of demands" (1960, p. 63). In this Jack succeeds whereas *TNW*'s Smith did not. To do so he must suspend his actual world—his image of thought, his identity—in order to take the leap into the virtual, responding to the call, the moment that calls him into the vastness of time, or perhaps outside of time. Or as Kierkegaard might say, he must allow the eternal to live within the finite, to give an infinity to time. Smith could not do this—abandon his predetermined, ethical time of obligation—while Jack could. And yet each film offers a similar mnemonic gift to each character, whether conceived as lived within or as a persona for one who lives outside. Cinema *is* the repetition, one built upon the activity of recollection, reverie, and imagination that creates it. It gives life to the repetition that, in Malick's characters, struggles to live. Both films repeat for those who cannot, those who stand fixed at the chasm, incapable of making the leap. Perhaps it is for the *Malick* who could not, but is surely for all of us who have felt a similar dilemma. As his characters shift into and move along the ruptures of recollection and reimagining, so do we, which is what Malick's cinema enables. Devoting oneself to such thinking within recollecting, as Heidegger wrote, is what seeds poetry (1968).

Malick's Time and Becoming

David Hume writes that ideas (thoughts, memories) are fainter than impressions (what one sees, hears, etc., in the present) (1977). Fainter perhaps, but ideas are what give impressions their value. Their gathering builds what is meaningful within the present-actual. This folds back and resonates in a

---

[19] His comments in this regard are readily available through popular film websites, as are the critiques of reviewers.

continuing cycle that gives significance to any impression within a state of affairs. If we then take both such notions as axiomatic, we find that Malick flips Hume's equation in order to flip it back again for the audioviewer. He intensifies the ideas of thought and memory, while impressions of the past and present take on an arbitrary emergence. The multiplicity of both coexist in a forward progression, opening a theater of ideas that then *become impressions* for the audience. The reality of the film for the audioviewer, in other words, is the idea, the thinking that unfolds. This elevates the *intensity* of ideas, to use Hume's term, to a higher level than the state of impressions. This is how Malick's cinema unfolds—by conjuring repetitions of ideas into the simultaneity of impression through the course of the film. Here the audioviewer finds *her own* ambiguity of simultaneity and coexistence. It is also where we find Malick's metaphysics and ethics as revealed in *The Thin Red Line, The New World*, and *The Tree of Life*.

Beginning with *TTRL*, and becoming more pronounced in the latter two works, there is no single line of *mythos* in Malick. As a world that unfolds through its *logos* of unseeing relations, *mythos* in the Aristotelian construct does not exist in its linear causality and changes in character based on (mis)fortune. The *pathos* is in a sense already occurring and is unceasing, drawing forth durations within the whole of time. This whole is expressed in the various ways in which *logos* gathers such durations in its acts of taking account. Each Dasein is a being in relation to his or her own world through *logos*, as a relation to one's past that projects into an open future.[20] The question with Malick is to what immeasurable degree the *logos* is heard, listened to, attended to. As his films progress, this attention and lack thereof become the very *pathos* of the film. Each is a series of percolations[21] in time, which draw together into an undulating meditation on what it has meant, what it means, to live. Continuing and expanding most profoundly with *The New World*, Malick does not present a progression of events nor a purposely fragmented time for reflexive effect, as so many filmmakers do today. In Malick, the film is a persistence of memory

---

[20] Deleuze has an oblique and effective way of describing the particular entrances into the totality of cinematic time, which finds resonance in Malick's approach: "As long as the whole is the indirect representation of time, the continuous is reconciled with the discontinuous in the form of rational points and according to commensurable relations. ... But, when the whole becomes the power of the outside which passes into the interstice, then it is the direct presentation of time, or the continuity which is reconciled with the sequence of irrational points, according to non-chronological time relationships" (1986, p. 181).

[21] I am referencing here Michel Seres's concept of time, from a 2013 EGS lecture by Elie During.

that one gathers in various durations and extends as a time of thinking, emerging in variable threads that long for the time of unification. This is not a *unity of thought*, nor a specific time—neither back to the past nor forward to the future alone. In Malick it is, rather, the *thinking of unification*—its eternal duration, the repetition that reaches into the infinite. It is not an arrival, the finality of the grand cosmic answer, but an ideal duration created through the regaining of lost time. The temporal and immanent thinks toward, arcs toward, the eternal and the infinite. Time draws forward a prior time of authenticity, projecting in a coexistence rather than a single line with a single *terminus*.

In this sense, Malick's characters over the course of the three films emphasized in this chapter are often, though not always, profoundly uplifting. We are given a self who is truly alive in this time of taking account, reforming the past, which is at the same time an awareness toward death. This does not make Malick's films *about* death; rather, they are about the death that lives within every soul's finitude and the redemptive possibility this offers prior to one's end. Resisting the authority of any human subject, his Spinozan sense of spirit moves through the relations of persons and nature, as all are attributes of God's thought. Sinnerbrink writes of *The New World* that its audacity "is to allow, through cinematic poetry, nature to reveal or disclose itself as a 'subject', as a participant in this mythic history. This is a perspective that Malick's cinematic romanticism expresses affectively and sensuously; an experience of cinematic thinking that evokes the possibility of another way of thinking, being and dwelling—if only we are open to this possibility" (2011, p. 192).

The Thin Red Line took up the issue of death and the emergence of a *logos* relation from various viewpoints, including nature itself. "*What's this war in the heart of nature? Why does nature vie with itself? The land contend with the sea? Is there an avenging power in nature? Not one power, but two?*" These questions, the first words spoken in the film, are Heraclitean: a harmony of strife and opposition, a game played among gods. As the *logos* permeates all in this world, men are the ones who must play out the clashes conceived by their immanent gods, their commanders and politicians. Soldiers, young men, have been assigned the sentence of carrying out execution without judgment. As in Greek myth, alluded to in the conversation between Capt. Staros (Elias Koteas) and Col. Tall (Nick Nolte), gods play among gods, men among men, nature with itself, and yet each dynamic affects the whole. *TTRL* presents the *question* of being-toward-death as a broad inquiry that could never be voiced in the moment; rather, it is from some timeless aspect of this ongoing strife.

Fragments of Unseeing: The Thin Red Line *Through* The Tree of Life

The bulk of the first hour of *The Thin Red Line* is a hyper-attentiveness to the now of audible unseeing, a constant state of waiting. People rarely speak to each other and instead listen and learn their environment, thinking through this present time. After the noise and fractured confusion of the main battle sequences, the film moves into states of reverie and the sphere of time widens to incorporate yet another kind of audibility—that of one's past as one lives in waiting. Pvt. Jack Bell (Ben Chaplin) is one character who opens us to coexistence as his life of combat shares his time with his wife Marty (Miranda Otto). As he leaps into coexistence, linearity is broken, yet the present remains through his hearing. Malick does not establish a hard cut between then and now, but blends hearings as Bell blends his virtual and actual coexistence. This first happens as Bell moves up the hill alone in an attempt to see the Japanese position; he looks for what he cannot see and the camera cuts to Marty at the ocean. The hearing of grass follows into the cut, and we know he is not back but has lifted her into his time, creating the coexistence. The hearing of the ocean emerges and then, back with Bell at Guadalcanal, the ocean blends to become the hearing of tall grass again. This continues in other temporal shifts as we remain unsure whether ocean or grass is being heard, the ambiguity in the drawing forth that paints its strokes of audibility across the borders of time. Bell's voice remains in the present tense as he declares his love for his wife in thought. "*I wanna stay changeless for you. I wanna come back to you the man I was before.*" This is not a diegetic now, a present of narration that recalls imagery of the past. We come to understand this because the shifts in time begin to change their vector. Rather than remaining in Bell's recollections, the camera begins to move into another now—*coexistence shifts into simultaneity.* Remember that coexistence is the sharing of multiple durations in one space, while simultaneity is a single time that shares multiple, discrete spaces. Who is this who stirs in her bed? Who is this man walking toward her? Is he still in his recollective coexistence or is she in *her now* of a simultaneity—a separation not in time but in the now of spatial distance across the ocean between the two. We come to learn through a letter that she has met another man she wants to marry. The spiritual bond between them was rendered in coexistence and faith; but its treasured recollections and hopeful imaginings become supplanted by the actuality of simultaneous time: she has found another man while he remains at Guadalcanal. From the point of his reading her letter onward, we hear no further thought as voice narration from Bell.

This ambiguity of time that creates the new image is dilated by the disjunction of space, which becomes even stronger in Malick's films that follow. In *To the Wonder* (2013), Neil (Ben Affleck) overlaps his hearings of travel—trains becoming cars becoming trains. It evokes a similar thematic sensation as *TTRL*, of one's *logos* hearing between time spaces within the film's world. Bill in *Days of Heaven* and Capt. Smith in *The New World* begin their stories by emerging from a dungeon into a new world reborn. And Pocahontas rises from her own world into a new one, carrying the memory of her timeless culture with her. As cinema establishes its connections between actual and virtual, organic and crystalline, it stretches itself into broader ideas beyond concepts and becomes its own form of philosophy. Such expression is neither of nor in language but is in and of such ineffable connections. Perhaps this is why *TNW* expresses itself best in its wordless moments that are interlaced with Wagner's *Das Rheingold*. As with much of Malick's choice in music, it is neither diegetic nor its negation but an idea of the eternal, the timeless, that is real within the world of the character who cannot explicate such feelings. "Music" disappears as an expression of "*the metaphysical in relation to all that is physical in the world*" (Nietzsche, 1999, p. 77). Or as Nietzsche writes in his post-Schopenhauer stage: "What is it that my whole body really expects of music? ... My melancholy wants to rest in the hiding places and abysses of *perfection*" (1974, pp. 324–325). Such expression evades what language brings and what it leaves wanting. Many reviewers questioned the point that Malick was trying to make in this film; it seems clear, in all its lack of exposition, that this *is* the point: to rest in the hiding places of perfection—the projection forward into an idealized whole, the eternal.

The New World is a film about many "worlds" within its world, encircling and overlapping each other, penetrating each other, in this Bergsonian sense of the struggle between logic and intuition toward essences. This is not the "intuition" of popular New Age literature, but the entry point other than analysis, logic, and language. Here we return to Heidegger's Aristotelian appropriation of *logos*. For Aristotle, *logos* meant many things, but Heidegger concentrated most of his writings on one aspect, the one Aristotle's method gives the most attention as well: speaking. In Heidegger's readings of Aristotle's rhetoric and logic, *logos*-speaking is what lies between nature and man (Heidegger, 2010). But for Aristotle, rhetoric is also what distinguishes animal from man, and more to the point, non-Greek from

Greek, savage from rational man. This is a tension implied and acted out in *TNW* through Pocahontas and Smith, the presumptive archetypes of the "savage"—the word is voiced often—and the cultured Englishman. What is offered through their interaction is another aspect of *logos*, a hearing that joins nature and ethics in a shared learning that leads to a more intuitive listening. Arendt writes that intuition, which is guided by our senses, is the highest means toward truth and where the tension between vision and speech need not enter (1978). Rather than a division, the signs of shared humanity create connection points and possible affective openings—a look, a smile, a sense of trust, a calmness, a spirit, an ability and willingness to hear and to listen, a *feeling*—all of which creates the dream of the idyllic that returns. Smith and Pocahontas learn to understand each other through such receptivity—a shared *logos* that brings together world (*phusis*) and person (*ethos*) in their widest possible spheres. Curiosity and openness, rather than attainments and pragmatic ends, allow the attraction to unfold, before and in the midst of trying to come to a shared way of speaking and listening. Elizabeth Walden writes that Malick's attempt in this film is to approach that which cannot be spoken, that although we come to know the world materially "the world is nevertheless irreducible to their terms and, importantly, this ought to be a cause of wonder, even humility, before it" (2011, pp. 197–198). Only when language finally comes do the expressions of discord and distrust emerge through the necessities of rhetorical *logos*. Reasoning percolates in fragments of misunderstandings and violence when intuition and the signs of humanity and love have broken down to what is necessary, the duties that rationalize love *out* of *logos*.

As mentioned previously, *The Tree of Life* narrows the question of authenticity and finitude through the Dasein of Jack. He gathers as he lives in his concrete and glass world, conjuring childhood memories and metaphors of the infinite as he works his job. Architect that he is, he begins to build a vision of another time, an imagined time. Bachelard writes that imagination does not form an image but deforms it (1988). But one might also claim that time is what deforms images, while imagination, this new time, reforms them. Here we have a reformation, an engagement that seeks along the limits of all known horizons, reaching a timelessness when all is forgiven.[22] This for Kierkegaard is what releases time from presence. There is no present *in time*, he writes, while the eternal *is* time, the making

---

[22] "And now the moment. Such a moment is unique. It is, of course, brief and temporal, as moments are, ephemeral, as moments are, passed, as moments are, in the next moment,

of time by annulling succession, the succession that defines finitude and the demands of succession (1980). The eternal goes forth without the body having to leave. Because it has no past nor future, the eternal is the perfection of itself; its emergence is expressed in the coexistence of time—the moment that activates the eternal. As Kierkegaard writes, spirit is the synthesis of the temporal and eternal. Spirit enters not from presence but from the moment that becomes present.[23]

Jack's moment of authenticity comes in his struggle within such forces that intersect and complicate his unidirectional listening, his singular sequence of thought. His consciousness is brought forward into a new relationship to what has been closed, reforming in a spiritual vision of the future that takes on the quality of a dream. For Bergson, the dream state contains in its designs the totality of a person's past. Any dream is not only a relation to memory but also a resurrection of this past. "But it is a past we sometimes fail to recognize" (1920, p. 114). He goes on to say that memories are not only of events but also of memories themselves. While one's understanding may remain out of reach, nothing is entirely effaced through forgetting. Everything one has perceived, willed, felt, and experienced is there in memory. The connective tissue between memory and its dreaming is sensation;[24] the two work together to reinforce each other.[25]

Pages of a Life: Memory and Dreams in Coexistence

Schopenhauer would probably not disagree, yet he sees dreams as both memories of the past and projections forward. In *The World as Will and Representation*, he writes that "Life and dreams are the pages of one and the same book" (2010, p. 39). As awake we read the book from beginning to end; in dreams we randomly open to various pages, landing here and

---

and yet it is decisive, and yet it is filled with eternity. Such a moment must have a special name. Let us call it: the fullness of time" (Kierkegaard, 2009, p. 95).

[23] From Kierkegaard (1980): "Man, then, is a synthesis of psyche and body, but he is also *a synthesis of the temporal and the eternal*" (p. 85). "As soon as the spirit is posited, the moment is present" (p. 88). "The synthesis of the psychical and the physical is to be posited by spirit; but spirit is eternal, and the synthesis is, therefore, only when spirit posits the first synthesis along with the second synthesis of the temporal and the eternal" (p. 90–91).

[24] "When this union between memory and sensation is effected, I dream" (Bergson, 1920, p. 117).

[25] "Sensation longs for a form into which to solidify its fluidity; memory longs for matter to fill it, to ballast it, in short, to realize it" (Bergson, 1920, p. 118).

there. Sometimes we read a page that has already been read and other times we jump to what has not yet been read. This future-oriented gathering into the moment again calls Kierkegaard to mind. He writes that the past is a part of the eternal while the future signifies its *entirety* (1980). There is an availability to the future that is open to signification and *also includes* the past. The content of the future is wide open because time has not yet doled out its events. This is why our gatherings as recollection are only an accounting of the what-has-been. But an account of the future opens to a true repetition—a gift from the unknown, an epiphany, a revelation.[26] In this way, dreaming, memory, recollection, and repetition find themselves sharing a similar activity, which Malick is able to draw forth in *TToL*.

For Schopenhauer, life is lived in its sequence, as in the reading of a book. This linear progression and logic of page-turning is what cinema usually attempts to do. It adopts the real-world laws of causality to recreate the feeling of the common—a *logos* forming from and conforming to logic, rather than the other way around. Under such cinematic laws, the audience can accept the renderings given to the screen and loudspeakers. Malick plays with this *common*, pushing forward within the common—an intermingling of what was and what is not yet. To again paraphrase Schopenhauer, no matter where we are, in the past or future, we are always in the same book. The only difference between dreams and reality is sequence and causality. But in Malick, the sequence loses its necessity as the unfolding becomes increasingly coexistent. One other important point to emphasize with Schopenhauer's metaphor brings us to the level of the *film*: If one were to stand outside of a book (or a single page, as he later visualizes it) there would be no way to distinguish what is dream and what is real. Here "we must concede to the poets that life is an extended dream" (Schopenhauer, 2010, p. 40). This is also the folding/unfolding relation of the audioviewer. The distinctions among dream, reality, memory, reverie, and understanding become blurred and rather than such distinctions, we are given the opportunity to build relations in the unraveling of an original experience, a *story*, which takes on the quality of a dreamer's images and echoes.

The oneiric aspects of a film such as *The Tree of Life* are this between or overlay of dream, memory, projection, and reality. Who is to say what the collisions are that break through the common? Do they happen now? Are they being remembered by someone? Perhaps it is all of it, various relations,

---

[26] I paraphrase here from Edward F. Mooney's wonderful introduction to *Repetition*. See Kierkegaard (2009, p. viii).

signs, circuits, and threads that constitute the whole of the story, one not spoken of but evoked. Each of us lives in relation to one's past and one dreams the dream of his own time. While *TToL* is the adult imagining the child, it is through Malick's singular approach a spiritual imagining. Dewey writes of the spiritual dimension of childhood recollection and notes that he cannot explain why experiences become deeply spiritual, "except on the basis that there are stirred into activity resonances of dispositions acquired in primitive relationships of the living being to its surroundings, and irrecoverable in distinct or intellectual consciousness" (1934, p. 29). He adds that "There is no limit to the capacity of immediate sensuous experience to absorb into itself meanings and values that in and of themselves—that is in the abstract—would be designated 'ideal' and 'spiritual.'" The sonic-events of *Days of Heaven* clearly came from material relations (object-events), as an invitation in hearing; the audible-events of *TToL* are not so easily delineated. Is this hearing gathered as a call that comes from sensory-motor conditions in the immediacy of the moment? Or is it a movement within, the call from another time as oneself, the "folds and foldings that together make up an inside...the inside *of the* outside" (Deleuze, 1988, pp. 96–97). Perhaps it is entirely other, the call of transcendence, a duration outside of time, which can only call along the barest *perhaps* of the *logos*'s audible threads.

Malick judiciously leaves such a question open. But if Jack is a metaphorical dweller of our shared cave, his emancipator is *his logos*. His gathered imaginings are a *rupture*, thrust upon him from some Dionysian aspect of himself. It arrives in signs, incorporeal rumblings that conjure a vision and fragment the mundane as a reminder to remember to re-form and *reform*. This is not just recollection, but as Bachelard writes, the reverie of childhood that does not recount and instead aims to eradicate history, "to rid us of our names" and to seek out the "original solitudes" (1960, p. 99). "Childhood knows unhappiness through men. In solitude, it can relax its aches. When the human world leaves him in peace, the child feels like the son of the cosmos." Jack the child imagines dinosaurs and only wonders hesitantly about what the world is. Adult Jack pulls such feelings from child Jack and projects them as a cruel, overbearing father. He draws forth early curiosity into a boldly rendered visual question about the origins and fate of life in the universe. This is a cosmic reverie that can only be listened to in the solitude of childhood regained.

Virginia Woolf writes often of childhood in a way that reads as cinematic, as *Malick*.[27] "Many bright colours; many distinct sounds; some human beings, caricatures; comic; several violent moments of being, always including a circle of the scene which they cut out: and all surrounded by a vast space—that is a rough visual description of childhood. This is how I shape it; and how I see myself as a child, roaming about, in that space of time" (1985, p. 79). Such reverie is, again, not an arrival but a means toward rebuilding, rehabilitating. Memory for Bachelard is a "field full of psychological ruins" that must be reimagined as a form of *recovery*. This is the oneiric power of *The Tree of Life*, that it gathers overwhelmingly within the virtual field of memory in crystalline durations that project forward along the newly made idea. Tarkovsky writes that childhood memories are the most vivid ones (1989). Reflection, he adds, doesn't bring one back to the thing as it is but calls forth an idea of what it was as it now lives and creates anew.

Without stating so outright, Silverman makes a connection between Andreas-Salomé and Rilke in a similar way. The former wrote that "we *all* 'live through more than we are,'" not only because the past lives on in the present but "because the present has a transformative influence over the past."[28] In reading Rilke, Silverman later offers a notion that reminds one of Schopenhauer but is quite different: one's history is not a book but rather one chapter, whose writing is not entirely one's own nor graspable. The book itself has lived prior to oneself and continues on after. "This volume is written from the inside, through the analogies we acknowledge and those we refuse. Its production is also a collective process, in which everyone participates and everyone is implicated. ... The Book of Life is forever in the making, and *later chapters have the capacity to rewrite other ones*" (2009, p. 65, emphasis added). The emphasis added here brings us back to Andreas-Salomé. Insofar as film *is* a narration, it is in its idea. Its author may be Malick, but the characters' attention as *logos* makes the history that is already past. The present, whatever one takes as the reality of now, is the coloring, distorting, and reforming of the past and the future into what is unfolded cinematically.

Malick's films offer us an unfolding of what one is capable of becoming when a life, this particular life, is lived authentically and in a state of won-

---

[27] Of course, the reverse might actually be the case, if Malick is a reader of Woolf.
[28] Silverman (2009, p. 45). She also quotes Andreas-Salomé that one is not a writer of one's own story but a "listener" to it (p. 62).

der in repetition. What is the best aspect of one's character? It lies in one's willingness to seek out a time most authentic to one's own sense of self—the openness of a gathering that *takes account*. In *Badlands* (1973), Holly (Sissy Spacek) narrates: "*Something must've told him that we'd never live these days of happiness again, that they were gone forever.*" This theme is found throughout his films. The past is gone. The film becomes the safekeeping, the Heideggerian holding in thanks. It is the widest possible scope of what we name as "thinking" that takes account, that gathers and reforms. Malick's films express a listening to the past that reimagines and preserves, which saves the future. Salvation is possible in *logos*, as one both recalls and imagines one's life as a gathering toward a future ideal time. It is felt in the soldiers' togetherness in battle as they found themselves through each other. Violence is imbued in all of Malick's films, but the violence of *Badlands* and *Days of Heaven* becomes transformative after those films. If *DoH* is a failure to listen within the open field of hearing, *TTRL* begins to seek along the opening that is listened to and accounted for in his films that follow. Continuing through *TToL*, Malick presents a deeply hopeful unraveling in the sense that one finds the best aspect of one's character at the precise moment when one should find it—the one who emerges in an open, authentic relation with life that leaves itself continuously open. Each film is a potential awakening.

Early in *TTRL*, Witt (Jim Cazaviel) stares at a lighted match for a long time and finally says "*I love Charlie Company.*" Witt, as much as Bell, lives within two realms, as most of Malick's protagonists do: a zone between the accepted and the ideal, or Kierkegaard's time and the timeless. In *TNW*, Malick paints a contrast. While Smith bears some resemblance to Bill of *DoH*—destroying the ideal of repetition in favor of recollection—we find more sympathy with Smith's condition. His *ethos* is torn between the activation of love/grace/eternity and duty/state/time. He chooses the latter and love is abandoned, to his regret and her dismay. Pocahontas is the authentic individual, maintaining her sense of wonder throughout her own regrets and deceptions. She takes account of such failings and learns to live between and within worlds, even of past and present, never forgetting Smith nor her people. She implores Smith at his lowest point with a single word: "*Remember.*" This urge from her is in many respects the *essence* of the film that is sometimes encircled, other times penetrated *by its characters' relations*—to each other, to their time and place, and to the obligations of love and duty. Each one is a question of choosing time or eternity. Transcendence is given life in her embrace of eternity, her refusal to forget him, and at least here in her repetition, time cannot be erased and love lives on.

Silverman writes that what sets Malick apart from Heidegger is that the latter is about anxiety whereas the former is about wonder (2009). This may be true in the more hopeful, authentic aspects of all his characters, particularly in *TTRL*, which is her film of study. But Malick's cinema absolutely embodies its anxiety, less in Heidegger's use and more in Kierkegaard's future-oriented existential condition that becomes one's "serving spirit that against its will leads him where he wishes to go" (1980, p. 159). What makes Kierkegaard's anxiety so cinematic, which Malick manifests, is its dynamic quality. Malick's anxiety emerges in its constant twists and pulls of authenticity and inauthenticity, appearances and silences, possibilities and closures, often in the same moment. This is what allows coexistence to emerge with such potency. Anxiety, as Wahl writes, brings one into contact with something, sharpens one's individuality. As Malick's cinema progresses, we find that there remains within his characters their propensity for despair as much as a movement to the higher callings of grace, wonder, glory. Like Bill, Capt. Smith falls back tragically into who he had always been, retreating to prior identity in spite of his better self.

After The Tree of Life: *Adrift in the Repetitions of Habit*

This fragmentation and disassociating tendency in Malick becomes more amplified in *To the Wonder* (*TtW*; 2013) and *Knight of Cups* (*KoC*; 2016). Both films continue the temporal coexistence from *TToL*, but the gravity of loss pulls the threads of gathering out of reach. In *TtW*, Neil is trying to hold on to that which cannot remain, a love that is distant in its nearness, felt but always in elsewheres, at other times, even in co-presence with his beloved. In *KoC*, Rick's (Christian Bale) disassociating—a dissociation that is an act—is dilated to the point where love becomes a series of losses that can barely be felt. As another film of recollecting, our protagonist's memories are so broken and drug-addled that he cannot find himself within his re-imaginings. No longer even the wistful poet of Kierkegaard's recollection, he has given up entirely. Instead, he moves through the joys and sorrows as a kind of penance. Themes of *TToL* return, as Rick harbors the remembrance of a brother's death, not through his own efforts but through recollections of his other brother and father, depicted through settings that are more like dreams than any actual event of the past. As cinematic, they are both: the metaphorical dilapidated, neglected, and rejected home interior. Rick dresses to his class but dreams within a squatter's reality, again suggesting not only his fissures but also the gaping chasm between economic success and spiritual failure that is both real and symbolic of Los Angeles.

From the standpoint of unseeing, *TToL* marks the close of an era. *TtW* begins a new period, running at least through *Song to Song*.[29] This period remains wide in temporality, but such heightened dispersion has eroded *logos* through its failure to gather what is meaningful in time. We may recall again the problem of habit in Kierkegaard, which takes over when repetition has abandoned eternity. Without the originality of eternity in repetition the threads of *logos* have stretched too far, as coexistence becomes *separation* in his characters, an abandonment of the eternal to randomness. In Kierkegaard, such abandonment is what drives people to run around in haste, and perhaps this is the intercessional dance of character, actor, and director that Rick and Malick engage in *KoC*. The thinking that strives has given way to the dreaming that longs for peace, as Kierkegaard wrote, but that also fragments to such degree that gathering becomes lost. In dreaming, the difference between oneself and other becomes "an intimated nothing" (Kierkegaard, 1980, p. 41). We may recall as well what Kierkegaard said about the transcendental conditions of sinfulness, that *as selfish*, sin becomes "entangled in indistinctness" (p. 79).

Deleuze's concept of repetition is aligned with Kierkegaard on this problem of habit, in which repetition fails to create newness. We may here consider Deleuze and Guattari's idea of *assemblages*, which are based on the fluid, molecular (and "molar") interplay of deterritorialization and reterritorialization (1987). This concept is usually regarded for its mechanical interplay of relations; but if we carry it to the activity of unseeing, there is also in Deleuze's solo writings the concept of the *circuit*. As a circuit widens, the potential newness of deterritorialization also has the potential to fall into sameness in repetitions. If the circuit (time's cycles) widens too far, it cannot reterritorialize. In other words, the expansive verticality of time's cycles leaves nothing new to make. Nothing positive adheres as forces fail to establish points of contact that intensify into new planes of potentiality. Teresa Rizzo summarizes this well in writing that "while a body may be powerful as a result of certain relations, it may at the same time be ineffectual through other relations that recompose it in ways

---

[29] *Song to Song* (2017) is Malick's most recent film at the time of this writing.

that diminish its power to be affective" (2012, p. 64). Rizzo is conceiving the power of reterritorialization in cinema as a relation of the body/visuality/audience in creating new assemblages, yet this is applicable to Malick's unseeing *logos* as the process of actualizing thought.

We can turn as well to Deleuze's Spinozism and the passions that contribute to one's *conatus*, or power to act (1990). In *TtW* and *KoC*, one finds downtrodden protagonists, dwelling in the sad passions of *passivity*. Passions, in Deleuze's readings of Spinoza, affect a person through one's collisions with bodies or forces. Deleuze expresses this passion as passive because it needs a relation to what is outside the self—this body or affection. But when a passion is joyful, it aids in one's capacity for both imagination and action. A sad passion comes through affectation that is disagreeable to one's *conatus*. Partial and indirect joys arise from contempt of what gives one sadness, even hatred. This path creates only a *fleeting* joy, which masks the sadness that remains. At such a point, "We now seem farther than ever from coming into possession of our power of action: our capacity to be affected is exercised not only by passive affections, but, above all, by sad passions, involving an ever lower degree of the power of action" (Deleuze, 1990, p. 245). In a sense, one is made to watch, or listen to, one's own incapacity to act, express, utter. We see this expressed often in *TtW* and *KoC*. Although there are moments of joy and wonder, they mask the sadness that has been amplified within the self.

This is another entry point into why *logos* is not antithetical to, but adds vitality to Deleuze's concept of difference in repetition and the virtual/actual milieu. Conceived as a *made* rather than *prior* structure, *logos* territorializes thought into its own new actualization. By the time of *KoC*, however, Malick's unseeing cinema has reached the opposite—a state of near total destruction. *Logos* gives way to chaos through a lack of care, a listening that cannot hear. Rick separates from his *sophronesis* (good sense) in favor of a private *phronesis* (discernment), which in Heraclitus is the dangerous split. Such a separation is an act of self-alienation from the common of mankind.[30] This is not an act of negation but, rather, one of having lost one's attunement to the *logos* relation. We may conceive of Rick as the inward expression of the Farmer in *DoH*. Both listen without hearing. What is different in the expression is that Rick's process of failure is given rather than seen from a distance. To find himself he must go on a

---

[30] This is informed by Kahn (1979). See also Heraclitus' D2 and D114.

journey, to seek out his *hodos* (path) toward the common of humankind, finding perhaps a not a place but a divine timelessness.[31]

This condition, this alienation, is not madness but despair. More than any of Malick's prior protagonists, Rick fails to listen to his *conatus*, fails to make *logos*. The noise of his deterritorialization cannot find itself reterritorialized in sense.[32] He is therefore Malick's least sympathetic character, not in deeds—for Kit and Bill were physically and unrepentantly violent—but in his seeming apathy, a desire that is unwilling to gather. He is lost and defeated, journeying without any hope of finding an opening. We are reminded of Deleuze and Guattari's writings on Beckett in *A Thousand Plateaus*: "The knight of the novel of courtly love spends his time forgetting his name, what he is doing, what people say to him, he doesn't know where he is going or to whom he is speaking, he is continually drawing a line of absolute deterritorialization, but also losing his way, stopping, and falling into black holes" (1987, p. 174). There is kinship here with Kierkegaard's knight of infinite resignation, who feels the *pathos* but gives up on the real, choosing to disconnect from the possibility of love. Again we hear, as Rick does, the imperative: "*Remember*." In *The New World*, it was Capt. Smith's beloved who said it almost as a mystic's *suggestion*. This time it is Rick's father; but half of what his father speaks is unheard and therefore unlistened. Rick asks, "*Begin? Begin where?*" As with any failure to listen for what is lost, the question has no answer, for we are already within. "*Begin*" is also the final word of dialogue in the film. But *the film* has no beginning nor any end, and is instead this particular series of failures to take account. Rick is stuck in the drifting currents of time perhaps because his condition offers no *real* movement, no joyful path, nothing outside the demands of time and the time of demands.

If the four films accounted for here—*Days of Heaven* through *The Tree of Life*—are a gathering in the account, its fragmentation by *KoC* has become adrift. Composition has ceded its power to decomposition as his *logos* disintegrates through his failure to affirm, to activate, *to make logos*. Malick's *nomos* is now forgotten, unreachable in its dispersion, and his *logos* increasingly disengages as his characters give in to despair. With his characters' lack of power to create imagery from thought, imagery lies scattered. This is the danger of the untethered thought, of pushing the metaphysical "limit" but without the belief or faith needed to bind oneself to the move-

---

[31] For a contemporary Kierkegaardian take on *Knight of Cups*, see Logan (2016).
[32] I am informed here by Deleuze and Guattari's writings on Kafka (1986), but as audible relations rather than sonic de/reterritorialized as language or music.

ment forward. Out here in the field of disengagement, there remains much to account for but little activation. The everyday of *DoH*, evident through *TToL*, has by *KoC* become inaccessible, *unassociable*, and his characters are becoming lost because of it. Instead of riding the new idea available in a gathering, Neil and Jack find themselves lost in time.

Perhaps destructions such as these are necessary in the art of filmmaking, and perhaps time will treat this era of Malick's more kindly. Mitry writes of a critic who claims that a filmmaker has overthrown the rules of cinema, to whom he says: What rules? "They may be overthrowing conventions… but only to replace them with other conventions…. Since all art is necessarily conventional, all artists have the right—and, I maintain, the duty— to manufacture the conventions they find necessary, i.e., necessary to the expression of the ideas and feelings they may wish to communicate. Provided, that is, that they do communicate them" (1997, p. 373). What is important, Mitry emphasizes, is that in the effort to communicate, one's technique submits only "to the requirements of the expression." But what if the very effort of art is to express what cannot be communicated? Deleuze and Guattari write that "Communication always comes too early or too late" (1991, p. 28). When one's experience is a gathering in the present—taking account as a relation to the past within the continuance of time—the struggle lies in the incapacity to remember at play with the incapacity to forget. Art works in zones of indeterminability, the affect that expresses prior to any communication. "Life alone creates such zones where living beings whirl around, and only art can reach and penetrate them in its enterprise of co-creation" (1991, p. 173).

Malick is careful to avoid communicating any particular argument or agenda in his films. Within each film we often find that there are multiple paths overlapping toward authenticity, fallenness, wonder, despair, or violence. Are Bill and the Farmer not on the same quest? What of the various ways in which the soldiers of *TTRL* are coming to terms with the violence and mortality they face, particularly in the antagonistic brotherhood of Witt and Welsh? The former dies and the latter lives, something Welsh reminds him of at his funeral; but which of the two lived in wonder, in "*the glory*," as Malick writes? Pocahontas and Smith find themselves an idyllic timeless eternity before violence and duty forces each in different directions. If their love is itself a soul, it is like Plato's chariot, whose horses have shattered it by pulling in opposite directions (2002). And Jack is a struggle within himself, a man who must fracture his world in order to hear what has been unlistened in the midst of all his listening, opening to an unseeing in the midst of all his seeing. Keeping in mind that in Heidegger authenticity is an engagement with *hearing*, we should remember again that "hearing" has many meanings. In Malick, authenticity is not an achievement of lost understanding, but an opening to move forward.

Narration: Layering Time, Speaking the Unspoken

In his second cinema book, Deleuze uses the term "voice-off" to describe the narrative voice (1989). This word reveals another visual bias in Deleuze, one in which the voice is bound, much like sound effects, to the image, stating that without the image the voice is not "on." If we were to be audiovisually egalitarian, the term "image-off" is the same thing, because the image is off of the voice. Even "voiceover," *de rigueur* in film studies, implies that the imagery is that which is to be inscribed over. Could one not say instead that the image-over is the montage element that supports the literary voice (or artistically conflicts with it)? In *Last Year at Marienbad* (Resnais, 1961) and *The Usual Suspects* (Singer, 1995), which is "off" or "over"—the voices or the images? And in films like *Klute* (Pakula, 1971) or those of Malick, when is the voice over or off the montage and when are the two embodied? When it comes to narration as often conceived, we find two biases: the first, described earlier, is a Deleuzean image bias while the second is a Heideggerian *logos*-as-speaking, diegetic bias. In an image bias, both "off" and "over" emphasize the dominant state of the image, which fits Deleuze's conception of narration as defined by images rather than as language. In Deleuze's cinema books, he attempts to overturn the language-as-prior film semiology by claiming that an image "description" defines the narration. Rather than montage falling into its existing language, the images effectuate what language then expresses from them. This is why narration for him is "off" the images. What, then, of this language-as-prior that he aims to discount? This brings us to the second bias, which brings us back to film theory's application of *diegesis*.

Remembering that Heidegger's *logos* aims to give sight to what is unseen through the statement, we may note as well that *diegesis* presumes that language is what discloses imagery. Think of the oral tradition of storytelling, where the exposition, often in verse form, conjures the images that carry the story in one's imagination and memory. The cinematic version of this concept would be that exposition-as-vocalized is either effaced or merely implied and the images alone tell the story. In other words, the speaking is muted because the orator is absent, leaving only the imagery born of such unheard speaking. This is the *poeisis* in which a mimetic *diegesis* functions, because the film is the time of the narrative disclosure through the voice.[33] If the ideal of Heidegger's speaking is to reveal the image of truth, then film does its visual reveal in a way that erases the uttering of language. Therefore, even as textually driven, such thinking does not even grant the voice its expression that gives rise to imagery. Occasionally some of this voice that labors forth images is given its actual *sound*; yet it is regarded as voice "over" rather than voice as genesis.

Moving beyond these two ways of thinking through narration, if the voice is instead considered as one attribute *within logos*, then neither image nor voice is "off" and rather displaced from each other in time while sharing the same world. To say that the voice is off or over necessitates some image or language ontology prior to experience. But in experiential cinema, as we find in Malick, there is nothing prior to the unfolding of *logos* in time, a *logos* made through its unfolding. The voice is given its own expression and its own hearing within the *logos*. Herein lies its potentiality, and indeed its tendency when used well, to go beyond what is both seen and unseen. Rather than voice-off or -over, better terms would be "voice narration," *diegesis* (were it not already occupied), or even better, "voice."

Repeating an earlier claim, we see that too much exposition is the enemy of good filmmaking. "For the poet himself ought to speak the least, since it is not by this that he is an imitator" (Aristotle, 2005, Section 24, p. 59). Even more relevant in cinema than in Greek poetry (theater), a film rarely requires spoken explanation. The medium offers its story in the relationships of image and sign, sound and silence—the indices, vectors, and layers of cinema and what can be inferred within a multidurational unfolding. What has come to be named "voiceover" too often becomes yet another application of *sound*—in this case, the voice—to suture the failings of content and story. Even in situations in which explication, voiceover or otherwise, is well written, "wording that is too brilliant pushes character and thinking back into obscurity" (Aristotle, 2005, p. 60).

Malick's Voices

Malick's use of voice narration is both effective and *affective* not because it is needed but because it is integral. Narration is not an exercise in paraphrasing, whereby it ties together elements along the straight line of

---

[33] For more on this, see Plato's *Republic*, Book III (2004).

events, nor does it explain what is not seen or heard. Rather, it functions in two ways: (1) It is the consciousness, or thinking, of the film in prose, and in this is one of several forms of expression. (2) It offers a time for such expression. On this second point, an important change occurs between *Days of Heaven* and *The Thin Red Line*. One could consider *DoH* and *Badlands* before it as a Heideggerian *logos*-as-disclosure of images or a Deleuzean after-image. Yet they are closer to the former, as narration unfolds *the time* of events. Starting with *TTRL*, however, neither description fits. No longer can the voices be considered *the* time of events but, rather, a multiplicity of events that unfold threads of time. After *DoH*, each voice-event establishes its own duration that expresses within a coexistence. Voices gain freedom from presence and take on a multiplicity of thought vectors as various expressions of time. Such speaking unravels additional layers of *ethos* and *pathos* without needing to adhere to any authoritative or objective *chronos*. This is not *logos*-as-statement but, instead, an expression that thinks, perhaps without a sound—the utterable of thinking.

Classic voice narration commonly establishes a film's time for the audience. There is usually an assumption of a present narrating activity in relation to past images: a distinctly diegetic storytelling. In *Badlands* and *Days of Heaven*, the voices of Holly and Linda assume a present disclosing—in the Heideggerian sense of images *from* speech—of events that happened prior, which in terms of the film's *poiesis* is the means of artistic presentation for an audience. Here the voice is gathering from memory to make an account in images that unfold. *Badlands* as told and seen seems to occur at some present unfolding after Kit's arrest. It is not Kit's time but Holly's; her voice is the *time that discloses* through the narration *of* her past events. The melody of her voice suggests a private and written narration, perhaps in a teenage diary. She is less drawing from memory in recollection, and more recollecting from the just-occurred in order to preserve it as memory. In this sense, her images are born of her writing. The narration in *Days of Heaven* is again from a female nonprotagonist: the observer and storyteller Linda. Manz's rich, largely improvised expression of events, with its mystical elements of folklore, sounds not written but told to someone. This reflects her character well. Perhaps, unlike the schoolgirl Holly, Linda can't write and instead tells stories. Hers is therefore recollected and embellished from recent memory and is public rather than private. As with *Badlands*, the imagery that unfolds is hers.

In each of Malick's later films, the time of voice narration becomes increasingly multilayered as voices gain their independence and take on an interplay with the fragmentations of memory. Voices gain their own expression as they flow within various indiscernible durational states of now-then, now, and even now-future. Such percolations of image- and voice-time find a cohesion that feels lived.[34] There is a double complexity here: each now may express the past and future within itself, while all nows of the voices together express various overlapping presents. The distinctions of event states become tensions within the interplay of image montage and sound montage and the montage that brings the audiovisual experience together.

The Thin Red Line thus marks the pivot not only in its shifts in time but also in acts of narrating time. The voices in *Badlands* and *DoH* are bound to the imagery that unfolds. But *TTRL* is fixed to no linearity; it moves in its own time, *in play* with its imagery, unfolding in an indiscernibility of past-present-future. One might claim that the film is future-oriented because in the beginning we hear musings on "*this war*" while viewing soldiers who have not yet fired a shot. The ending imagery features extended reflection about the brotherhood of Charlie Company: "*Where is it that we were together?*" Of course, this could all be a future reflecting into the past as with Malick's two previous films. What is different here is that we get the now of thought, beginning with Col. Tall's grumblings on the deck of the ship and continuing throughout the film in the soldiers' unspoken inner selves. Pvt. Bell's expressions are similarly in the present, since the man who learns halfway through the film of his wife's infidelity couldn't possibly express his love for her. The expression of emotions and the expression of imagery are bound together in ways that are not unidirectional. Such employment of the voice creates a new audible-event, which gains independence from both cinematic image-events and material object-events through the character who speaks.

Perhaps it is no coincidence that *TTRL* is also Malick's first use of the Steadicam, which enables the camera operator to move into and through the *mise-en-scène*. With the Steadicam, Vertov's eye finds its embodiment, as Elie During writes. "By inventing a new body, an imaginary body, the

---

[34] "Thus narration will consist of the distribution of different presents to different characters, so that each forms a combination that is plausible and possible in itself, but where all of them together are 'incompossible,' and where the inexplicable is thereby maintained and created" (Deleuze, 1989, p. 101).

cinema can unveil a new nature: the universe in itself, seen from nowhere and by no one" (2015, p. 1). This body moves through spaces as much as the voices move through times. *Badlands* and *DoH*, by comparison, were shot from various fixed angles in a more distant presentation. Both early films are thereby more reflective in their voice narration (in fixed time) and their images (in fixed space). His later works, by moving *through* spacetime both in narration and in imagery, become mobile as the *logos* frees itself from a grounding to the time of object- and sonic-events. Mobility also frees up the thought of his characters. Malick's films begin from this point to unfold the nonlocalizability of space but also time *because* the relations are mobile.[35] This mobility of thought opens toward a *mobile subjectivity*, for which a writer like Woolf is famous in her narrative shifts from character to character. But because it is cinema, the multiplicity, simultaneity, and coexistence continually fold and unfold through affects and various durations, recollections, and repetitions.

There are times when Malick breaks the now and creates ambiguity of the extended events that are depicted. When Pvt. Witt returns to his idyllic world of nature, he is shunned by its native inhabitants. The imagery holds on his bewildered face as we hear "*We were a family. How did it break up and come apart?*" He could be speaking as much about C-Company in a future gathering as his adopted family of natives in the image-present. But as the voice continues—"*So that now we're turned against each other, each standing in the other's light*"—the time takes shape as now. To add further complexity, the narration also foreshadows Malick's next film. Taken in its entirety, the monologue could have come from *The New World* as much as from *TTRL*: "*We were a family. How did it break up and come apart? So that now we're turned against each other. Each standing in the other's light. How did we lose the good that was given us? Let it slip away? Scatter it careless? What's keeping us from reaching out? Touching the glory?*" Indeed we can find such themes continuing to echo in *The Tree of Life*, *To the Wonder*, and *Knight of Cups*. Malick carries himself, *his logos*, continuously through the various voices that emerge within theirs.

---

[35] Melberg writes that Kierkegaard's *Repetition* is an allegory for mobility. The text is always "moving, like Diogenes, back and forth between eye and ear, between irony and pathos, between past and present time, between concept and story" (1990, p. 81). We might say that Malick does the same through the camera and the durations of sonic- and audible-events as relations of coexistence.

Ruptur*ing the Authority of the Voice*

There have been complaints from critics that the voices in *TTRL* are too poetic for young, working-class soldiers, and therefore are unrealistic. This assumes that the speaking of unseen thoughts in a film is a testimonial, as in a courtroom where a statement is authoritative and evidentiary, under punishment of perjury. Such criticism feels distinctly American, America being a system that controls itself through an ever-present threat of punishment. It pervades the psyche, unacknowledged, that every person must obey the same codified laws. When one suspects another of a false, misleading, or somehow not logically constructed testimonial, the superego reels. Deleuze similarly writes of truthful narration as testimony, or that which falls into the "legal connections" of the organic relation (1989, p. 133). Narration in this stratum becomes referential to a "*system of judgement*" based on chronological relations of time. This is perhaps why a film like the previously mentioned *The Usual Suspects* led to such utter confusion upon its release. Most of the film is a lie, its images fabricated and spoken with authority. Even with acceptance of the "unreliable" or even "implied" narrator notion,[36] film convention recoils at the impression of a continuous false testimony because of the tacit agreement of trust in the legitimacy of the voice and the responsibility of the storyteller to be truthful. In Malick's poetic *diegesis*, therefore, one finds it difficult to imagine expressions that live outside this rule, as chronology loosens and testimony devoid of a clear subject abandons its hold on evidence.[37] Such a dynamic *poiesis* requires a release of the demand for testimony, but more important as well, the notion that what is heard is always stated. We in the audience may hear an abundance of voices speaking, but Malick's *logos* is deterritorializing narration, rejecting it, as he creates *collective assemblages* that carry and move thinking.[38]

---

[36] Sinnerbrink challenges whether cinema needs the concept of a narrator, even an "implied" one, as suggested by Seymour Chatman (Sinnerbrink, 2011). Sinnerbrink is correct when he states that a camera zooming out from Marion Crane's eye in *Psycho* is not engaged in any kind of narration, implicit or otherwise. Yet even in Sinnerbrink's critique, it again reminds one of the problem of visual veracity, the reification of a necessary distance between film and audioviewer.

[37] "Malick's narrators are never obviously authorial and often evince views shaped by limited or transient perspectives" (Walden, 2011, p. 197).

[38] Deleuze and Guattari state that as Kafka's literature develops, he will "reject the role of the narrator… There isn't a subject; *there are only collective assemblages of enunciation…*" (1986, p. 18).

This returns us to the utterance and the utterable. For the characters of *TTRL*, narration is the thought that lives within them, but that has not yet found voice outward into the world and perhaps never will. If language is the limit of the sayable, as Wittgenstein suggests, then this is some other description, another expression of thought in which Malick's *logos* has exceeded Wittgenstein's limit. Cinema verbalizes not evidence but thought, even the thought that struggles to find its time of saying and further, thought along multiple streams of emergence. The play of virtual and actual, utterable and utterance, is what injects a *logos* with its width, its mutually resonant streams of becoming that gather and also give various accounts. The narrators convey their brotherhood of one mind—"*features of the same face*" as the words say. This soul or this wholeness speaks through them. This is not to suggest that the characters are some kind of medium or that they are being channeled. It is them, their *logos*. But the *logos* speaks *them*, their community, rather than the other way around. It is the horror, beauty, and brotherhood of their world, their presence within the world, that speaks through the *logos* that offers another voice. It unbinds the virtual to give something more to the actual of thinking, emerging in moments of clarity that would otherwise never find language on its own.

Yet another turn occurs in *The New World*, a film whose time and utterance also lacks specificity. Smith speaks of the past in how the relationship developed and how he felt for her: "*I loved her.*" He also speaks in the now, "*We will*" build a better society in America. Rather than some single thread of nostalgia, or the diegetic narration of Holly and Linda, Smith's voicings offers a wider coexistence that expresses his inner turmoil at multiple points: his present pragmatism overlapping with his regretful recollection of a lost eternity.[39] Pocahontas's voice narration is even more complex; she speaks of the image-present in clear English, a language which, at the point of image-time, she has not yet learned.[40] He is present and reflective, while she is displaced in time, like a spirit that seeks out its place along the hodology of time, and which she crystallizes and accounts through her utterances. Perhaps it has followed her death and she speaks not from any now but within eternity. *The New World* is a film that is both the memory and the

---

[39] "Characters are of the present, but feelings plunge into the past. ... And feeling is that which is in continual exchange, circulating from one sheet to another according to what transformations occur" (Deleuze, 1989, pp. 124–125).

[40] This is different from *To the Wonder*, in which Malick allows the French to remain, translated in subtitles. Perhaps it serves a different purpose—a simultaneity but one separated by language and physical distance.

fragmented now of love itself, combining into its restoration and repetition. This is their search for an eternity outside of time as much as ours *in* this time; their signs lead us in different directions, giving the film its oneiric reverie.[41] This again brings forth the irrelevance of establishing a single time and instead presents through her the thought that speaks in words that are not yet speakable. We regularly find her in an ongoing dialogue with "*Dear Mother*," invoking a relationship with nature as life-giving, transcendental, and timeless. Through such expressions, her *logos* carries her across worlds to encompass the one, eternal, and infinite world that she lives in relation to Dear Mother. Not only her individual self but also her entire culture crosses such boundaries. It is not "I who rose" of the past, nor "I rise" of the present; it is "*We rise, from out of the soul of you.*" As with *TTRL*, this authenticity of being present in Dasein comes through and belongs to Charlie Company or tribe. Yet in some respects it is the inverse of *TTRL*: rather than the whole coming through the voices of the many, the one, formed by the many, carries the many through her singularity of expression. Through this she preserves her culture, her world, and through her, it continues beyond both the time of the film and her brief life.

The Tree of Life is a return of sorts to *TTRL*, in which the characters aren't speaking so much as their being is expressed, and words are its vehicle. Voices are more expressive but also more tentative; we hear muted cries of anguish and whispered words or short phrases to no one.[42] Here a voice does not so much recount or take account as in *TNW*, in which the voiced expression is what pulls one through. In *TToL*, utterances are born of being affected, of coming to terms, a failed striving to put into words. As with *TTRL*, *TToL*'s narration is not just a character in the world, and not simply about how the world is. Jack is grappling with Malick's unseen forces through father and mother: nature and grace. It is not dialectical but, rather, two lines of flight, each opening to different imagery. Returning us to Heidegger, the former is the world as given (*phusis*); the second is the self in a relation to virtue (*ethos*), or one's ethical being.[43] Grace is in one respect divine but also one's responsibility to oneself and others in any

---

[41] Sinnerbrink, writing about *The New World*, says "This is a film that is not only about time but which reveals time, provided we are open and receptive to the kind of temporal transformation that it seeks to effect" (2011, p. 180).

[42] "In its very essence, memory is voice, which speaks, talks to itself, or whispers, and recounts what happened" (Deleuze, 1986, p. 51).

[43] See as well, Leibniz (1934), Sections 85–88.

human relation and the manner in which one enacts such responsibility. Nature is what it is, marking the point of antagonism between father and son and the source of sorrow, strife, grief, and violence that comes.

In all such wonderings about the fluidity of time and disclosures through words, we cannot forget of course that the film has its own disclosure. In this another time is gathered, one that lies with the empathetic relation between character and audioviewer that here unfolds as pure simultaneity. Malick's voices do not explain but, rather, express, taking shape as *his* expression. Ultimately, every character who speaks through his *logos* is Malick's muse, the one who is telling him the story as he writes it. In writing and filmmaking, he feels it coming through to audience. This again is how we find empathy with the film, this simultaneity and coexistence, the overlaps of relations where one and the other—filmmaker and audioviewer—disappear, much as sound disappears in an extended audibility; in both, film and sound become immaterial as empathy subsumes reason. Deleuze asks: Can the present stand for the whole of time? If so this moment lives in the multiplicity of events that stretch in all directions. "Adopting St Augustine's fine formulation, there is *a present of the future, a present of the present and a present of the past*, all implicated in the event, rolled up in the event, and thus simultaneous and inexplicable" (1989, p. 100). This is also an apt description of Kierkegaard's *moment*. The time as material gives way to its utterable, unspoken, which speaks outside of time and thereby creates the infinite. This is a filmmaker's right, and as Mitry suggests, her or his duty: the material cedes its dominance, loosens its grip over spatiotemporality, to allow the empathetic relation to breathe.

REFERENCES

Texts Cited

Agamben, G. (2002). Difference and Repetition: On Guy Debord's Films. In T. McDonough (Ed.), *Guy Dubord and the Situationist International* (pp. 313–319). Cambridge, MA: MIT Press.

Andreas-Salomé, L. (1990). *Looking Back: Memoirs* (B. Mitchell, Trans.). New York: Paragon House.

Arendt, H. (1978). *Life of the Mind*. San Diego: Harcourt.

Aristotle. (2005). *Poetics* (J. Sachs, Trans.). Newburyport: Focus.

Bachelard, G. (1960). *The Poetics of Reverie: Childhood, Language, and the Cosmos* (D. Russell, Trans.). Boston: Beacon Press.

Bachelard, G. (1988). *Air and Dreams: An Essay on the Imagination of Movement* (E. R. Farrell & C. F. Farrell, Trans.). Dallas: Dallas Institute Publications.
Badiou, A. (2000). *Deleuze: The Clamour of Being* (L. Burchill, Trans.). Minneapolis: University of Minnesota Press.
Bergson, H. (1920). *Mind-Energy* (C. H. Wildon, Trans). New York: Henry Holt.
Bergson, H. (1988). *Matter and Memory* (N. M. Paul & W. S. Palmer, Trans.). Brooklyn: Zone.
Bergson, H. (1999). *An Introduction to Metaphysics* (T. E. Hulme, Trans.). Indianapolis: Hackett.
Deleuze, G. (1983). *Nietzsche and Philosophy* (H. Tomlinson, Trans.). New York: Columbia University Press.
Deleuze, G. (1986). *Cinema 1* (H. Tomlinson & B. Habberjam, Trans.). London: Continuum.
Deleuze, G. (1988). *Foucault* (S. Hand, Trans.). Minneapolis: University of Minnesota Press.
Deleuze, G. (1989). *Cinema 2* (H. Tomlinson & R. Galeta, Trans.). Minneapolis: University of Minnesota Press.
Deleuze, G. (1990). *Expressionism in Philosophy: Spinoza* (M. Joughin, Trans.) Brooklyn: Zone.
Deleuze, G. (1994). *Difference and Repetition* (P. Patton, Trans.). New York: Columbia University Press.
Deleuze, G., & Guattari, F. (1986). *Kafka: Toward a Minor Literature*. Minneapolis: University of Minnesota Press.
Deleuze, G., & Guattari, F. (1987). *A Thousand Plateaus*. Minneapolis: University of Minnesota Press.
Deleuze, G., & Guattari, F. (1991). *What Is Philosophy?* (H. Tomlinson & G. Burchell, Trans.). New York: Columbia University Press.
Dewey, J. (1934). *Art as Experience*. New York: Perigee.
During, E. (2015). Turning Movements: Fragments on Mark Lewis. In F. Bovier & H. Taieb (Eds.), *Mark Lewis*. Geneva: Métis Presses.
Elsaesser, T., & Hagener, M. (2010). *Film Theory: An Introduction Through the Senses*. New York: Routledge.
Heidegger, M. (1968). *What Is Called Thinking*. New York: Harper Perennial.
Heidegger, M. (1969). *Identity and Difference* (J. Stambaugh, Trans.). New York: Harper & Row.
Heidegger, M. (2010). *Logic: The Question of Truth* (T. Sheehan, Trans.). Bloomington: Indiana University Press.
Hume, D. (1977). In E. Steinberg (Ed.), *An Enquiry Concerning Human Understanding*. Indianapolis: Hackett.
Kahn, C. H. (1979). *The Art and Thought of Heraclitus*. London/Cambridge: Cambridge University Press.
Kierkegaard, S. (1980). *The Concept of Anxiety* (R. Thomte, Trans.). Princeton: Princeton University Press.

Kierkegaard, S. (2009). *Repetition and Philosophical Crumbs* (M. G. Piety, Trans.). Oxford: Oxford University Press.

Leibniz, G. W. (1934). The Monadology, 1714. In M. Morris (Trans.), *Philosophical Writings* (pp. 3–20). London: J. M. Dent & Sons.

Logan, T. (2016, March). *Kierkegaard in L.A.: Terrence Malick's Knight of Cups*. http://www.curatormagazine.com/trevor-logan/kierkegaard-in-l-a-terrence-malicks-knight-of-cups/

Melberg, A. (1990). Repetition (In the Kierkegaardian Sense of the Term). *Diacritics*, *20*(3) (Autumn), 71–87.

Mitry, J. (1997). *The Aesthetics and Psychology of the Cinema* (C. King, Trans.). Bloomington: Indiana University Press.

Nietzsche, F. (1974). *The Gay Science* (W. Kaufmann, Trans.). New York: Vintage Books.

Nietzsche, F. (1996). *Human, All Too Human: A Book for Free Spirits* (R. J. Hollingday, Trans.). Cambridge: Cambridge University Press.

Nietzsche, F. (1999). *The Birth of Tragedy* (R. Speirs, Trans.). Cambridge: Cambridge University Press.

Plato. (2002). *Phaedrus* (R. Waterfield, Trans.). Oxford: Oxford University Press.

Plato. (2004). *Republic* (C. D. C. Reeve, Trans.). Indianapolis: Hackett.

Plato. (2005). Meno. In R. Waterfield (Trans.), *Meno and Other Dialogues: Charmides, Laches, Lysis, Meno* (pp. 97–143). Oxford: Oxford University Press.

Rizzo, T. (2012). *Deleuze and Film: A Feminist Introduction*. London: Continuum.

Schopenhauer, A. (2010). *The World as Will and Representation* (J. Norman, A. Welchman, & C. Janaway, Trans.). Cambridge: Cambridge University Press.

Silverman, K. (2009). *Flesh of My Flesh*. Stanford: Stanford University Press.

Sinnerbrink, R. (2011). *New Philosophies of Film: Thinking Images*. New York: Continuum.

Tarkovsky, A. (1989). *Sculpting in Time* (K. Hunter-Blair, Trans.) Austin: University of Texas Press.

Wahl, J. (1969). *Philosophies of Existence* (F. M. Lory, Trans.). London: Routledge.

Walden, E. (2011). Whereof One Cannot Speak: Terrence Malick's *The New World*. In S. Kendall & T. D. Tucker (Eds.), *Terrence Malick: Film and Philosophy* (pp. 197–210). New York: Continuum.

Woolf, V. (1985). A Sketch of the Past. In *Moments of Being* (pp. 61–160). San Diego: Harcourt Brace.

Films Cited

Jonze, S. (Director). (2013). *Her* [Motion Picture]. USA: Annapurna, Warner Bros.

Malick, T. (Director). (1973). *Badlands* [Motion Picture]. USA: Warner Bros.

Malick, T. (Director). (1978). *Days of Heaven* [Motion Picture]. USA: Paramount Pictures.
Malick, T. (Director). (1998). *The Thin Red Line* [Motion Picture]. USA: Geisler-Roberdeau, Phoenix Pictures / 20th Century Fox.
Malick, T. (Director). (2005). *The New World* [Motion Picture]. USA: New Line Cinema.
Malick, T. (Director). (2010). *The Tree of Life* [Motion Picture]. USA: River Road Entertainment.
Malick, T. (Director). (2013). *To the Wonder* [Motion Picture]. USA: FilmNation Entertainment, Redbud Pictures / Magnolia Pictures.
Malick, T. (Director). (2016). *Knight of Cups* [Motion Picture]. USA: Dogwood Films, et al. / Broad Green Pictures.
Malick, T. (Director). (2017). *Song to Song* [Motion Picture]. USA: Buckeye Pictures, et al. / Broad Green Pictures.
Pakula, A. J. (Director). (1971). *Klute* [Motion Picture]. USA: Gus Productions / Warner Bros.
Resnais, A. (Director). (1961). *L'Année dernière à Marienbad* (*Last Year at Marienbad*) [Motion Picture]. France/Italy: Cocinor.
Resnais, A. (Director). (1968). *Je t'aime, je t'aime* [Motion Picture]. France: Les Productions Fox Europa, Parc Film.
Singer, B. (Director). (1995). *The Usual Suspects* [Motion Picture]. USA/Germany: Bad Hat Harry Productions, Blue Parrot / Spelling Films, et al.
Soderbergh, S. (Director). (2002). *Solaris* [Motion Picture]. USA: Lightstorm Entertainment / 20th Century Fox.
Vallée, Jean-Marc. (Director). (2014). *Wild* [Motion Picture]. USA: Pacific Standard, River Road Entertainment / Fox Searchlight Pictures.
Villeneuve, D. (Director). (2016). *Arrival* [Motion Picture]. USA: FilmNation Entertainment, Sony Pictures.

CHAPTER 6

Listening to the *Logos*

The almost inexpressible feat that Malick accomplishes in his best moments are when he levitates experience out from the cinematic confinements, categories, and conventions of time, dialogue, image, sound, dream, memory, flashback. One's unseeing, in its most meaningful moments, finds new expression when it finds its *own* air, its own line, veering from its expected trajectories of the systematic, expository, or material. Here, its translucent tethers to the world become stretched and come alive with energy. Unseeing audibility at this level ignites time and spreads out into near infinite potentialities of hearing and listening. When one is hearing, one expects, seeks, or disregards based on one's own sense of acceptance or will in any situation; when one is listening, one flows among shifting states of believing, doubting, and questioning; and hearing and listening find themselves entwined with one another in time, weaving each other's resonance, distorting and reforming. In Malick's worlds, his *logos* becomes a widening interplay of hearing the finite and immanent that reaches out to the folding of the infinite and the eternal.

Hearing that Listens; Listening that Continues to Hear

Listening is the *active* engagement of audibility. There is always a question of the predicate of listening: a listening for, listening to, listening into, listening through. Jean-Luc Nancy writes, for example, that listening is a "straining toward" meaning and sense in the present. He adds that this straining moves along horizons and margins and always arcs back to oneself. "To be listening will always, then, be to be straining toward or in an approach to the self" (2007, ebook). In such a return to the self, we might also ask what listening *is* as *itself*. What is listening alone, a pure listening? Barthes writes that listening is a psychological act while hearing is physiological (1991). This presumes that a sound mind need only listen. But if one takes listening on its own terms, neglecting its own hearing, one finds an act of enclosed rationality, a rationality that excludes the resonances that are not only a *deeper psychology* but also, to again borrow Bergson's use of the word, "intuitive." It is a listening that is open, that resonates its hearing, maintains its *logos* relation, and is able to seek out new times, new streams of thought. This dilating and constricting of the relation of one *within* the other is a significant theme in Malick's cinema.

Perhaps this is another reason why people speak very little in a Malick film. Those voices that do give sound in their speaking tend to break apart in audibility, as its listeners (including the self who speaks or thinks) seek other openings or conjure a recollection that mostly forgets the words. If we think for a moment of cinema as art, we can consider Deleuze and Guattari's definition of art as blocs of sensation, "*that is to say, a compound of percepts and affects*" (1991, p. 164). Any such bloc can be thought of as the becoming of that which gives sense a relation; it reaches beyond its material aspect and affects us because of this. In other words, cinema need not continually *reference* things through language and objects. Silence is a major component of this. The authors note that "blocs need pockets of air and emptiness, because even the void is sensation" (p. 165). With silence an opening forms, a disclosure to a new engagement. Returning again to *Stalker* (1979) and continuing the scene,[1] Tarkovsky rides us noisily into the zone, and after the train car stops he gives us some 30 seconds of absolute silence, an eternity in film time. A spoken comment finally breaks the suspension: "*How quiet it is. This is the quietest place in the world.*" We have come to a new time, perhaps even a rebirth. The absolute silence returns when the decision is made to not detonate the bomb. Again, the Stalker says: "*It's so quiet.*" Here we have another change, another new opening.

Malick's silences are more internal, in a nearly constant relation with forgetting. Any of the multitude of his variable and temporally layered silences is both, by necessity, an abandonment and an opening. The first invites the second in the ongoing cycle of continual death and rebirth of

[1] See Chap. 3.

thought and listening. In this way, silence as forgetting is a regenerative force, whose role is "supporting consciousness and renewing its freshness" (Deleuze, 1983, p. 113). Malick's silences are not thematic or symbolic and are instead that which gives new life to what has been left behind through the necessity of forgetting. Increasingly his silences widen to such magnitudes that they come to form the lattice-like nature of his work. The openings, contractions, and abandonments of the faintest threads weave a web of various strands: engagement and disengagement, noise interjecting with clarity, stunted listenings overcome by new hearings. As Kierkegaard writes, silence tests one's endurance, a silence that "is the most penetrating and acute questioning" (1980, p. 125). Perhaps for this reason, Deleuze gives a positive quality to the relation of silence and forgetting, which is, as he writes, a positive power. Silence also leaves a time-space for music, which in a cinematic *logos* is not sound but an expression of emotion, thought, reverie. Music is the suspension that sustains the reverie within, but also the opening of a new path of thought for the audioviewer, bestowing on her an opening to think and feel in a way other than through language.

As any character finds an opening, he may enter into a mode of *listening-for*, the event which is not yet present but expected. Here we arrive at an *aporia* in language, in which listening, as both word and concept, has taken on too much responsibility. Listening-for devoid of any sonic-event is hearing that reaches out along its opening. Similar to what Sartre writes about the image–object relation, one is both absent a percept (object) and empty of intention (image) (2004). It is all expectation prior to an arrival that may never come, a circuit that awaits its signal, an arcing into the unknown future of self and memory as it precedes disclosure in anticipation. Listening-for is the unseeing that also carries the *feeling*, the *parouisa*, that it is both immanent and *imminent*—both here and about to come. It is the terror or the desire that can only wait. This is why its engagement attempts to bridge a gap in time by traveling blindly along the dismissal of hearing, between the *passive* openness (the willingness of hearing) and the *active* openness (a striving that is not yet an act of *listening-to*). Listening-to can in one respect be a wish or need to find meaning within the act of listening. One lives inside the event of disclosure and the event of thinking; there is something there to which one is listening. A listening-for is a reaching out to what is not only absent but also what is not conceptually available and may never be, neither present nor known. This is its spiritual component, a believing that waits for a sign, salvation, angel or demon, an *apocalypse*. Listening-for is not a gathering but a reaching out along an unknowing field of hope, desire, or faith. This listening-for is a *hearing-toward* that is unseeing at its most alive due to such absence. Unseeing becomes the force of necessity. It moves toward the un-visible—the unimaginable within unseeing—as it waits for the future to emerge, to "appear."

This waiting, the interval, threatens to drop one deep within one's sense of lack. Looking-for also arises from a lack, but it manifests as an act of will, a presentation of self forward, taking charge, grasping the moment. But as Heidegger reminds us, this unidirectional striving is Dasein's inauthentic desire, as "What is striven for is not *had*, but on the contrary *has* the striver" (1988, p. 154). True to the hegemony of vision, the word *for* is a modification of *before* or *fore*, which expresses what is *in front of*, either in place or in time. But listening-for is holding still within the omnidirectionality of hearing, an expectation of future reception from anywhere, at any time. Often it is a bodily expectation, as one stands waiting in readiness for an arrival of what will, possibly, come to the fore. Dasein's *authentic* striving for Heidegger thereby reads more like Nancy's listening: "the striving self does not strive away from itself but rather back towards itself, i.e. in order that, in this striving, it may gain its own self" (Heidegger, 1988, p. 154). Whereas the past is drawn into a particularity of image in order to form what is needed, the *for* of the future and frontal is a wide-open hearing that expects the particularity to come, the engagement of the relation. It is not vision's longing for object attainment but, rather, that which waits for a *sign*, here an absolutely material index that one may then infer within a sonic-event toward some event of the world that is meaningful to oneself. This audible waiting reveals, even more than in visuality, which side of the fulcrum the weight of one's attention lies—toward authenticity or inauthenticity. Much like Heidegger's waiting upon and waiting for (1966), listening-for finds one either in the openness of the moment forward or the fallenness of everyday closure and expectation. The latter risks an inauthenticity of Dasein and the lack threatens to stretch one out across expectation, exposing the potential for despair. Perhaps this is why this aspect of what we name as listening—the aspect that is qualified so strongly by this particular preposition—is associated with madness. But unlike being "touched *by*" madness—an event outside of one's control—this listening-for is a madness in waiting that has already found itself.

In addition to the listening-for that has not yet arrived is another listening-for, one nested inside the listening-to. As one listens (to a sonic-event, hallucination, echoic return, voice from the beyond) and the presumed percept sustains but is unseen, one may take on an even more active role, moving from interpretation toward investigation, a seeking of *nomos* within *logos*. This is the listening-for *within* the event of listening-to. In the speaking of another to whom I listen, I also listen for a particular word or vocal inflection, the opening of an idea. Within any sonic-event of the world, I might listen for a particular element, perhaps a shift, some aspect that I can act upon. If listening-to is phenomenological, listening-for within the same event is the fallen desire to attain a previously conceived element—an *identity* that is not yet present. This is the inauthenticity of waiting, the inauthenticity of despair. Or it may also be the anticipation of a moment of affirmation, a new activation, the anxiety that as Kierkegaard suggests, presses forward. In either case—the not-yet-audible listening-for and the within-audibility listening-for—the arrival or attainment either becomes the *terminus* of thinking or opens a new beginning. And here we find ourselves at the core of an audible epistemology. If listening-to is an act of moving along belief or action, listening-for is faith in the absence of evidence. Along one circuit of listening-for is faith in identity, the same; along another is faith in the emergence of a new idea, a moment of genesis, perhaps eternity. The subjective variable, at least as an entry to thought, is one's attention.

The Thin Red Line: Listening for the Now

In 1998, two powerful and deeply affective war films were released to great acclaim: Malick's *The Thin Red Line* and Steven Spielberg's *Saving Private Ryan* (*SPR*). The latter is regarded highly in the community of film sound designers for applying a "subjective" and "realistic" treatment to the soundtrack. The advance on Omaha Beach was offered as an *experience*, a feeling of being there. Bullets whiz by a POV camera that adheres visually to POA[2] shifts between air and water as characters emerge and submerge; first-order hearing collapses into single lines of listening attention. Indeed, the mix by Gary Rydstrom is brilliant and justifiably celebrated for its visceral connection between audience and character. Malick's *TTRL* also featured an arrival of soldiers from boat to land, but in a completely different way. The early tactical objective of the two films is similar—take out the big guns. *SPR* has them in full sight while *TTRL* has them hidden and unseeable by all who hope to overcome them.

---

[2] Point of audition; see again Chap. 2.

After its prologue scene at the gravesite, *SPR* drops its characters—and the empathetic "us"—straight into the violence of a chaotic hearing. The door to the amphibious vehicle opens and the threat is fully present in hearing and vision. The massive guns sitting atop the bluffs are the known threat, the object seen in a frontal orientation. In *TTRL*, the unit hits the beach tense and ready for a fight. Malick sets up the landing almost as a promise of immediate action. His characters are nervous, revealed in close-up shots that show their wide-eyed intensity. Yet when they land, nothing happens. Instead of confronting the enemy, these men must wait for them.[3] Malick subsequently moves his characters into an audible expression of Heidegger's angst or anxiety that is the hearing of nothing and nowhere as they move through the jungle. Following Kierkegaard, in Heidegger's angst there is no entity, no object; rather, it is a condition of possibility.[4] It is the anxiety of waiting, an openness to the not-yet. Spielberg's waiting comes later, yet in his dialogue-heavy scenes no one seems to be open and there is no anxiety; there is neither hearing nor a listening-for, and instead, there is talking over the waiting, an ignorance of waiting as itself. In Malick, waiting comes first. His characters must silently confront the realities of nature, this unfamiliar world, before they can deal with their antagonists. They move through forest and swamp, quietly, inexorably. The film's early hearings are continuous, expected, natural, even peaceful. There is no noise of violence or machinery; instead, they hear insects and birds. But more important, they hear their bodies moving in response to this unexplored world. They also see the effects of violence prior to their cause, in mutilated bodies and the shell-shocked soldiers they are to relieve. Malick brings the violence forth only in signs, simultaneously pointing to the past and promising a future engagement. This is one plane among many for Malick—here of a past and future that is negotiated in the duration. Such visible signs are gathered by the main company in what is not yet seen or known, an anticipation of what for their brothers has already been revealed. In these men there is a hearing and waiting that anticipates a future listening-for and listening-within—a time of understanding that does not yet know.

As with *SPR*, *TTRL* is an invasion, but of a different kind. It is not an above-ground chaos of images, noise, and terror, but of relationships within this first-order hearing. This deeper, unseen chaos is slower, quieter, opening

---

[3] Deleuze points out that this is common in war films, the "interminable waiting and its permeations of atmosphere on the one hand and on the other its brutal explosions and its acting-out" (Deleuze, 1986, p. 160).

[4] See section 40 of Heidegger (2010).

to angst and anticipation that constitutes an extensive listening-for. One's listening is open within the moment at the same time one attempts to reach out beyond the horizon of knowability. Here we can think of a "region" or opening, a *standing open*[5] to what is to come toward the possible arrival of listening, a striving toward the reveal that takes time to arrive. Malick's relative silences open various temporal paths of attention to this world they are fully in. The characters live within this hearing always alert to the necessity of *noticing*; their immediate sensorial attention lies ahead of itself, toward the signs of the future in hearing more than in seeing. As Heidegger suggests, authenticity or inauthenticity comes to the fore within such states.

In *TTRL*, the unit's advance has no visual verification as its men reach a point where they must occupy a hill. After looking through his binoculars and seeing nothing, Capt. Staros (Elias Koteas) says, nervously, "*I'm sure the Japs got something there to protect the approaches.*" Only then, after this statement, does Malick finally reveal—to viewers, not to his characters—the threat before them, in a hard cut to a massive gun in a bunker on the hillside manned by someone who remains unseen. We know someone is there because the gun moves just before the cut. The reveal is not an antagonist in personhood but a sign that someone is behind this technology, its violent power shining under the light of the sun. It aims downward toward its target who is also not yet seen, not yet known. This cut between shots—a visual reveal that occurs 40 minutes into the film—also features a dramatic shift in hearing. Whereas Staros and his men are encased in the hearing of life—insects, wind in grass, birds, nature—the cut to the gun is silent. One may consider this as a promise of an eventual approach toward death, but the open ambience and slight movement of the gun also suggest that this man is hearing his open; he is engaged in his own waiting, his listening-for. The shot therefore marks an empathetic shift toward the foreign other, mollifying at least to some degree a protagonist/antagonist divide for the audioviewer. Spielberg's German gunner slaughters a row of American troops and another soldier pats him encouragingly on the head. In this moment we are instructed to hate the Germans, unquestionably. Malick avoids such division. As Silverman correctly notes, Malick refuses to take sides, since all men and indeed nature itself are involved in the same struggle (2009). The gun joins space and time in the same interval that marks the distance between waiting and action, unseeing and seeing, listening-for and listening-to.

---

[5] See Heidegger (1966).

The first death finally comes 45 minutes in, when the first two men of Charlie Company are killed. The soldiers hear not a hail of noise but a simple series of quiet, unceremonious gunshots. Following their deaths is an extraordinary 50 seconds: The clouds part and the sun bathes the tall grass that sounds in the wind. It is a moment, a duration of nature's beauty that both honors the lives taken and harkens back to *Days of Heaven* and Bill's emergence from hell into heaven. The open ambience is similar in both: nature sounding its own eternity independent of the actions of men. But the characters and conditions within the two films couldn't be more different. This singular moment of bliss is the way up for one—remembering again Er's tale in the *Republic*—and the descent for the others, an anticipation of the roar. The *apocalypse* (arrival) comes, finally, in the explosive chaos of noise that brings the bloody advance up the hill. The enemy remains unseen, like a vengeful god roaring from above.

These dynamic shifts in audibility make us aware of the importance of a first-order hearing. One's audible being is bound to the ambience of the world into which one is thrown. This world is, like in all Malick's films, a new world to these characters, but an old one to the timelessness of nature. It has embedded within itself a sense of eternity, and its sound is their horizon, coupled with an audible presence that tries to reach beyond it. What awaits in *TTRL* is eternity itself, the gathering of eternity, and in this the *apocalypse* is a Kierkegaardian repetition—the moment in which eternity comes to coexist within the time of mortality. "The moment is that ambiguity in which time and eternity touch each other, and with this the concept of temporality is posited, whereby time constantly intersects eternity and eternity constantly pervades time" (1980, p. 89). The eternal is the repetition in the moment that strips time and inhabits it with the infinite. In writing of "the moment" Kierkegaard uses words like *invisibility, movement, vanishing*. The moment "is not properly an atom of time but an atom of eternity. It is the first reflection of eternity in time, its first attempt, as it were, at stopping time."

The New World: Listening to Meaning

As mentioned in the previous chapter, Deleuze describes the various durations of repetition and connectivity as a circuit in his image ontology.[6] A circuit in common usage is a signal whose route cycles and returns in

---

[6] We may remember again that "repetition" for Deleuze and Kierkegaard are not the same, but neither are they entirely at odds.

repetitions. In Deleuze, what feeds back is the moment affected by the activity of its relation to virtual images, which return, repeat, or cycle into any actual event.[7] Deleuze picks up here again from Bergson, who wrote of "two centres, one real and the other virtual, from which emanate on the one hand a series of 'perception-images', and on the other a series of 'memory-images', the two series collaborating in an endless circuit" (1994, p. 100). A moment is caught up in this process. The virtual is not what has passed but *how* its passing is synthesized into the real. The past is "contemporaneous with its own present, as pre-existing the passing present and as that which causes the present to pass." Any event is thereby a "passing through." It is modified by the circuit that cycles around the virtual realms that are themselves affected by other images and the activity of other circuits. In the vastness of a large circuit we have dream-images that connect to other image-relations in an array of virtual recombinations. Just as important is cinema's ability to narrow to the smallest circuit. This involves a path through which the differentiating element of the virtual interjects itself at the point when identification might otherwise take place in an association. This creates difference that supplants expectation and a new idea forms. Although Deleuze does not mention it, such an interplay of circuits is a useful way of considering a moment of heightened attention in one's listening—a crystalline duration—within one's territory of hearing. He attempts to place this in the category of *sonsign* (sonic), yet he never distinguishes it from the *opsign* (optical) (1989).

Michel Chion has conceived of a sonic concept that, although problematic, helps lead toward an audible circuit and its crystallization. This is the distinction of null and vast extension (1994, 2009). The word *extension* as used by Chion refers to the expansiveness or reach of *film sound* that takes an audioviewer far beyond cinema's frame (vast) or down to a narrow point (null). Vast extension is his way of expressing ambient sound beyond the frame that gives a width to space. The narrowing of null extension is instead an extreme attention; he mentions silence and other filmic techniques that offer a sonic "suspension" in the null point. The problem with these terms is that (1) they involve a relation of space more than time and (2) the frame is necessary to the concept. Null and vast are therefore

---

[7] The circuit is found most prominently in his second cinema book (Deleuze, 1989) but is found as well in other texts. His brief essay "The Actual and the Virtual" (Deleuze, 2002) is an unusually direct definition of the connection of the two and how circuits function in their operation. (See also Eliot Ross Albert's footnote on this text.)

conceived sonically rather than audibly. Yet these concepts of null and vast can be modified to become *relational* elements of memory and time in the instant of an *actual* moment that crystalizes through the temporality of circuits in their repetitions.

Consider, first, Chion's example of ambient sound, or in our case, the firstness of ambient hearing—both temporal and independent of the frame. As with *Days of Heaven*, ambience—the vastness of audible time—forms a matrixial topology of deep significance in *The New World* (2005). The film's natural ambience is the precognitive every day of the common. Thought of as audible, ambience is eternal, the timeless presence of firstness within any particular time of hearing. It is persistent audible presence—never turned toward, never questioned. It only calls attention to itself in its sudden absence or differentiation. Absence occurs if one were to somehow "mute" or silence *its* continuity—in a sense, silencing *one's own* unconscious, one's own link to memory. Such silence is jarring as it strips life from everyday hearing. Differentiation would occur if one were to notice a sudden change in ambient continuity.[8] "Natural" in this sense is an appropriate signifier, not for sound but for the condition of hearing, the "common" or universal of hearing.

In *TNW* specifically, one hears territories as fields of new conflict between the world of nature and the coming of industrialization. Smith and Pocahontas in the forest hear the sounds of birds, water, controlled fire, grass, stones, shells, and wind moving through nature's glory. Such ambient elements are the continuance of a harmony between *phusis* and *ethos*, which casts a wide (vast) dispersion and constitutes the audible horizon of this culture. Cinematically, it establishes the bed of continuity that lives through the leaps in recollecting-imagining their time together. Later in the film, ambient hearing establishes coexistence during a scene when Smith is remorsefully and contentiously trading with the natives and his mind turns toward Pocahontas. Echoing and deepening Pvt. Bell's ambiguous simultaneity/coexistence in *TTRL*, Smith's need for reverie pushes him into gathering both an image and a silence of her. His recollection hovers behind her, giving emergence to both his gaze of

---

[8] These two may occur in the same moment, typically marked by the arrival of some unseen entity. Examples are the jungle sounds that fade prior to the appearance of the tiger in *Apocalypse Now* (Coppola, 1979), the crickets that fade prior to the arrival of the UFO in *Close Encounters of the Third Kind* (Spielberg, 1977), and the cicadas that cease twice prior to the reveal of Frank (Henry Fonda) in *Once Upon a Time in the West* (Leone, 1968).

memory and his desire for approach. We know the scene has not changed because the time of present voices and ambience remains. Space matters little; in fact, it might objectively have the same "sound" because the environment is the same. What creates the recollection is that presence remains while giving birth to a moment of coexistence, an intersection of their time together within his time without her. In other words, the vastness of ambience anchors him in his present time while he draws forth the idealized image of her. Within this single coexistent moment, his recollection is a regret, a desire, a longing of the past that is also a projection forward, and a hope to be with her again. The leap into the circle is a "now" that resonates another time that makes the new image-event. Chion might conceive of such moments as null points of subjectivity given for the audience as a relation of the frame—a trick of the apparatus. But considered as unseeing, Malick has opened to a *moment* as the "fullness of time" that is filled by an intersection of the crystalline, the eternal.[9] Actual space becomes irrelevant, but as well, any *particularity* of time loses import—the crystalline time-with that is spatially absent takes over and cuts through the present event.

Capt. Smith gives birth to his coexistence through a retention of present hearing over the imagery of an imprecise time. Perhaps he has withdrawn into the fantasy or nostalgia of remembrance, born of longing.[10] But it may also be, or include within it, an imagined projection of memory into a line that pulls him forward. The coexistence is born out of the noise of chatter that opens to its flight, a silence that discounts sequential time to open a new time. Smith opens to a new expression: the coexistence of time that gathers the two types of love offered by Kierkegaard (2009). The struggle is of recollective love, here the regret over dwelling in "old man" love—seeing love through to its end. This is Smith's frequent state, which begins with and carries the idea of loss throughout the relationship and thereby has nothing to lose. In Kierkegaard the love of the poet is always closing the story, acting based upon the certainty that love will eventually

---

[9] "And now the moment. Such a moment is unique. It is, of course, brief and temporal, as moments are, ephemeral, as moments are, passed, as moments are, in the next moment, and yet it is decisive, and yet it is filled with eternity. Such a moment must have a special name. Let us call it: the fullness of time" (Kierkegaard, 1980, p. 90).

[10] "While thinking I am not where I actually am; I am surrounded not by sense objects but by images that are invisible to everybody else. It is as though I had withdrawn into some never-never land, the land of invisibles, of which I would know nothing had I not this faculty of remembering and imagining" (Arendt, 1978, p. 85).

come to its end. The love of repetition is where a different memory enters, the memory which Malick's cinema does so well. The film becomes an act of gathering, a remaking of the love that was lost. In this, love is created anew through this repetition, through the thought that creates from the past, that recalls the noise so that it may be forgotten, opening to the silence of a present that is a rebirth and a remaking as *logos*. Malick has created the thinking within cinema that opens the time and space for a repetition to live, to exist. Such complex layering of the present, the past, and their projection into the new is the opening of coexisting fields of time, something Malick does extensively. Cinema becomes through Malick the theater of movement that Deleuze describes through *his* concept of repetition, influenced by Kierkegaard— movement as the dramatization of Ideas.[11] The simultaneity and coexistence first employed in *TTRL* is by *TNW* layered across many scenes. It may take on a quality of ambiguity, but by now it is more like what Deleuze describes with Guattari as that of a movement between the planes of immanence and transcendence in Kierkegaard.[12] The movement of thought creates time, opens spaces as the theater of images. Malick's coexistence expresses the longing that Smith feels, but it also instills in the film the very thought of a redemption. The film makes its ideas through those who recollect, regret, take account. This is how *TNW* takes on its dreamlike state, forming variable differences of both *kind* and *degree*—the making that lies within and between the now of now, the now of then, and the now yet to be fully realized.[13]

In contrast to the place and time of spirit is Smith's other world: inside the walls of the Jamestown colony. Here the ambience is starkly different as everything narrows. Nature has ceased and within fixity we hear a hollowness. No birds sing and nothing grows. Water does not flow but is taken in

---

[11] Both Deleuze and Kierkegaard are countering Hegel's generality, mediation, representation. "When we say, on the contrary, that movement is repetition and that this is our true theatre, we are not speaking of the effort of the actor who 'repeats' because he has not yet learned the part. We have in mind the theatrical space, the emptiness of that space, and the manner in which it is filled and determined by the signs and masks through which the actor plays a role which plays other roles; we think of how repetition is woven from one distinctive point to another, including the differences within itself" (Deleuze, 1994, p. 10).

[12] In *A Thousand Plateaus*, they write that Kierkegaard's infinite plane "must become a pure plane of immanence that continually and immediately imparts, reimparts, and regathers the finite…"(Deleuze & Guattari, 1987, p. 282). This unmediated movement becomes the limit of the relation, "the presence of one haecceity in another, the prehension of one by the other or the passage from one to the other: Look only at the movements."

[13] In Deleuze's Bergsonism, there are several differences in kind (matter/memory, perception/recollection, etc.). But when recollection becomes actualized, differences in kind become "obliterated," leading to differences in degree between recollection-images and perception-images. See Deleuze (1988).

the plunking of buckets. Axes hack at the forest, dogs bark, children prattle mindlessly. The chaos of collisions that was layered and harmonious in the forest is now separated out into individuated and discordant objects, carrying the weight of divisible labor and identifiable concerns. It is the onset of industrialization, where such objects separate from one another, categories form, tasks are handed out, and audibly, one can acquire individual sonic-events and attribute them directly to their objecthood.

This contrast between worlds is achieved most effectively when Smith first returns to the colony from his initial time with the natives. He arrives, blindfolded, unseeing, and then is unblinded, forced to re-see and thereby re-know the sights and objects of his culture. The doors open and we feel as he does the change in sound, the change in hearing and the change in self, even as such change is not consciously regarded. Wagner's glory fades with the null creaking open of the giant doors of civilization, replaced by a plaintive, empty wind.[14] Audibly, it pulls us along with Smith, as he is dropped back into this state of affairs. Heidegger's *Verfallen* is usually translated as "fallenness," but Stambaugh translates it as "entanglement" and in a footnote connects the state to a variety of terms: "wasting away," "addiction" or "falling for someone."[15] In Heidegger there is a sense of "getting caught up" in something, she continues, "a kind of movement that does not go anywhere."

Fallenness is the familiar existential mode of Dasein and both the forest and the colony can be thought of as their own mode of *care*; what is at issue therefore is authenticity. Smith's existential conflict is a choice between one world or the other, one self or the other. This is the freedom that carries anxiety as an ongoing condition. In what Heidegger will echo nearly a century later, Kierkegaard writes that "Anxiety is neither a category of necessity nor a category of freedom; it is entangled freedom, where freedom is not free in itself but entangled, not by necessity, but in itself" (1980, p. 49). Here, upon his return to the colony, Smith finds a world of language, dispute, violence, and arguments driven forth by suspicion, acquisition, and ambition. Smith is made president of this world and eases into duty and despair. "*Tell her. Tell her what? I love you. But I cannot love*

---

[14] For another take on this scene, see Sinnerbrink (2011): "The music fades and finally stops as he is led into the grey, muddy, dispiriting fort, the Wagnerian Prelude replaced by the sound of barking dogs and whistling wind" (p. 185). Sinnerbrink's emphasis is on Wagner's music as transcendent and symbolic (audioviewer), whereas mine is on the immanently audible (character).

[15] Stambaugh, in Heidegger (2010, p. 130). It is worth noting as well that Macquarrie and Robinson employ the term "*entangled*" from Heidegger's "*verfängt*" (Heidegger, 1962).

you. It was a dream. Now I am awake." This despair is distinguished sharply by its contrast with his prior statements depicting his time with the natives: "*I was a dead man. Now I live. You my light, my America. Love. Shall we deny it when it visits us? Shall we not take what we are given? There is only this. All else is unreal.*" Although starkly different in mood, both reflect a characteristically "cultured" pragmatism, a musing over what is to be done in the now. Despair comes with having two wills,[16] and Smith's struggle is one of choosing which will to forget. This is why Pocahontas tries to remind him to remember. Later, when they are rejoined, he tells her: "*There's something I know when I'm with you that I forget when I'm away.*" He cannot make the repetition—make the memory actual—enough to maintain the love through the despair of duty. It falls on her to protect it, to build the repetition. Within the same scene, the next words spoken are by her as she slips into a future gathering of this image-time: "*True. Shut your eyes. Is this the man I loved? So long. A ghost.*" If there is a love to survive—a love that *survives*—its only chance may be in a memory that lives forward, which is perhaps what Malick's film is: not a layering of withdrawal in presence but a living *memorial* created through the affectivity of fragmented recollections that becomes repetition.

Tendere *and Tension*

We can now return to Chion's vast and null extension, but with significant modifications. First, we can consider extension neither as audiovisual nor material but in its etymology, as *tension*. From its Latin and Old French origins, *tendere* is "to stretch," and in this we can think of the widest possible tensions along *logos*—the interplay of *ex*-tension, *in*-tension, and *at*-tension. Space stretches its horizon but unseeing also stretches along the farthest reaches of transcendental and unknowable horizons. Second, and related, to move outside of the duality of thought and space, one can think of tensions and *tendere* as not relegated to what is outside but, rather, is a matrix of intensities, extensities, and attention as a relation of forces.[17]

---

[16] "Two Edifying Discourses in Various Spirits." See Kierkegaard (1946).

[17] For Deleuze, *intensity* is the movement that differentiates—singular, vertical, interpretive, spiritual. "One is extensive, the other intensive. One is ordinary, the other distinctive and singular. One is horizontal, the other vertical. One is developed and explicated, the other enveloped and in need of interpretation" (1994, p. 23). He continues in this manner, putting intensity in the activity of change, mutation, newness, in contrast to extension which is terrestrial and comparatively lacking in newness.

Third, therefore, is the tension of time as the plane of a generative relationality. If extension in Chion constitutes a present horizon, tension is stretched into infinity through the coexistence of transcendental threads: memory, time, place, and one's present-actual gathering as *logos*.

These various audible tensions resonate each other like circuits—large, small, vast, and null. This is how the small comes to modulate and change the whole. Vast extension is not the purely present materiality of a location. As a matrix of tensions, it is instead the vast interplay of forces that act upon one's failures and successes of gathering the eternal within the various circuits of time. This is the *logos* of openness that listens to thought, emotion, and recollection, as well as the breadth of a space, in a time unified by coexistence. Null extension becomes the contracting of audibility to its singularities of listening, whose differentiation ruptures time and opens the possibility of the crystalline. Within the field of an open hearing, a null listening in Malick becomes an interjection—an *interstice*, as Deleuze would say—within the sensory-motor, which implores attention to the audible-event in its singularity. This is how eternity comes to live within finitude: the null tension of the *moment* intercedes and is made within the vastness of presence, opening to the vastness that is virtual, *transcendental*. In both the vast and the null, one hears in fragmented associations, not only in a relation to time but also in relation to Malick's image circuits, which *also* break apart as they attempt to unify. Taken altogether, audibility and imagery fly free from one another, seeking out and *cycling through* different times as the consciousness of the film attempts to bring them together and make thought. This is the struggle of *dis-associating* that becomes so concentrated in *TNW*, yet begins to pull apart in *TtW*. It gives Malick his experiential depth, but as *pathos* expresses the various struggles his characters endure.

Null audibility need not negate the vast field; listening need not close all hearing. In fact, it becomes the very complexity of audible thinking. When done artfully, the null or contracting circuits become audible singularities that develop *within* the vastness of any whole. It does, however, have the effect of dividing consciousness *ideologically*, creating from the audible-event a truth or a lie in consciousness. Sometimes the sound is a repetition with variation, sometimes it is a new sound, but it only becomes null when one's audibility decides it must be *tended to*. For example, in a sonic-event produced with the intent to be heard (such as the ringing of a bell), the sound effectuates a rational choice in its listener about what to believe from the audible. It may be gathered through its difference or it may be ignored through cycles of sameness or habit. In other words, such a sonic-event only becomes an audible-event when its differentiation is noticed, tended to, given attention. At this point it is not only an index taken as a sign but also a duration of significance for one to act upon. In this way they are not given to be found but an invitation to follow, to create a new idea. It breaks the ideology of sameness and habit. This is how Deleuze's signs are different from, say, Heidegger. For the latter, the sign is an indication, a pointer to its identity, and this is the danger of ideology—identification. For Deleuze, a sign is an aspect of experience, itself an engagement as an opening to thought. As audible, signs draw together into a matrix of tensions—the incomprehensible array of intensions and extensions that one may or may not *attend* to in hearing.

One of the elements heard often within Jamestown that offers this distinction is a church bell. In one hearing, the bell is an unquestionable tether to its identity of place, territory, ideology. It is made for such a purpose. But in another hearing the bell finds its resonance within the questioning of its broader significance, an index not material but meaningful. Within a vastness, it identifies with the space that is always present; its repetition here has no differentiating element. To the colonists, its sound, sign, and symbol mark an *identity* to their religion and culture and a passive psychological nurturing through indoctrination. R. Murray Schafer notes that the church bell was central to rural life in European Christendom (1993). Not only this, he adds, it attracted, defined, and unified the community through its hearing as centripetal, drawing man and God together into a shared horizon of worship and devotion. "Wherever the missionaries took Christianity, the church bell was soon to follow, acoustically demarking the civilization of the parish from the wilderness beyond its earshot" (1993, p. 55). It gave order to the day by presenting clock time that signifies without the need to be seen. "The clock bell had a great advantage over the clock dial, for to see the dial one must face it, while the bell sends the sounds of time rolling out uniformly in all directions" (p. 55). Its hearing helps these men of Jamestown to remember their identity to God and community, to not go astray, to retain and maintain the teachings of Christ. In *TNW*, it mnemonically but unconsciously places them in a temporal life-world that is familiar because the spatial life-world is distant, strange, new, fearful, and permeable. As a sonic representation of the church, it keeps the unfamiliar and exotic at bay in favor of the fixed identity to Christ's transcendence.

This same bell, the same sound, finds another hearing and listening in the *pathos* of Pocahontas after she is captured and must live in the colony. She hears this bell and looks up to the sky above her new home, seeking an understanding. She cannot see it and only wonders at it. She may not understand its objective significance, and thereby in her particular audible-event the same object- and sonic-event takes on a new inference: rather than acceptance of the colonists, forgotten and uneventful, it becomes for her a new opening, a duration of wonder. Through her, the ringing of a bell invites significance through her process of being "touched." This touch is the *intensive moment* of audibility's transition point. This touch is not object-to-object but, rather, a moment of having been touched in the mind, an act that attaches to the sonic-event. Etymologically, *teched* (touch) is a touching of consciousness, a touching from the inside. The Vulgur Latin *toccare* (not to be confused with its current Italian usage) is a tapping sound, such as the ringing of a bell. It implies not the activity of ringing but of having been rung, the gathering from the touch.

The touch as the striking of the bell also brings to mind a Buddhist metaphor for perception. Of Buddhism's six mental factors, the first is *vitarka*, which is, as in the Latin "touch," a striking of a bell. *Vitarka* marks the moment of contact between nonthought and thought. In Buddhist philosophy, the *vitarka* is the initial strike, but the strike does not live in isolation; it carries with it the *vicara*, the resonance of the bell that relates to the resonance in the mind *as* thought. *Vitarka* always *becomes vicara*: the initial strike, the impact that sparks the audible-event, becomes its resonance. This is Buddhism's moment of selection: that which triggers the application of thought then becomes thought itself. The strike resonates and its sustain is that which is "discursive" or scrutinizing, known in Buddhism as sustained thinking. Audibility functions similarly. One's openness in the firstness of hearing—if you will, one's access to the bell—is what allows the strike of the bell to be listened to. Without the bell there is no true sound; but without hearing there is no true listening. We can therefore think of *vitarka* as that which emerges within the already of hearing—the bell as that which always existed in a state of readiness. *Vicara*, as listening-to, is the metaphorical resonance of the bell, the thought that remains from the strike that occurs and continues within its event of occurring.

For Pocahontas, this event of listening-to is also her listening-for, which is a reaching out, a *tendere* or stretching of the mind that is attention within extension. The gathering of being touched wants to respond, to *give* account, to return the touch that touches, reaching toward the eternal and spiritual vitality of the man she has loved. Time passes and this listening follows her as she now lives within its deeper significance, changing her name, donning the clothing of its culture. It strikes again when her life changes and she marries John Rolfe (Christian Bale). Her next significant life change is when she arrives in England and hears the bell at the boat docks at her moment of arrival on the shores of England.

Such listenings are null in extension. But taken in a series of evolving repetitions, they differentiate through her changing audibility and expanding world as the tether widens. Once an index is learned it becomes referential and the index disappears. At the point of accepting the reference, ideology takes hold. But in her listening, this does not occur; the index never becomes *symbolic*, never loses its inferential aspect of curiosity, learning, and questioning. In her, understanding the reference does not efface the inference, so each new listening enters into a play of thought that moves forward. Each new emergence evades the immutability of things and symbols and develops, through time and in her repetition, a relation to the expanded history and forward progression of her character. This finds its culmination when she finally arrives in her new world of London. Her journey, which began with the single bell at Jamestown, now rings out in a clamor of bells at a grand church where "Rebecca," designated princess of her world, is to meet this new world's king and queen. The significance of the bell has *extended* to such a degree that she and we have found Deleuze's spider, for better or worse—the unseen source and the fullness of its concept. She has left the *inference* of England, the farthest thread of its reach, and found herself deep within the center and its activity. Through her hearing and listening, the child, Jamestown, has come back to *its* mother—the part joining the whole, the singularity ringing the infinite, the settlement returning to its originating culture. The meaning has changed through this other kind of ex-*tension*: The question that arose within the first event, which gave way to an idea in the next, now finds its home in understanding. Pocahontas is the spirit of the film because she manages this dual role of learning and repeating, each in concert with the other. Her journey is a movement from essence to essence, from hearing her own culture to listening to another to understanding this other. But, as is a theme in Malick's *logoi*, this understanding is not the end but a continuance. She carries her own culture as she learns another, but she also carries and lives the memory of her loves. She reforms and redeems them through her creative repetition that saves what Smith can only recollect.

The Tree of Life: Listening Beyond Memory

The New World's bell in listening invites a new understanding by both tracing and widening its circuit. Yet within such resonance this learning is *indexical* because, although the bell gives way to a new idea, its object-event propels the circuit. The movement maintains its inferential quality, but it unfolds in a forward direction *in time*. By the time of *The Tree of Life* (2010), Malick's audible design becomes an expression of pure nonassociative virtuality. There are few indications to material causes in the soundtrack, seen or unseen, and no objects are to be found in attended listening. Audible thought defies unidirectional and unitemporal indices and takes on its omnitemporal potential. This is not an index but movements through various openings that are neither causal nor spatial; rather, they are intersections of time with eternity and its ideas. Audibility moves and lives freely from image-space and object-events without abandoning its *logos* relations. Unseeing in this *independence from the present-actual* and *inseparability from logos* has abandoned its need for attachments and can seek along its own time, associating with and disassociating from the dominance of object-events and learning that has already decided. What is aural becomes a call from the decomposition of visuality and statements, a zone independent of space, causality, sensory-motor, and readiness-to-hand. Freed from object and image, the tone of a bell here resonates more deeply, with more *vicara*. This invites its listener toward *idea*, without the need for any actual strike, visual embodiment, nor even of a particularity of recollection. This is because the audibility in *TToL*, unlike his previous films, is not only a connection of memory but also one that as itself is the idea of a projection forward toward unseeing, toward what has never been heard or seen. The time of audibility must seek along its own tethers to form new crystals of thought.

The film presents four main temporal regions to consider.[18] It begins entirely in hearing, with a sound whose *sound of* (object-event) is unseen but feels like a slow burst of nature: perhaps a seaside, but perhaps as well the arrival of thought from the ocean of thinking. It is materially indefinite and imageless, the unseeing of what might be the imagining of a time or place that is tidal, oceanic. Greater specificity begins to form into whispered voices, the faint call of seagulls, and the emerging image of a single swath of light. This light is rendered as coexisting within a border space

---

[18] There are more than four, as audibility and its time-images are indeterminate. But for the purposes of description we will limit ourselves to four.

between image (candle/flame) and idea (ritual). The *logos* moves to Time 1,[19] childhood, through Mrs. O'Brien's (Jessica Chastain) meditation on the ways of grace and nature. The *logos* then leaps to Time 2, and the affection-images reveal to us an unknown tragedy. Malick's following camera is an unseen witness behind Mrs. O'Brien. The ambient hearing gradually dissolves to an almost silent return of the surf, allowing her scream to punctuate the *logos*. Space shifts suddenly to airplane noise that masks communication (as it did for Bill in the coal factory) in Mr. O'Brien's (Brad Pitt) reception of the news. His "*What?!*" is inaudible and the noise around him gradually dissolves to a variation of the near-silent surf. We then receive the previously mentioned tone of a deep, resonant bell in three occurrences as he gazes soundlessly out to the sunset. Here the bell does not point toward any understanding; rather the transcendent idea intercedes. We come to learn through affect alone that the O'Briens' son R.L. (Laramie Eppler) has died in some tragic or unexpected manner. This is revealed not through depictions or exposition but through affected faces and interactions, brief dialogue, cries, and muted screams from somewhere. Eleven minutes in, Malick's *logos* moves forward to Time 3, Jack's adult life, as the hearing of a surf reemerges. In so doing, however, Time 4 emerges, a time that has no time and is embedded in its *relation* to all other time regions. Time 4 is the spatiotemporal region from which the hearing of the surf has gained its *independence with inseparability*. The image of thought is created from hearing—a seaside, whose own time is unknowable. It is a where/when Jack is able to take account in a full sensory imagining.

At the 13-minute mark of film time, Jack lights his ritual candle and from this point on, *logos* becomes a coexistence that moves entirely through him. The only physical (extended) space from this point is his apartment and his office. Everything else weaves his overlaps of virtuality, expressed in time and attention, drawing his childhood forward into the ideal of reconciliation. The hearing of this world of Time 3 is hollow, vacant, an abundance of space encased in glass where all is visible and known. Audibility is disjointed, fragmented into unseen durations of dialogue from Jack, something about "*bumping into walls*." The camera swoops into business relations and ducks away. Dialogue from any "company man" in business dealings is muffled, unlistened, just like Christopher Plumber's company man of *The New World*.

---

[19] It is not yet clear who is hearing or thinking. It is another example of Malick's Woolf-like floating subjectivity.

Such idle talk is the accounting of material concerns, business dealings, and the incessant mutterings of *Das Man*—the everyman or common man.[20] This listening must cease so the unlistened *logos* of signs may emerge.

The hollow tone returns and morphs back into a synthetic sea moving us again to Time 1 beside a river. This shifting of sounds, unsteady hearings, unconscious and broken associations are all Jack by this point. He hears from nowhere R.L.'s whispered call: "*Find me.*" Something is happening to him in spite of himself that engenders unsteadiness and questioning, taking shape as fragmented recollections and imaginings as they occur. This is Jack in the midst of a shudder within his fallenness, an invitation to listen to the *logos*. Heidegger writes that Dasein in thrown projection is "constantly 'more' than it actually is," not factically but in the sense of "one who lets *go*—and *becomes*."[21] The authentic understanding in attention is one that originates from oneself and opens to the possibility in this projection.

Heidegger refers to such a break as an *immediate summoning* (2010), "the call."[22] Jack is being invited, perhaps forced, to stop listening so that he may hear. Heidegger writes that Dasein "*fails to hear* [*überhört*] its own self in listening to the they-self," (Heidegger, 2010b, p. 261). But we have to remember the dual meaning of hearing; *überhört* is a failure to *understand* through inauthentic listening. Instead, Jack's Dasein is within a failure of listening owing to a closure of first-order hearing. Put another way, he cannot hear other than what his Dasein believes is understanding. Authentic audibility, then, is a process in which understanding requires no terminus, no concept, and instead maintains this open virtual, transcendental hearing that works along other threads of time. Although Heidegger moves toward the truth that already exists (*aletheia*), he also writes that listening must be stopped so that "another kind of hearing" can emerge, one that interrupts one's listening to the *they*. Heidegger's is an arrival, but what is needed is a *paracusis*, a clinical word that means "audible hallucination," but here is a disruption that offers a new beginning. Malick is offering an opportunity for Jack to relearn where his Dasein stands, to *attend* (stretch) his Dasein. This can only come if there is something broken or

---

[20] *Das Man* comes from Heidegger, but it is surely influenced by his readings of Kierkegaard. "There is a restless activity which excludes a man from the world of the spirit, setting him in a class with the brutes, whose instincts impel them always to be on the move" (Kierkegaard, 1946, p. 24; *Either/Or*).

[21] Heidegger, 2010, p. 141 (see also footnote on that page).

[22] See as well, Ronell (1989).

released in his listening to "the publicness of the *they* and its idle talk"—an opening to lose himself. Heidegger describes this idle talk as a "groundless floating,"[23] and what we find in this call is another flow that intercedes within fallenness. It is a call to consciousness through hearing. Heidegger writes that what is most distant is often what is nearest,[24] and here such a distance is vast, unfamiliar, outside of facticity. "The call is precisely something that *we ourselves* have neither planned, nor prepared for, nor willfully brought about. 'It' calls, against our expectations and even against our will" (2010, p. 265). The call and the caller are the same: "The call comes *from* me, and yet *over* me."

What is this call that is not spoken, the one that arrives in sign rather than words, which drives one to take notice? Heidegger writes of the "step back" into essential thinking. "The step back points to the realm which until now has been skipped over, and from which the essence of truth becomes first of all worthy of thought" (1969b, p. 49). Heidegger's *difference* then allows a re-entry into lost essence. "The step back goes from what is unthought, from the difference as such, into what gives us thought" (p. 50). The stepping back is at the same time an approach, the perdurance of essence via transcendence (transition) to presence (arrival). Deleuze thinks in terms of an *intensity* of difference as itself that carries over to imagination. "Something in the world forces us to think," he writes in *Difference and Repetition* (1994, p. 139). This force is the repetition that binds in memory, implored through the newness of difference—the jaggedness of time, recollection, and nonassociable sound. This for Deleuze is the "encounter" that arrives in "affective tones: wonder, love, hatred, suffering." An encounter involves a faculty other than sense, that which is "not a quality but a sign. It is not a sensible being but the being of the sensible. It is not the given but that by which the given is given. It is therefore in a certain sense the imperceptible [*insensible*]" (p. 140).

---

[23] In both Macquarrie-Robinson (Heidegger, 1962) and Stambaugh (Heidegger, 2010). See section 38 of Heidegger (2010).

[24] This is something Malick himself recognized. See his written introduction to his translation of *Essence of Reasons* (See Heidegger, 1969a). The distance that is near is found throughout Heidegger's writings, but see in particular his *Letter on Humanism* (Heidegger, 1993): "he at first fails to recognize the nearest and attaches himself to the next nearest. He even thinks that this is the nearest. But nearer than the nearest and at the same time for ordinary thinking farther than the farthest is nearness itself: the truth of Being" (p. 235). Heidegger writes that this nearness comes through the "essence" of language as the house of being, whereas I am writing of another kind of being.

Jack's unfolding is neither representation nor recognition—both of which require understandings through preformed images of thought—rather, it is a firstness that invites (or in this case *forces*) an audibility that pulls along reason's limit or horizon. The Malick who translated Heidegger's limits of world has offered it through his cinema. The limit is found in the sign, born of a hearing that has no sound and as such has no sense. "Sensibility, in the presence of that which can only be sensed (and is at the same time imperceptible) finds itself before its own limit, the sign, and raises itself to the level of a transcendental exercise: to the 'nth' power. Common sense is there only in order to limit the specific contribution of sensibility to the conditions of a joint labour: it thereby enters into a discordant play, its organs become metaphysical" (Deleuze, 1994, p. 140). Deleuze continues that at this edge, the encounter "moves the soul… forces it to pose a problem." This is Deleuze's transcendental-empirical memory that can be grasped in the immanence of recollection. This, he adds, is not a contingent past but a "being of the past as such and the past of every time. In this manner, the *forgotten* thing *appears* in person to the memory which essentially apprehends it. It does not address memory without addressing the forgetting within memory."

The pure audibility of this hearing, devoid of any identification or recognition of sounds, is the *abandonment* of listening, a beyond-listening. This path opens to Jack a silence to actively engage what is not recognizable or referential in the *common* but, rather, a new listening.[25] In short, Jack does not reach out to a belief in anything given, but takes a leap of faith. Such an abandonment is not necessarily an abandoning *to* any existing divine entity but, instead, to that of a relation that lives within the indiscernible order of time. Such relationality as itself is neither succession nor interval, but the "internal relations of time" (Deleuze, 1989, p. 274). The sheets of time, the memory that is "world-memory," true and false, become indiscernible: "[T]he before and after are no longer themselves a matter of external empirical succession, but of the intrinsic quality of that which becomes in time. Becoming can in fact be defined as that which transforms an empirical sequence into a series: a burst of series" (1989, pp. 274–275). The internal relations here are not internal to "the film," nor the work of art, but the self made in memory, expressed in one's own multiplicity of time that unfolds. Breaking from the sonic world's simultaneity, audibility wanders freely in this burst, playing within

---

[25] "The subconscious is ceaselessly murmuring, and it is by listening to these murmurs that one hears its truth." (Bachelard, 1960, p. 59).

its own independence and inseparability, extending what is seen and building projections from forgetting.

This is not a destruction of memory, but as Kierkegaard, Heidegger, and Deleuze are all suggesting, it is an excitation, a movement, a thought that breaks habit and moves along other currents. Kierkegaard's problem of anxiety is finding oneself stuck in the wrong kind of movement, the entanglement or *Verfallen* that Heidegger picked up. When one is in sin, one becomes stuck, incapable of recollecting, incapable of accessing eternity. The inwardness becomes so acute that one is given to public acceptance.[26] Jack, like many of Malick's characters, feels stuck in time, but also stuck in time's acceptance, made by oneself through others. Thought struggles between closure and reaching out to eternity through the call. "If the eternal is posited, the present becomes something different from what a person wants it to be. He fears this, and thus he is in anxiety about the good. He may continue to deny the eternal as long as he wants, but in so doing he will not be able to kill the eternal entirely" (Kierkegaard, 1980, p. 152). Because people live in fear of eternity, Kierkegaard adds, they "preach the moment" while they rush around in a terrible haste. Yet in anxiety, to flip the familiar reading of Nietzsche, the eternal continues to return. Those bound up in listening to time will never hear the opening of eternity that calls at its farthest edges. This is Jack's situation: the choice to maintain closure or to open. The "eternal is the boundary of the temporal, but he who lives energetically in temporality never reaches the boundary."

As his hearing flows across time, Jack searches within his susurration, moving through tentative and whispered states of openness and closure. The seaside is a fragmentation of the wholeness of the present and the past. This duration from the whole, the eternal, is the virtual creating its own actual as an extensive, indeterminate duration—the infinite that lives with finitude. Sea and noise have always had a close relation in philosophy and literature—noise, nausea, seasickness—but also as the sound of tiny singularities whose horizons constitute the infinite, the whole, the indistinct, the eternal that moves in waves, nausea. For Leibniz, the noise of the sea is indicative of the confusion that the universe makes within us in our impressions (1934). The noise is Jack's nausea. He needs this disruption in thought to make this unseeing become *logos* in listening. The "hearing" of this wholeness draws Jack forward into the audible crystalline wave that cuts through and flows with the most distinction across time. It is a wordlessly cast invocation, a suggestion to come forward, to take account.

---

[26] See Kierkegaard (2009b).

The Act of Transferring and the Limits of Logos

In addition to the sea, this nausea, the other element from Time 4 that recurs is the call from the bell that remains unseen. It is another means of being "touched," affected—a found resonance in one's own *vicara*. In this resonance lies the call that carries the sign, not the sound but the hearing that wants to carry Jack into new thinking. As with a church bell, it is a call to salvation, a way home. Returning again to Heidegger's call (1968), it shares with *vicara* the element of sustain. As Heidegger continues to dissect his own question of *what calls* for thinking, there is a *something* to be found in the call, a calling to Being. In this seeking that finds, memory is given an etymological hearing in *thanc*, or the giving and receiving of thanks. Memory, through recollection, becomes for Heidegger an act of "devotion," a "prayer" that brings the past into the present toward the future. Such devotion "upon the holy and the gracious" (p. 145) is "a constant concentrated abiding with something—not just with something that has passed, but in the same way with what is present and with what may come. What is past, present, and to come appears in the oneness of its own present being" (p. 140). Thinking then, a new thinking, is for Heidegger done in devotion to grace that abides in the present withdrawal. Such withdrawal overcomes the distance and draws memory close through recollection. The soul "then pours forth its wealth of images—of visions envisioning the soul itself." Here there is the "contrast…between oblivion and retention," which Heidegger calls "*memoria tenere*," the keeping and holding of memory. The element of sustain is what continues the call of audibility to preserve the actual/virtual relation forward. But to hold the relation, audibility must come not only in response but along action: the *vicara* of thought is the *listening to* one's hearing that reaches no object. For Heidegger it is again the seeking *that finds* Being.

The resonating suggestions Malick employs pave a new clearing in the matrix of audibility and thereby take on a significance, entering Jack into the time of the sublime, which is itself a projection. For Deleuze, destiny lies within a spiritual dimension of Nietzsche's *return*. Although Deleuze is writing within his experiential semiotic framework, he might as well be describing a Malickian destiny that in its active disassociating is distinctly audible: Destiny, he writes, "implies between successive presents non-localisable connections, actions at a distance, systems of replay, resonance and echoes, objective chances, signs, signals and roles which transcend spatial locations and temporal successions. We say of successive presents which express a destiny that they always play out the same thing, the same story, but at different levels: here more or less relaxed, there more or less contracted. This is why destiny accords so badly with determinism but so well with freedom: freedom lies in choosing the levels" (1994, p. 83). The present point becomes an instant that resonates the whole of life, or in Deleuze's words "the sign of the present is a *passage* to the limit" (p. 83).[27]

The question one may ask with Malick and Jack is the opening of a passage to where? There are many ways to think this. Heidegger's call is authentically answered in understanding what *is*, and yet his *thanc*, the *giving thanks* that is memory, lies within. "The *thanc* means man's inmost mind, the heart, the heart's core, that innermost essence of man which reaches outward most fully and to the outmost limits, and so decisively that, rightly considered, the idea of an inner and outer world does not arise" (1968, p. 144). The reaching out is some kind of *trans* in thought and spirit—travel, a journey, a mutation—a transmutation that moves. Bachelard writes of the Jungian forces *animus* (man within woman) and *anima* (woman within man), involving an *Übertragung*: a transfer, but more a transferring *over*.[28] Here through Bachelard, the familiar significations become flipped when taken to the audible dimension: the *animus* of thinking in fallenness is the state of nature that listens, while the *anima* of reverie leaves open a state of grace: a time-space to hear that opens an *Übertragung* of new listening.[29] "*Uebertragung* is, as it were, a transfer *over* the most contrasting characteristics. This transfer passes over the detail of everyday relationships, over social situations to link cosmic situations. One is then urged to understand man not only from the basis of his inclusion in the world but by following his impulses for idealization which are at work on the world" (1960, p. 78). Jack comes to a crystalline audibility that leads to a different kind of hodological transfer: not space to space via audible-event to object-event; rather, it is the audibility that works through the gathering that takes account in a repetition, a transformation as a new formulation of eternity. This *trans* invites the outside

---

[27] For Heidegger, destiny is coupled with freedom, the abyss of Dasein, which provides it a "'potentiality for being,' with possibilities which gape open before its finite choice, i.e., in its destiny" (1969a, p. 129).

[28] Both Jung and Freud applied *Ubertragung* as what became known in classic psychotherapy as "transference," a projection of troubling aspects of identity onto another. Here I mean instead an affirming, transformative aspect.

[29] This is a diversion as well from Heidegger's *animus* (1968), which is more aligned with the Latin use as soul and yet for him is the striving along and attuning to what is.

within, the eternal in time. One can interpret God or spirit or grace, but whatever "it" is, is not a static, determining Being but a movement within *logos* that ruptures territory and carries life to a new territorialization. This new listening is both independent and inseparable from the moment that arises. In lucid reverie, "we know a sort of *interior transfer*, an *Uebertragung* which carries us beyond ourselves into another ourselves" (Bachelard, 1960, pp. 81–82). The line of transferring over takes on a verticality, the "celestial vertical" of transcendence that inscribes itself on the immanent plane of thought (Deleuze & Guattari, 1991, p. 89).[30]

One may turn to Spinoza as well, who conceives of a third kind of knowledge, one of the most challenging aspects of his *Ethics*. The real, unmediated experience of God is to live the limitless attribute of God in alignment with the limited attribute of oneself—God's idea as inseparable from one's own. By Deleuze's description, to achieve this third knowledge, beyond imagination and reason, is "to form the idea of ourselves as it is in God. This idea is just the idea that expresses the body's essence; to the extent that we form it, to the extent that we have it, we *experience* that we are eternal" (1990, p. 315). This is *logos* that for the moment must disregard *nomos* and move beyond sound, beyond understanding. It is the unseeing that one might name as transcendent but that maintains immanence in the necessity to return again to life. In Deleuze, Spinoza, and Kierkegaard, the eternity that one experiences is both duration with eternity and eternity within duration. We can think as well of Plotinus, for whom time is the image of eternity, and for whom the task of time is to gain an understanding of eternity. Here is not only the eternal within time but also the *work* of time, the work of finitude, to gather the eternal and make the account. This is the walk along the shore, but also the repetition of lost love (*The New World*) and the time of brotherhood in war (*The Thin Red Line*). The notion of "transcendence" becomes an immanent, creative act of faith, undetermined and willfully made.[31] Here we find Malick's limit of *logos*.

---

[30] Revisiting a theme from *A Thousand Plateaus*, they write : "Kierkegaard's 'knight of the faith,' he who makes the leap, or Pascal's gambler, he who throws the dice, are men of a transcendence or a faith. But they constantly recharge immanence: they are philosophers or, rather, intercessors, conceptual personae who stand in for these two philosophers and who are concerned no longer with the transcendent existence of God but only with the infinite immanent possibilities brought by the one who believes that God exists" (Deleuze & Guattari, 1991, p. 74).

[31] See James (2002).

The seaside is a fragmentation of the wholeness of the eternal in the images of time projected forward—the virtual creating its own actual. The hearing that draws Jack forward into the audible crystalline duration is recollection given rise from the call that creates newness as repetition. Kierkegaard describes these dual states of recollection and repetition as "auditive." Noise and silence are brought together into the sublime moment that is both nonverbal and "pure sound."[32] But it bears repeating: What Kierkegaard writes of is not sound but a hearing, with a listening-to that that is not verbal. For Kierkegaard and for Malick, language must be transcended, silenced, to reach out along the newness of unseeing. Kierkegaard writes, and James would agree, that in the becoming of its event, belief "believes what it does not see; it does not believe that the star is; it sees that; but it believes that the star has come to be. The same thing is true in relation to an event" (2009a, p. 148). To become this movement, this action, this choice that is believing, one must resonate the unseeing that lives within and outside of seeings and statements. One must *trans*—find the movement within that is the fold of the outside that is most near. Jack's hearing is not an understanding because there is no sound *of*. It is the pure audible-event, immanent to itself, from which he listens and creates the path. Jack, as with Pocahontas, is Malick's knight of faith who must *trans* alone, resonate the eternal within time—Dear Mother and the seaside. This knight is not the common tragic hero of cinema, the hero of ethics who within his struggle gets help along the way. The knight of faith is no hero; he, she, cannot gain assistance because she, he, is in another relation, one set apart from the sequence of universal ethics. This knight of faith is immersed in a journey that is entirely in conflict with himself, one who gains no help along the way and whose faith is continually tested. Jack's guide toward the seaside is himself, the self reformed by the past who leads the present into the new. The self is a constant flux of foldings and unfoldings. But through this, through such living, the call, the sound, the hearing, came from within.

---

[32] See again, Melberg (1990) for more on this audible aspect of Kierkegaard: "What is remarkable is that the young man describes his expected experiences in auditive terms: ideas are about to 'spume,' thoughts to 'arise noisily'; and he also expects a 'stillness like the deep silence of the South Sea' [186/221]. Noise as well as silence indicate that the young man's expectations of the sublime point to the nonverbal or to pure sound (that is, language without purpose or meaning). Or to deep silence. The desire of this text for a privileged now can be realized only beyond a language of meaning" (p. 77).

Malick's Ethics: A Time of Forgiveness

So much has been said up to this point about all these collisions: collisions of objects that make sound, of time that ruptures the now, of recollections within repetitions. These are not Hegelian collisions but, rather, Heraclitean ones: the *logos* that maintains as it changes in its making. Before ending this *diegesis*, this exegesis, we must at last come to the collision of immanence and transcendence in Malick. It is the question of limits, the most ineffable of inquiries. Here in the limits of language we have reached the dangerous point of claiming, stating a thesis, providing an argument. Because here unseeing confronts what it must in these ineffable moments: it makes a determination about *meaning*. And as Kierkegaard reminds us, only the subject can decide.

What lies in this limit, Jack's metaphorical time-space? Is he in the realm of spirit, God, death, rebirth? If one listens to Heidegger, perhaps he has transcended by reaching his own-most Being: a return to the same in the giving of thanks. If one listens to Deleuze, perhaps he has never left and the only finding is the emergence of the singular event that activates the new: an eternal recurrence of difference that mutates into infinity. If one listens to Kierkegaard, then perhaps Jack, as the knight of faith, walks along the authentic Christian ideal moving into the unchangeableness of God's eternal Love. What I wish to suggest, what I wish to determine from my own subjective immersion into Malick's worlds and *logoi*, is that perhaps these ideas are not in opposition and are various expressions of the whole, a multiplicity of thinking the ineffable thought of life, any life. One may recall that unseeing is a condition of life that is with us at every moment, a moment in which nothing is known so nothing is dictated. Audibility as an expression of such living opens oneself to the freedom of choosing within hearing—the time of now, the time of the past, perhaps even the time of the future. This continues to invite these irresolvable questions of within, beyond, outside, self, other, madness, redemption. Philosophers may quibble over the details of metaphysics, but what especially concerns all mentioned here is ethics. Perhaps more important is not what *is* but what is gathered in the encounter, what is made in *logos*, and this is the real of what one may name as spirit.

What is made—in Kierkegaard, Deleuze, Heidegger, Malick—is the creative activity that redeems the past. The time of memory is not about what has already happened; it is a question of how one lives *now*. What will *logos* gather, what will become expressed? Will now be a recollection of the past, its sad passions, or a repetition that reforms the future, igniting the joyful passions? In his closing words about Spinoza, Deleuze expresses the journey of Malick's intercessors: "Most men remain, most of the time, fixated by sad passions which cut them off from their essence and reduce it to the state of an abstraction. The path of salvation is the path of expression itself: to become expressive—that is, to become active; to express God's essence, to be oneself an idea through which the essence of God explicates itself, to have affections that are explained by our own essence and express God's essence" (1990, p. 320). In creating a place without space, a duration that intersects time, Malick has expressed rather than stated such a philosophy. It is a philosophy that, through cinema, collides both repetition and recollection to shape an ethics of forgiveness, salvation, reformation, and redemption.

This is my determination and only mine, for each one who experiences Malick's cinema will have her and his own gathering, including Malick himself. In *TToL*'s penultimate scene, Jack moves willingly within this active zone of forgiving, where grace finally permeates all and clears a path *toward* forgive*ness*. In this zone at the furthest reaches of *logos*, Jack's body does not sit and contemplate; he engages with family in the act of gathering forgiveness. The call is not a demand to *forgive*. It is not an end but a process, a place to gather, an opening—the sea as a vast image-less space and time. Unseeing, Jack's unseeing, *has made this place*, the nonplace he envisions from his hearing. As Agamben writes, the imagining that is free of images is Mnemosyne's ideal: "the farewell—and the refuge—of all images" (2011, p. 79). Understanding has no terminus here, the images of recollections have faded, and guilt enervates under the light of such forgiving.

We must return then to the question of unity, the time of unity. Plotinus, as a good Platonist, gives to the universe a desire. Eternity, not content with itself, desired an unfolding, a stirring toward the ever-newness of *difference*. This is why, he claims, time was created. But from this desire to "uncoil," unity became lost. It can never be regained, for that would be the end of difference, the end of time. But if time is eternity's imperfection, the fragmentation of all imagery, hearing seeks to answer the call to eternity, this imageless, timeless, and unchangeable whole. It is no end; rather, it is the continual ebb and flow in the account. Writing of the unchangeableness of God, Kierkegaard conceives, as does Andreas-Salomé, the place of unity. It is not arrival so much as "an accounting in eternity, where nothing is forgotten, not even a single one of the improper words that were spoken" (Kierkegaard, 1946, p. 476). Forgetting gives way, in this eternity, to a repetition that remembers the entirety of life and remembers it forward, free of such worldly burdens. Yet within this zone we can think as well of the event that mutates the whole, a redemption not only of the self but of all that moves forward, all who move forward.

The struggle to make amends with family is a condition that runs deep because it is the nearness that feels most distant and the distance that feels most near. Words and recollections are not enough when they aim toward rational and worldly *references* to events, *sources* of pain. Poetry and cinema at their most expressive move instead toward suturing the gaps of lost unity—seeking out the thinnest of threads that can begin the process. Through Jack's journey, and the finding of his timeless forgiveness, *now* has necessarily lost its source of sorrow that has passed. Causes become streams untethered, adrift in the ineffable currents of regrets, misunderstandings, all that may have been said and unsaid in a time when language was uncertain and its intent long since faded. "The elemental and intimate do not declare themselves openly. As a result, what is truly essential remains unsaid" (Andreas-Salomé, 1990, p. 124). There is too much to say and no means to express rationally. It only matters because the love is real, and this is what both transcends and repeats.

As Jack responded to his call, so too did Malick. One may take note of the final words of *Essence of Reasons*, in which Malick takes leave from his scholarly work on Heidegger and finds his own new path toward cinema: "And so man, as existing transcendence abounding in and surpassing toward possibilities, is a *creature of distance*. Only through the primordial distances he establishes toward all being in his transcendence does a true nearness to things flourish in him. And only the knack for hearing into the distance awakens Dasein as self to the answer of its Dasein with others. For only in its Dasein with others can Dasein surrender its individuality in order to win itself as an authentic self" (1969a, p. 131). Thus the call: maybe it is destiny, a dream, a vision, an apparition, a new creation. Maybe such words do not matter. The vastness itself calls and has no other shore, no destination. It is a call with no objective, a call to some higher state within that lives on and continues to take account. The mind is released from its need to rationalize, control, hold on, free to wander without consequence or judgment: a time and space to forgive, and a new opening to continue.

REFERENCES

Texts Cited

Agamben, G. (2011). Nymphs. In *Releasing the Image: From Literature to New Media* (pp. 60–80). Stanford: Stanford University Press.

Andreas-Salomé, L. (1990). *Looking Back: Memoirs* (B. Mitchell, Trans.). New York: Paragon.

Arendt, H. (1978). *Life of the Mind.* San Diego: Harcourt.

Bachelard, G. (1960). *The Poetics of Reverie: Childhood, Language, and the Cosmos* (D. Russell, Trans.). Boston: Beacon Press.

Barthes, R. (1991). Listening. In *The Responsibility of Forms* (pp. 245–260). Berkeley: University of California Press.

Chion, M. (1994). *Audio-vision: Sound on Screen* (C. Gorbman, Trans.). New York: Columbia University Press.

Chion, M. (2009). *Film: A Sound Art* (C. Gorbman, Trans.). New York: Columbia University Press.

Deleuze, G. (1983). *Nietzsche and Philosophy* (H. Tomlinson, Trans.). New York: Columbia University Press.

Deleuze, G. (1986). *Cinema 1* (H. Tomlinson & B. Habberjam, Trans.). London: Continuum.

Deleuze, G. (1988). *Bergsonism* (H. Tomlinson & B. Habberjam, Trans.). Brooklyn: Zone Books.

Deleuze, G. (1989). *Cinema 2* (H. Tomlinson & R. Galeta, Trans.). Minneapolis: University of Minnesota Press.

Deleuze, G. (1990) *Expressionism in Philosophy: Spinoza* (M. Joughin, Trans.) Brooklyn: Zone.

Deleuze, G. (1994). *Difference and Repetition* (P. Patton, Trans.). New York: Columbia University Press.

Deleuze, G. (2002). The Actual and the Virtual. In *Dialogues II* (E. R. Albert, Trans.). New York: Continuum.

Deleuze, G. & Guattari, F. (1987). *A Thousand Plateaus.* Minneapolis: University of Minnesota Press.

Deleuze, G. & Guattari, F. (1991). *What Is Philosophy?* (H. Tomlinson & G. Burchell, Trans.). New York: Columbia University Press.

Heidegger, M. (1962). *Being and Time* (J. Macquarrie & E. Robinson, Trans.) Oxford: Basil Blackwell.

Heidegger, M. (1966). *Discourse on Thinking: A Translation of Glassenheit* (J. M. Anderson & E. H. Freund, Trans.). New York: Harper & Row

Heidegger, M. (1968). *What Is Called Thinking.* New York: Harper Perennial.

Heidegger, M. (1969a). *The Essence of Reasons* (T. Malick, Trans.). Evanston: Northwestern University Press.

Heidegger, M. (1969b). *Identity and Difference* (J. Stambaugh, Trans.). New York: Harper & Row.
Heidegger, M. (1988). *The Essence of Truth: On Plato's Cave Allegory and Theaetetus* (T. Sadler, Trans.). New York: Continuum.
Heidegger, M. (1993). Letter on Humanism. In D. F. Carell (Ed.), *Martin Heidegger: Basic Writings* (pp. 213–266). San Francisco: Harper.
Heidegger, M. (2010). *Being and Time* (J. Stambaugh, Trans.). Albany: State University of New York Press.
James, W. (2002). *The Varieties of Religious Experience*. Mineola: Dover.
Kierkegaard, S. (1946). In R. Bretall (Ed.), *A Kierkegaard Anthology*. Princeton: Princeton University Press.
Kierkegaard, S. (1980). *The Concept of Anxiety* (R. Thomte, Trans.). Princeton: Princeton University Press.
Kierkegaard, S. (2009a). *Repetition and Philosophical Crumbs* (M. G. Piety, Trans.). Oxford: Oxford University Press.
Kierkegaard, S. (2009b). *Concluding Unscientific Postscript to the Philosophical Crumbs* (A. Hannay, Trans.). Cambridge: Cambridge University Press.
Leibniz, G. W. (1934). Principles of Nature and Grace, Founded on Reason, 1714. In M. Morris (Trans.), *Philosophical Writings* (pp. 21–31). London: J. M. Dent.
Melberg, A. (1990). Repetition (In the Kierkegaardian Sense of the Term). *Diacritics, 20*(3) (Autumn), 71–87.
Nancy, J. (2007). *Listening*. [Ebook]. New York: Fordham University Press.
Ronell, A. (1989). *The Telephone Book: Technology, Schizophrenia, Electric Speech*. Lincoln: University of Nebraska Press.
Sartre, J. (2004). *The Imaginary: A Phenomenological Psychology of the Imagination* (J. Webber, Trans.). London: Routledge.
Schafer, R. M. (1993). *The Soundscape: Our Sonic Environment and the Tuning of the World*. Rochester: Destiny.
Silverman, K. (2009). *Flesh of My Flesh*. Stanford: Stanford University Press.
Sinnerbrink, R. (2011). *New Philosophies of Film: Thinking Images*. New York: Continuum.

Films Cited

Bergman, I. (Director). (1966). *Persona* [Motion Picture]. Sweden: AB Svensk Filmindustri.
Bresson, R. (Director). (1956). *Un condamné à mort s'est échappé ou Le vent souffle où il veut* (*A Man Escaped: or The Wind Bloweth Where It Listeth*) [Motion Picture]. France: Gaumont Film Company.
Coppola, F. F. (1979). (Director). *Apocalypse Now* [Motion picture]. USA: Paramount Pictures / American Zoetrope.

Leone, S. (Director). (1968). *Once Upon a Time in the West* [Motion Picture]. Italy, et al: Rafran Cinematografica, et al. / Euro International Film, Paramount Pictures.
Malick, T. (Director). (1998). *The Thin Red Line* [Motion Picture]. USA: Geisler-Roberdeau, Phoenix Pictures / 20th Century Fox.
Malick, T. (Director). (2005). *The New World* [Motion Picture]. USA: New Line Cinema.
Malick, T. (Director). (2010). *The Tree of Life* [Motion Picture]. USA: River Road Entertainment.
Spielberg, S. (Director). (1977). *Close Encounters of the Third Kind*. USA: EMI Films / Columbia Pictures.
Spielberg, S. (Director). (1998). *Saving Private Ryan* [Motion picture]. USA: Amblin Entertainment / DreamWorks Pictures.
Tarkovsky, A. (Director). (1979). *Stalker* [Motion Picture]. Soviet Union: Mosfilm.

CHAPTER 7

Continuer

The Tree of Life does not end at the shore, with Jack wandering the eternal, the transcendent. It returns him to time, the *time* he never left, and life continues: reborn, transformed. The seaside is not arrival, finality, death—not a conclusion. Malick drops Jack, literally through a descending elevator, back to the city, back to finitude. Kierkegaard, if we recall, does not want one to sacrifice the finite for the infinite. The finite is the time of life within the *transcendental*, a continuance. In a life, nothing concludes. Jack, Malick, myself, any life—we are the continuers of time. When this film ends, one leaves the *reverie* and continues on in one's world, where one is given a silence to think.

This conclusion will therefore not summarize but, instead, will offer a brief continuer of thought, a moment to step outside and speculate. If one did wish to conclude with any statement about Malick's unseeing, it would be tempting to run with the thought that all thought in his films, his *logoi*, is the gathering of Malick. Is this not what lies in any story, any experience, that it is the account of its author? One can conceive of the director of any film as its god, a Platonic *demiurge*, or even more appropriate, an Aristotelian *nous*, the latter as the divine thinking that thinks itself: the god who thinks. But such a conclusion does not satisfy. Why would a divine creator fragment his perfection? Malick is not the divinity of his cinema; rather, Malick seems to understand this key aspect of Spinoza that Deleuze and Kierkegaard recognize as well: insofar as one may wish to conceive God, God's knowledge and power is infinite while one's own is finite.

Lives live time *in time*, not outside it. This is the limit that fragments in the attempt to strive and gather, to wonder and reform, within absolute and eternal perfection. What resonates out of Malick is neither cause nor the art but, instead, the *account*, through his characters, that resonates us, the audioviewers. This is not *nous* but *logos*, in its failures and attentions. Amending from Barthes, the experience, not the image, is what remains. Cinema is an experience, the expressions that become an expression, reaching a point when one names it art for its imperfection. The great accident of art is that these resoundings, these echoes of its creator, are usually, at best, unconscious. What resonates is not this but what is folded within the selves who live the experience.

Great works polarize those who engage with them, and Malick is a polarizing filmmaker. Those who analyze, who distance, who expect, cannot resonate. The Malick who makes films is not Socrates, Seneca, Heidegger, or Wittgenstein. If one were to compare him to any philosopher, one might do well to name Kierkegaard—for his subjectivity in the making, for his faith, for his storytelling. Kierkegaard is the most cinematic of philosophers when his writers tell stories through his characters within *their* settings, their relations. He does not reference storytellers—as Deleuze might do with Godard, Carroll, or Proust—he produces the act of thinking through the stories of his intercessors. Kierkegaard's characters, as Deleuze said early in his career before he abandoned him, follow authenticity by following the question to its end; this journey is one that cannot be said, cannot be reasoned, breaks apart; the conclusion of the path of passion in Kierkegaard is the shock of loss and the threat of one's own destruction.[1] This is the fragmented journey that Malick puts himself through, puts his characters through, puts us through—the wild struggle to get beyond the limitations of self,[2] to open the true infinite, returning and repeating.

This returns us to the "conceptual persona," who for Deleuze and Guattari carries out the *activity* of a philosophical concept (1991). It is neither representation nor metaphor, and instead the bestowment of life upon one who lives the concept of the philosopher, making the immanent plane that realizes it—or, making the *logos* they make. They write that this

---

[1] I am appropriating here from Deleuze's early classroom lectures compiled in *What Is Grounding?* (2015), several pages of which center on Kierkegaard.

[2] "Repetition is too transcendent for me. I can circumnavigate myself, but I cannot get beyond myself. I cannot find this Archimedean point" (Kierkegaard, 2009b, p. 50).

persona, an intercessor, is like a heteronym—words that look the same in text but sound differently in speaking.[3] In its appearance, a word has no differentiation; only when it is sounded is the expression made. Both philosophers and artists live the *reality* of the concept. They create personae who live the idea. Dionysus, they write, was not a philosopher, but through Nietzsche he becomes one; or to state it more finely, Nietzsche becomes through Dionysus. As Pvt. Bell becomes a poet and philosopher through Malick, Malick becomes through Pvt. Bell. A work of art provides the field (the plane) for action. One may recall as well that Socrates had his interlocutors, but we cannot forget that they become philosophy through Plato the writer. This is an important distinction, one that also applies to cinema: Socrates and his men lived the dialogue, made the *logos*, as it were. The dialogue becomes the written work, which becomes the story, which becomes the idea from any reading. Whether its actors are real or fictional matters to the historian, but not to the philosopher.[4] Even more prevalent in cinema than literature perhaps, because the form itself moves rather than speaks, we find Malick the thinker—indeed, the philosopher—coming thorough the lives of those who gather what has been lost and who express the very real joys and sorrows under constant threat of destruction, of forgetting. Deleuze and Guattari write that personae work within a field of sensation, in "philosophical sensibilia." Such personae are "the perceptions and affections of fragmentary concepts themselves: through them concepts are not only thought but perceived and felt" (1991, p. 131). What Pablo Neruda wrote of thinking—a fish caught in the wind—Heraclitus suggested much earlier: "what we see and catch we leave behind; what we neither see nor catch, we carry away."[5]

We can return here to Malick's cinema after *The Tree of Life*, but now to wonder why Malick's personae, those who intercede and create his *logos*, began slipping away from him. *To The Wonder* is perhaps his most personal film, at least one that seems to most reflect his actual life rather than that of his personae. Malick on occasion likes to "torpedo" his actors, as he puts it, to surprise them, catch them off guard in an effort to render

---

[3] We may recall as well the "heteronym" of Kierkegaard, mentioned in the introduction.

[4] "The destiny of the philosopher is to become his conceptual persona or personae, at the same time that these personae themselves become something other than what they are historically, mythologically, or commonly (the Socrates of Plato, the Dionysus of Nietzsche…). The conceptual persona is the becoming or the subject of a philosophy, on par with the philosopher" (Deleuze & Guattari, 1991, p. 64).

[5] Pablo Neruda, "Los Enigmas." For Heraclitus, see Kahn (1979, p. 111).

them more real.[6] But from a standpoint of unseeing, this quest for real experience through the *profilmic* real sacrifices the cohesion of *logos* and world as *made* real, not by actor but by intercessor. Perhaps in the growing proliferation of profilmic real, his characters' *logoi* began to thin to such a degree that the account fell into an indulgence of habit. Perhaps this again is where the *tendere* of *logos* is stretched too far, as habit takes over eternity in repetition. One may recall Kierkegaard's concepts of anxiety and sin, which compose the conditions between possibility and actuality. The path out of sin, according to Augustine and others, is redemption. The gathering of redemption needs a tether, a movement or line of flight, within the fragmented effort to take account. If sin is the condition of anxiety, and anxiety opens the path of temptation or redemption, maybe the former is what we find Malick's characters falling into more and more. Perhaps, for one cannot yet say, this is Malick's intent, a brief and quick period of loss. There are signs that Malick may have seen this approach through to its artistic end. As of this writing, there are reports that Malick's next film may again take a linear approach.[7] Regardless of these more recent shifts, *Days of Heaven* through *The Tree of Life* indeed define an era of unseeing. This is not a static one but one that moves, a progression that composes a whole, before breaking apart in the films that followed.

One may also, if the intent now is to question, call Malick to task for creating personae whose appearances are predominantly white and male. Yet one could convincingly argue that Malick's highest ideal is carried by neither: Pocahontas, of *The New World*. Rather than function as the other to John Smith's story, she is authentic because the new world is hers, a world that is not *oppositional to* but that *includes* Smith, Rolfe, and others. In Smith's recollection she becomes his poet of Kierkegaard's *Repetition*; but as herself, she lives repetition that *becomes* in cinema. We might say that both she and Jack have transcended, transfigured, lived the eternal; but whereas Jack heeded the call, Pocahontas *chose* to live in faith. She is the one who lives eternity without leaving time, without abandoning the Deleuzean transcendental infinite of earth. She has done so not by maintaining her identity but by continuing to listen. Listening and faith share a characteristic of striving, but they take on an "ethics" by detaching from any single line of causality—the listening that continues to hear and the

---

[6] This comes from a session Malick gave at the European Graduate School in summer 2015. Thanks to my friend Jonathan Bennett Bonilla for reminding me of it.

[7] See Sharf (2017) about *Radegund*.

faith that continues to expand. As Kierkegaard reminds us, the world tells us many things, but it is up to the person to decide. She decides by going beyond herself, traversing a new world of surfaces while carrying the depth and wholeness of Dear Mother that lives in her above and below worlds and outside of time's sequence. The transformation is subjective but within such an act of creativity she has transformed the whole, given spirit and culture an expression and an opening for repetitions in other forms, manifestations, emergences. This is cinema's capacity—to create the unseeing circuit that continually divides while it traverses. Like a vine that multiplies as it wanders, cinema—Malick's unseeing cinema—extends thought, activity, affect, and sign beyond all prior expression without leaving *logos* behind. She is the authentic character, but subjectivity is not exclusive to her. Smith gives her up and in this becomes the Kierkegaard, perhaps even the Malick, who rationalizes love out of his life for some other calling along the march of sequential time.[8] Who is to say with Malick? The answer is unimportant, for his characters live the truth of the fiction.

The distinctions between filmmaker and character, the intercession between and inclusive of the two, fade when one comes to feel that the indiscernibility is what makes the expression, not the answer of whom. The character makes the film when she or he makes the fiction that becomes the truth of the film. The truth of cinema emerges when its characters are the producers and creators of truth. This is how cinema becomes its own unspoken thought, its unseeing understanding: when the intercessor lives the life that reaches out along the truth within itself. The filmmaker "becomes another" when he "takes real characters as intercessors and replaces his fictions by their own story-telling" (Deleuze, 1989, p. 152). Like Woolf through literature, Malick through cinema evades a singular subjectivity by *moving* the expressions—their thoughts, their acts of gathering and taking account. It is not only a collectivity but also an activity of collecting and recollecting that moves "from place to place, from person to person, from intercessor to intercessor" (p. 153). The *intercession*, a word that also means "prayer on behalf of another," is a communal prayer. The two conjoin through the action and thought that together reach out along the same expression—fictional if we wish to see it that way, but real in the act of being made.

---

[8] He also faked his death and left her to marry another—additional themes found in Kierkegaard's life and/or his story of repetition.

Kierkegaard needed a *diegesis*—a story in prose in the persona of a poet—to express repetition. He could not explain repetition and chose instead a double of a double: an invented poet and his invented storyteller. In giving his philosophy a writer and a poet, a knight of faith and another of infinite resignation, he has chosen to give *choice* to his philosophy. His personae must choose, must decide. Malick is doing something of the same, but if so, I wonder who is writing whom. Perhaps his characters are whispering in his ear things he does not know. This is the suggestive sorcery of filmmaking—that nothing needs explaining or describing because its unseeing, their unseeing, emanates in signs, in emergences. Kierkegaard creates his concept through the words of others because that is his medium. In Malick's cinema, perhaps the expressions of his characters move through him, the audible gatherings which create the repetition. This is the indiscernibility, the independence and inseparability of flight, that Malick's cinema unfolds. The repetition, for every Malick film is an attempt at repetition, unfolds as the indiscernibility of Malick and his personae who intercede. The repetition that creates, imagines, and moves into a future was an impossible task for Kierkegaard to describe in prose because the task is impossible to write, impossible to remember. A repetition cannot recreate by revisiting. Constantin could not repeat in Berlin by going to the same places and altering his patterns. Repetition is the metaphysical solution that cannot be controlled. In short, it is an event, a lived event given rise from the condition of possible change. "Repetition is the solution in every ethical contemplation, repetition is the *conditio sine qua non* for every dogmatic problem."[9] It is a shock, a shudder, a rupture, an event that opens and continues.

Cinema is not writing, not *diegesis*. Through Malick, repetition becomes real because he gives life to it through the action that his characters live in their process of being alive. Malick engages in a true art of repetition, not by revisiting his dilemmas and settings of the past but by creating their redemption through his personae, their worlds and their *logos* that gathers. They live the repetition; they open or close their hearing; they divide time, and in their *unseeing* imagine, recollect, remember, forget. As we think through the increasingly layered folding, unfolding, unearthing, lifting, recreating that occurs from *The Thin Red Line* through *The Tree of Life*, it is not actual events that emerge but the events that have been reformed through repetition. What is repeated is this reformation, *this redemption*.

---

[9] Kierkegaard (2009a, p. 19). "*Conditio sine qua non*" is something like condition of necessary or essential action.

In this, Malick repeats for us as well. We live through our involvement in the repetition—an involvement that gives birth through empathy of our own redemptive possibilities. One is affected as one embraces the *logos* made by his personae, the thoughts born of their unseeing and the hearings of silences and signs that open it. The unseen, in acts of seeing, must be called, drawn forth into a gathering. We remember again that visuality is Heraclitus's fire; but the heart of *logos* is cinema's other: audibility. Beholden to neither images nor things, it conjures its own thought, takes life as a spirit that flies from actual presence in its gatherings. Like a visit to Heraclitus's Oracle who emits only in signs, a cinema as *logos* allows sonority and one's audibility to roam free, to detach from things and concerns, objects and language, without abandoning them—to be a sonic shadow now, to become its own light then, or to find its own dark expression, not necessarily as dour or malevolent but living within its own fragments. One might think as well of Echo's call. To attend as *logos* would require Narcissus to stop listening to himself in hearing her, to cease the narcissism of his images, opening to an Echo that is *herself*. Perhaps here he may find a new listening in his unseeing, a new understanding, before he ever turns his head to the sound.

* * *

"*My Dear Reader*!—Forgive me for speaking confidentially to you, but we are *unter uns*.[10] Despite the fact that you are an imaginary person, you are in no way a multiplicity, but only one, so there is only you and I."[11] At the end of *Repetition*, Kierkegaard lifts himself out of the young man persona, out of even Constantin, and address the reader as Søren. The life of the poet, he says, works through the struggle of all existence. Through the poet, actuality becomes repetition, but specifically in the sense that consciousness in its "exponential power…is repetition. … He has preserved an ideal picture of the whole love affair, to which he can give whatever expression he wishes, but only in terms of a mood, because he has no facticity." It is a fact of consciousness which in the poet has no consciousness-fact. It is a "dialectical elasticity" that is "ineffably religious." In this eternal state, finitude matters little, actuality matters little, and words cannot gather. "It is characteristic of this young person that, as a poet, he can never fully understand what it is he has done, precisely because he will

---

[10] "just you and me."
[11] This quote and from here onward are found in the closing pages of Kierkegaard (2009a).

both see it and yet not see it in the external and visible, or will see it in the external and visible, and therefore will see it and not see it."

Søren writes to the reader, of the young man who struggles, the poet in conflict with the man of faith. But perhaps one can say as well that this is Rebecca, Smith, The Farmer, Bill, Witt, Bell, Jack—the intercessors, the thinkers, perhaps even the poets, who leave time in seeing to listen in unseeing.

REFERENCES

Texts Cited

Deleuze, G. (1989). *Cinema 2* (H. Tomlinson & R. Galeta, Trans.). Minneapolis: University of Minnesota Press.

Deleuze, G. (2015). *What Is Grounding?* (A. Kleinherenbrink, Trans.). Grand Rapids: &&& Publishing.

Deleuze, G., & Guattari, F. (1991). *What Is Philosophy?* (H. Tomlinson & G. Burchell, Trans.). New York: Columbia University Press.

Kahn, C. H. (1979). *The Art and Thought of Heraclitus.* London: Cambridge University Press.

Kierkegaard, S. (2009a). *Repetition and Philosophical Crumbs* (M. G. Piety, Trans.). Oxford: Oxford University Press.

Kierkegaard, S. (2009b). *Concluding Unscientific Postscript to the Philosophical Crumbs* (A. Hannay, Trans.). Cambridge: Cambridge University Press.

Sharf, Z. (2017). Terrence Malick Vows to Return to More Structured Filmmaking: 'I'm Backing Away from That Style Now'. *IndieWire*. Retrieved online April 6, 2017 at http://www.indiewire.com/2017/04/terrence-malick-radegund-screenplay-style-1201802506/

Index[1]

A

Acousmatic, 37, 38, 43
Affection-image (Deleuze), 10, 77, 98, 100, 101, 119
Agamben, Giorgio, 51n4, 116, 184
Ambient sound/ambience, 67, 96, 100–103, 106, 107, 126, 161–166, 174
Anagnorisis, 105, 106
Anamnesis, 13n17, 115
Andreas-Salomé, Lou, 120, 121, 136, 136n28, 184, 185
Anxiety (Kierkegaard), 12, 38, 65–68, 102, 103, 111, 112, 119, 138, 159, 167, 178, 192
Apocalypse, 103, 112, 157, 162
Apocalypse Now, 37, 164n8
Arendt, Hannah, 36n5, 132, 165n10
Aristotle, 10, 16, 29, 39, 56, 106, 106n8, 106n9, 131, 144

Audible-events, 41, 42, 51, 58, 61, 69, 72, 76, 93, 96, 106, 108, 119, 135, 146, 147n35, 169–171, 180, 182
Authenticity, viii, 12, 13, 91, 129, 132, 133, 138, 142, 143, 150, 158, 161, 167, 190

B

Bachelard, Gaston, 26, 52, 53, 81, 83, 126, 127, 132, 135, 136, 177n25, 180, 181
Badlands, xi, 91, 92, 95, 137, 145–147
Balázs, Bela, 31, 32, 35, 81
Barthes, Roland, 26, 27, 81, 156, 190
Benjamin, Walter, 25, 81
Bergman, Ingmar, 79, 83

---

[1] Note: Page numbers followed by 'n' refer to notes.

Bergson, Henri, 27, 38, 53, 55n8, 62, 63n16, 68, 69, 71, 83, 93, 120, 121, 123–126, 133, 133n24, 133n25, 156, 163
Blade Runner, 27, 44
Bresson, Robert, 54, 58, 60, 60n11, 73, 79n27, 80
Burgin, Victor, 26

C
Cavell, Stanley, 2, 3, 44, 44n13, 77
Chion, Michel, 35, 36n6, 37, 40n8, 56n10, 73, 73n24, 75n25, 94, 163–165, 168, 169
Circuit (Deleuze), 62, 68, 123, 124, 139, 162, 163, 163n7
Coexistence, xi, 6, 7, 20, 21, 25, 27, 29, 33, 38–40, 44, 51, 59, 70–74, 76, 78, 80, 84, 85, 94, 117–130, 121n12, 123n17, 124n18, 133–139, 145, 147, 147n35, 149, 151, 164–166, 169, 174
Conceptual personae, 11, 11n14, 181n30, 190, 191n4
   See also Intercessors
The Conversation, 74–77
Coppola, Francis Ford, 37, 74–77, 164n8
Cronenberg, David, 68
Crystalline audibility, 72, 74–77, 122, 123, 178, 180, 182
Crystalline/crystal-image (Deleuze), 10, 68–70, 72, 75, 83

D
Dasein, 81, 87, 104, 127, 128, 132, 150, 158, 167, 175, 180n27, 185

Days of Heaven (DoH), xi, 3, 13, 45, 91–113, 117, 119, 131, 135, 137, 140–142, 145–147, 162, 164, 192
Demiurge, 7, 29, 120n10, 189
Deterritorialization/ reterritorialization, 8, 19n25, 76, 125, 139–141
Dewey, John, 135
Diegesis/diegetic, 3, 29, 30, 36, 37, 43, 44, 55, 55n8, 86, 122, 130, 131, 143–145, 148, 149, 183, 194

E
Eraserhead, 96
Ethos, 66, 81, 109, 118, 132, 137, 145, 150, 164
Ettinger, Bracha, xii, 43
Events, x, 5, 25, 39–43, 49, 93, 119, 157, 194

F
Fallenness, *see Verfallen*
Firstness (Peirce), 100, 101
Fold (Deleuze), 12, 12n16, 16n22, 62–66, 70, 82
Forgetting, ix, 3, 62–64, 80, 84, 96, 97, 99, 122, 122n15, 133, 137, 138, 141, 142, 151, 156, 157, 168, 177, 178, 185, 191, 194
Foucault, Michel, 4, 18, 57, 58, 62–64

G
God, 15–17, 20, 29, 39, 65, 66, 66n21, 82, 92, 102, 102n5, 103, 116, 116n2, 118, 129, 170, 181, 181n30, 183, 184, 189

Grace, 13, 17, 91, 113, 116, 126, 137, 138, 150, 174, 179–181, 184
Guattari, Félix, x, 8, 10n9, 10n10, 11, 11n13, 16n21, 19n25, 21, 41, 44, 139, 141, 141n32, 142, 148n38, 156, 166, 166n12, 181, 181n30, 190, 191, 191n4

H
Haecceity, 42, 54, 56, 96, 166n12
Heidegger, Martin, 4, 8, 11, 11n12, 12, 14n19, 16, 44, 50n1, 53, 57, 66, 81, 87, 108n11, 111, 116, 122, 123, 123n16, 123n17, 127, 131, 138, 143, 144, 150, 158, 160, 160n4, 161, 161n5, 167, 167n15, 170, 175–180, 175n20, 175n21, 176n23, 176n24, 180n27, 180n29, ss183, 185, 190
Heraclitus, 7, 16, 29, 30, 66, 66n20, 84, 84n31, 86, 86n33, 92, 93, 108, 112n13, 140, 191, 195
Heteronym, 11, 11n13, 191, 191n3
Hodological space/hodology, 69, 69n22, 75, 78, 80, 149
Hume, David, 100, 127

I
Identity, 10, 15, 17, 18, 20, 32, 33, 35, 42, 43, 51, 72, 97, 109, 113, 120n10, 125, 127, 138, 159, 170, 180n28, 192
Immanence, ix, 8, 10, 11n12, 15, 16n21, 44, 50–52, 70, 71, 80, 109, 117, 120n10, 166, 166n12, 177, 181, 181n30, 183
Independence and inseparability, 6, 178, 194
Index, 60, 74, 77, 95, 105, 158, 170, 172, 173

Intercessors, xi, 3, 11–13, 11n14, 181n30, 184, 190–193, 196
See also Conceptual personae

J
James, William, 4n6, 40, 40n10, 54n6, 100, 181n31, 182

K
Klute, 143
Knight of Cups, 138, 141n31, 147

L
Last Year at Marienbad, 143
Leibniz, Gottfried Wilhelm, 19n26, 62, 65, 82, 150n43, 178
Lewin, Kurt, 59, 69
Logos, xi, 2, 5–8, 15–17, 27, 49–87, 91, 117, 119, 155–185, 190
Lynch, David, 96

M
A Man Escaped (*Un condamné à mort s'est échappé ou Le vent souffle où il veut*), 58, 59, 73
Matrix/matrixial, 12, 39–44, 50, 51, 53, 59, 60, 62, 71, 77, 93–97, 104, 164, 168, 170, 179
Memory-image, 163
Metz, Christian, 21n27, 31, 32, 34, 60n12
Mimesis, 3, 29, 30, 35, 36
Mitry, Jean, 12n15, 31, 32, 142, 151
Mixing (sound), 94–96
Movement-image, 32, 62n13, 69n22, 100
Music, x, 7, 19, 19n25, 21, 35–37, 63, 81, 93, 96–98, 126, 131, 141n32, 157, 167n14

N

Narration (voice), xi, 30, 131, 143–147, 146n34
Nature, 14, 15, 17, 29, 33, 40, 61, 63, 64, 81–83, 85, 86, 91–93, 92n1, 101–103, 102n4, 102n6, 106–109, 112, 113, 129, 131, 132, 147, 150, 151, 157, 160–162, 164, 166, 173, 174, 180
  See also Phusis
Nietzsche, Friedrich, 13–15, 18n24, 57, 63n16, 81, 86, 92, 93, 116, 116n3, 125, 131, 178, 179, 191, 191n4
Nomos, 7, 16, 16n21, 30, 91, 92, 101, 107–113, 126, 141, 159, 181
Nostalghia, 79
Nous, 16n21, 29, 92, 108, 189, 190

O

Object-events, 5, 37, 41, 42, 53, 72, 76, 77, 93, 105, 106, 122, 173, 180
Offscreen sound, 37, 60, 60n12

P

Paripeteia, 106
Paris, Texas, 78
Park, Chan-Wook, 67
Parouisa, 103, 105, 107, 157
Pathos, 104, 116n1, 118, 128, 141, 145, 147n35, 169, 171
Peirce, Charles S., 60, 100, 101, 107, 109
Persona, 79
Photograph, 25–29, 44, 53
Phusis, 17, 81, 91, 92, 108, 132, 150, 164
  See also Nature

Plato, ix, 3, 13, 13n17, 29, 53, 86, 98, 99, 106, 115, 116, 120n10, 142, 144n33, 191
Plotinus, 116n5, 181, 184
Poiesis, 28, 119, 145, 148
Point of audition (POA), 75, 75n25, 159

R

Recollection-image (Deleuze), 10, 53, 62, 62n13
Reverie, 12, 25, 27–29, 44, 51n3, 52, 53, 79, 83, 84, 97, 98, 126, 127, 130, 134–136, 150, 157, 164, 180, 181, 189
Rilke, Rainer-Marina, 136

S

Sartre, Jean-Paul, 26, 117n7, 157
Saving Pvt. Ryan (*SPR*), 159, 160
Schaeffer, Pierre, 39
Schafer, R. Murray, 170
Schopenhauer, Arthur, 133, 134, 136
Scott, Ridley, 27, 28
Secondness (Peirce), 101, 107, 109
Semiology, ix, 10, 30–33, 36, 86, 143
Semiotics, 33, 35, 40, 41, 43, 44, 60, 71, 100, 179
Sensory-motor, 55, 55n8, 68–72, 74, 75, 85, 122, 127, 169, 173
Silence, 4, 10, 83, 91, 97, 99, 102, 138, 144, 156, 157, 161, 163–166, 177, 182, 182n32, 189, 195
Silverman, Kaja, 120, 136, 136n28, 138, 161
Simultaneity, 6, 27, 40, 44, 59, 60, 69–78, 84, 96, 97, 100, 118, 124, 128, 130, 147, 149n40, 151, 164, 166, 177

Sin (Kierkegaard), 65, 102, 111, 139, 192
Soderbergh, Steven, 123, 124n18
Solaris (Soderbergh), 124n18
Song to Song, 139, 139n29
Sonic-events, 37, 41, 42, 58, 59, 61, 67–69, 72, 74, 76, 77, 79, 93, 95–99, 105–107, 110, 111, 122, 125, 135, 147, 157–159, 169–171
Sound design, 19, 56, 72, 77, 94
Spider, 68
Spinoza, Baruch, 15n20, 42, 50, 82, 108, 118, 122n14, 140, 181, 184, 189
Stalker, 55, 156
Stoker, 67
Synchresis, 37, 38, 43, 72, 73, 73n24
Synchronization, 36, 37, 72, 73, 73n24

T
Tarkovsky, Andrei, 55, 55n7, 77, 79, 80, 85, 87, 136, 156
Tendere, 168–172, 192
Terminus, 54, 129, 159, 175, 184
Thanc (Heidegger), 53, 179, 180
The New World (TNW), ix, 45, 118, 119, 125–129, 131, 137, 141, 147, 149, 150, 150n41, 162, 164, 166, 169, 170, 173, 174, 181, 192
The Thin Red Line (TTRL), 12, 29, 45, 85, 109, 117–120, 128–133, 137, 138, 142, 145–150, 159–162, 164, 166, 181, 194
The Tree of Life (TToL), viii, xi, 44, 45, 85, 118, 119, 121, 122, 124, 126–128, 130–143, 147, 150, 173–178, 184, 189, 191, 192, 194
Thirdness (Peirce), 107, 109–111
Time-image (Deleuze), 39, 55, 55n8, 68, 69, 72
To the Wonder (TtW), 131, 138–140, 147, 149n40, 169, 191
Transcendence, 10, 11, 11n12, 15–17, 16n21, 29, 42, 44, 50, 52, 54n6, 67, 71, 79, 80, 83, 99, 117, 117n7, 118, 135, 137, 166, 170, 176, 181, 181n30, 183, 185
Transcendental, ix, 50–52, 64, 64n18, 66, 68, 83–85, 109, 116–118, 139, 150, 168, 169, 175, 177, 189, 192

U
Univocity, 17, 50, 120n9
The Usual Suspects, 143, 148

V
Verfallen, 12, 167, 178
Vicara/vitarka, 171, 173, 179
Voiceover, *see* Narration (voice)

W
Wagner, Kurt, 37, 131, 167, 167n14
Wahl, Jean, 38, 117, 138
Wenders, Wim, 77–80
Wings of Desire, 78
Wittgenstein, Ludwig, 4, 8, 20, 56, 97, 107n10, 149, 190
Woolf, Virginia, 84, 97, 116n5, 136, 136n27, 147, 174n19, 193

CPSIA information can be obtained
at www.ICGtesting.com
Printed in the USA
LVHW04*1243280518
578630LV00001B/1/P